Liners in Art

Dedication

I dedicate this book to Barny Vard, for bequeathing to me his appreciation of beautiful things.

*To Julie, my extraordinary and lovely Mother, for the faith she has in my abilities
that only she can see.*

To Simon, for his unstinted support, without which this volume could never have materialised.

*And to Anna, Daniel and Robyn, who represent the future and for whom there are
no more great liners to marvel at, this is a glimpse of glories past.*

Liners in Art

by
Kenneth Vard

HALSGROVE
in association with
Kingfisher Publications

Affinity

As a ship will seek shelter in its harbour, so too will you
It nuzzles the dock, its presence is felt
It becomes as one with its space and settles into familiarity
It takes in its lifes blood, moving slowly and restlessly
Till the time is right, then it is gone
Suddenly it seems as if it were no more, and never was.

You too are as real and as fleeting as a ship
Touching and leaving the harbours of your life
With nothing to prove you were there
Other than the reality of your being, as remembered by others.

Kenneth Vard

First published in Great Britain 1990
by Kingfisher Publications
Revised and reprinted by Halsgrove 2001

British Library Cataloguing-in-Publication Data
A CIP record for this title is available from the British Library

ISBN 1 84114 118 6

HALSGROVE
Halsgrove House
Lower Moor Way
Tiverton, Devon
EX16 6SS England.

Tel: 01884 243242
Fax: 01884 243325
www.halsgrove.com

Printed by
Amadeus Press
Cleckheaton
Yorkshire

Contents

Introduction

The great ocean liners were the largest moving structures ever created by man, they were designed as part of a transportation system which lasted a little more than 150 years. It hardly seems possible that such a complex and magnificent part of maritime history could simply come to an end at the blink of an eye, but incredibly that is what happened. The entire infrastructure supporting sea transportation seemed to crumble with the advent of the jet aeroplane, and one by one the great liners were sent to the scrapyards or sold to become cruise ships. With their going went also the last romantic era of gracious living and leisurely travel. Those marvellous ships should be included in any listing of mankind's most significant and noble achievements.

In the 1950s the continents were still bound together by a vast network of passenger steamships carrying millions of passengers. By the end of the 1960s everything had changed and the few liners remaining ploughed a lonely furrow sometimes crossing the oceans without encountering another ship – themselves sailing half empty. Such was the dramatic change in that decade of sad decline.

The ships which had once been so familiar survive now only as memories to those who knew them. The legends and stories which they produced today fascinate a new generation who are captivated by their aura of glamour and majesty.

Many books have been written about the great liners. Histories are available which tell the story of the famous shipping companies which existed then. Reference books dispense page after page of technological facts while decades of observation through the lens of the camera has produced illustrated journals which make the shape of those ships familiar to us all.

I love books and get great pleasure and knowledge from them. However, I believe that there is one great disadvantage in learning about any subject solely from the printed page, and that is their inability to convey that quality which we know as atmosphere. I was lucky to have been able to enjoy being around liners for most of my life, not out of necessity but out of choice, and the great impressions which live with me still are the unforgettable feelings of excitement which clung to them. Their great size and beauty, with the associated sounds and smells, make for a heady cocktail which few books can recreate.

Only one medium has, and that medium is art. It is a truism that one picture is worth a thousand words. If that is so with a photograph then it must be a thousand times more so when applied to a painting. An artist interprets what he sees and feels onto a plain surface, in a way that makes it appear alive to those who view it. Even if he paints from a sketch or uses photographs as his inspiration, a good artist can transform those images through colour, texture, composition and talent, into a painting in which the winds appear to be blowing.

It is not only a question of aesthetics. Great art has the ability to lift our spirits and illuminate our world which, at times, seems almost miraculous. Bad or indifferent art seems cold and has about as much impact on our senses as wallpaper. You don't need to be an expert to know the difference. No two artists will paint the same subject in the same way. Styles differ in interpretation, as much as we differ in our appreciation. Some pictures we like, others we don't. Nobody can teach us what to like or how to feel, too often an element of intellectual snobbery is present when art critics discuss the merits of one type of painting over another.

The pictures here are not highbrow, neither am I. However, the paintings chosen for this book are included because of their quality and the sensitivity shown by those who painted them. It has been argued that pictures such as these do not fit into any genre. I believe these paintings are though, the result of many years of inspired work. The traditions, techniques and teachings of great marine artists of the past are present in every one. The artists responsible have presented us with a wealth of beautiful paintings to enjoy and that is reason enough for them to be counted among the artistic treasures of our century. Of the ships themselves, more will be told later.

I do not intend to blind you with science. Where necessary, facts will be offered which have been fully researched and are, I trust, correct. However, mistakes do happen and if any are found within these pages I apologise. It is not my intention to offer a highly technical shipping book nor is it an intellectual treatise about marine art. It is simply a tribute to the ocean liners themselves and to the beautiful paintings which recreate their lives, presented here as fond memorials to an age which was filled with delicious experiences.

Introduction to the New Edition

It is with great pleasure that I introduce this 2001 edition of *Liners In Art*, to bring it into the new century. In the decade that has passed since the book was originally published, great strides have been taken in the development of passenger ships. When I originally wrote my book I thought the age of great ships had passed, and therefore the liners as pictured in this volume by maritime artists would never be equalled, I wrote then: "their like will never be seen again", but I was wrong. Their like have been seen again, though not as ocean liners intended to be part of a worldwide transportation system. They are now seen as glorious cruise-ships created to be part of a new world-wide leisure industry. Designers look back unashamedly to the elegance of the ocean-liner style and are in many instances recreating much of that beauty in the new ships, as well as creating innovative interiors appropriate to the future.

Today there are more extravagant ocean-going passenger ships sailing the seas than ever there were in the golden years of the liners. These new ships are the daughters of those fabled feminine and beautiful ships of yesteryear, some to be found here, living still as paintings within these pages.

The *Queens, Empresses,* the *Normandie,* and *Olympic,* the *Castles, Straths, Canberra,* and *Nieuw Amsterdam* have all gone, they live on in our memory, immortalised in books, photographs, models and artworks. They are replaced today by a new breed of wonderful ships, different in their form but now with a beauty that is all their own: stately vessels still, some bearing well-known names from the past sailing under familiar flags while others with inventive corporate names sail under the colours of shipping companies that did not exist at the end of the liner era.

The giants of yesterday are dwarfed by some of the new breed created to bring the pleasures and wonderment of deep-sea voyaging to another generation of passenger.

I am delighted that *Liners In Art* is again available, enabling a new audience to see what the past looked like as seen through the eyes of great contemporary maritime artists, but that is not the end of the story. Modern artists still paint the old liners as well as the new cruise-ships, and it is my hope that a companion volume will be published in the near future to bring alive the beauty of many more of yesterday's ships, as well as including today's great ships as seen by these artists of the twenty-first century. The story of ships is a never-ending saga, we are only at the beginning of a new age of passenger carrying floating palaces.

I have the continuing pleasure and honour to sail on many of these new cruise-ships as a maritime lecturer and can attest to the fact that they are equal to, and in many ways surpass, those fabulous liners of the past. Nothing can ever fully replace those special ships that were created to be the ocean-liners: the new cruise-ships happily continue where those liners left off and are in a class of their own, theirs is the future, I salute them all.

I re-dedicate this book to my parents' memory, to my now grown-up Anna, Daniel, Robyn and Linda, to my family of friends around the world and aboard the ships I sail on, and to all those passengers who support my speaking endeavours at sea, I also dedicate this volume to Cathal who keeps me steady when the seas get rocky.

Kenneth Vard
Hove, Sussex
March 2001

Foreword

by Captain John Treasure-Jones RD RNR Rtd. LLD (Hon) University of Wales

After a lifetime at sea, 47 years, starting as an apprentice in tramp ships and ending in command of Atlantic liners, my last ship and I both retired from the sea at the same time in December 1967. To me it seemed to symbolize the end of an era, not so much because it was the end of my career at sea, but because the ship I had brought to the end of her sea going life was none other than the great *Queen Mary*, perhaps the most famous liner ever built.

I had been her captain for her last two years in service, knowing that she would live on as a memorial to British shipbuilding and engineering at Long Beach, made her final voyage around Cape Horn to California from Southampton the most interesting and exciting voyage of my lifetime. It also made me a Cape Horner on my final voyage. It was, however, tinged with sadness but nothing like the feeling of melancholy which gripped me when I took the beautiful second *Mauretania* to her destruction at the ship breakers at Inverkeithing in 1965.

When I left her in that junk yard I felt that if I turned round and took a final look at her I would be turned into a pillar of salt. One by one the great ships were now disappearing as the final chapter was being written in the history of passenger liner transport. Today, those days seem to be receding ever faster into the realms of nostalgia. If it were not for books such as this and the growing interest of the general public, the entire history of the ocean liner could be lost forever.

I have known Kenneth Vard since he was introduced to me by a very great friend of mine in New York, namely Hymie Ross. I invited Ken aboard *Caronia* when we visited Belfast in 1955. I was staff captain of her at the time and he was a charming young man, he still is but 35 years older. He has sailed with me many times since that first meeting and we have discussed many things, in particular ocean liners, for which he always had a great love.

His plans to write this book interested me greatly, especially the idea of telling the story of liners linked with the reproduction of great steamship paintings. It is a recognised fact that paintings convey the essence of scenes much better than photography ever could.

I am delighted to write this foreword for a book written as a labour of love and produced with the same elegance and sense of dignity which surrounded those great ships of the past. It gives me great pleasure to commend this book as a tribute to all the ocean liners of yesterday and to all those who sailed in them.

J. Treasure-Jones
Chandlers Ford
Hampshire
England
1990

Preface - A Personal Note

When I think of my boyhood I think of ships – great vessels rising from the sludgy waters of Belfast Lough and encased in a web of cranes and gantries. Good old fashioned ships built of steel and pimpled with rivets. Familiar ship-shapes of masts and funnels, elegant bows and rounded feminine sterns. Their colours proclaiming their pedigrees – black hulls for the Atlantic, lavender grey for south of the Equator, or snow white for India or South America. They were the ocean liners, the aristocrats of the maritime world and many of them started life almost on my doorstep.

I was born and raised in Belfast virtually under the shadow of the great shipyards of Harland and Wolff. My first memory as a child was seeing cranes silhouetted like skeletons against flame, as the city was blitzed by German bombers in 1941.

Years later, as a teenager, I would sneak into those docks to watch the activities surrounding the building of ships. Those were the days when the ocean liner reigned supreme. While many famous ships had been destroyed and needed replacing after the war, others, used as troop ships, returned to their builders to be converted back into their original form, emerging better than ever and breathtaking in their beauty. Those sights made a profound impression on me and the impact has run like a thread through the fabric of my life ever since.

To a boy who lived in the claustrophobic atmosphere of a provincial Irish city the shipyards became a place where miraculous things were happening. The contrasts were startling. There, amid the grimy, grey and damp Victorian city, was a veritable industrial Disneyland, a vast factory where dreams were created. At that place, supported by the dirty waters surrounding the yards, were born some of the most incredible vessels ever seen. Witnessing the creation of these glamorous ships was a spur to my imagination which nothing has supplanted. On the one hand, Belfast, damp and dour, and on the other, the great liners. Both represented two extremes like fire and ice. Whereas in the city the phrase 'across the water' meant England, in the shipyards the same phrase meant exotic far away places with blue seas and white cities smelling faintly of spice.

When those lovely ships, with names of castles, countries and queens on their bows, finally sailed away down the Lough they left behind a kind of sadness. They looked like huge presents wrapped up in their newness and I wished I was sailing with them.

Within these pages you will find many ships. Some I knew only by reputation, others I sailed on, or have seen during the course of my travels.

My experiences have been the source of inspiration for this book. The era was exciting and beautiful, and my wish is to share it. I hope you will enjoy seeing some of it through my eyes.

Kenneth Vard
Hove, Sussex
Summer 1990

The Shape of Ships

The internal arrangements of any ship depends on its exterior design which takes its cue from the intended function of the vessel and the materials from which it is constructed.

The liners of the North Atlantic, as the name suggests, were intended to operate mostly through cold, wet and windy latitudes. Open decks were largely unused by the passengers, except when the weather was fine, and that was always problematical. Promenade decks had, by the 1920s, become long stretches of broad glass enclosed streets where people could sit in cushioned recliners or walk and gaze at the sea. Those decks were outside in feeling and though sheltered, they were subject to the temperatures prevailing outside.

Only when entering the ships interior did the passenger experience warmth and luxury. This feature in construction persisted almost to the end of the 1950s at which time public rooms placed within the superstructure were brought right up to the ships sides, resulting in the elimination of the traditional promenade deck.

Ships of the hot weather routes which sailed from the northern hemisphere to the Orient and Australasia, were usually built with many open promenade decks and terraces. These were designed to serve two main purposes: the obvious one being to provide places of shade cooled by the breezes whilst in tropical waters, the other reason being a financial ploy to cut down on operating costs. Both the Panama and the Suez canals charge dues on the gross tonnage of ships. Tonnage is not a matter of weight but of volume, it being calculated on the basis of 100 cubic feet of totally enclosed space being equal to one gross ton. Therefore, the more area of the ship which could be classified as unenclosed, the smaller the tonnage and subsequent charges.

These anomalies could distort the relative sizes of various ships on different routes. A ship of 20,200 tons built for the tropical service might have been physically larger, in fact, than a transatlantic liner of 21,600 tons.

For instance, the *Southern Cross* compared to the *Saxonia*: the former was actually 107 feet longer than the latter, but on paper *Saxonia* appears to be bigger. The soft curves and sweetness of line expected in great ships have today mostly disappeared. These have been replaced by ships with slab sided angularity, sawn off sterns and exaggerated bows. This is prompted, not only by a lack of aesthetic sensitivity but primarily by costs.

Prefabricated construction coupled with welding techniques and the use of aluminium has dramatically changed the shape of today's ships. When I talk of feminine curves, seen on countersterns, clipper bows and sensuous superstructures, all balanced by tall raked masts and massive funnels and built from steel plates that are pimpled with rivets, I am talking of ships constructed by old fashioned methods now outdated and impractical. But those methods resulted in a breed of aristocratic ships which were filled with character, quality and a great individuality. It was this combination of time-consuming labour and sheer weight of material which imposed a sense of permanence on those impermanent creations.

Those were the great liners which etched their existence on our minds. I don't believe there are many of today's cruise ships which will remain in the collective memory of the future, like those liners of yesterday. This is not to say that all of yesterday was good and all of today and tomorrow is necessarily bad, it is merely a change of function. The sea itself has not changed, nor has the salt air. The thrill and excitement of being aboard a great ship heading for the far horizon, always will be, an experience to savour.

The comforts provided on the new breed of ships are, in many ways, vastly superior to those that were provided on the ships of the ocean-liner era. Great advances have been made in technology and also the expectations of today's passengers. There is hardly a ship which is not fully air conditioned, providing accommodation even in the lowest price brackets equal to the best modern hotels. Therein lies the root of, what I think, is the sad difference.

Ships now are created to be massive, floating, moving leisure complexes. The ship herself being the ultimate destination for her passengers. Many of the ships of state of the 1930s have been surpassed in size by some cruise liners being built today, but even if the giants of yesteryear are surpassed in size, they will never equal their atmosphere nor their achievements and beauty. That which has been, is now gone, that which is now coming into being is for the future, comparisons cannot, and really should not, be made. We are talking of different periods and different functions. The breed ended with the *Queen Elizabeth 2*. She was the last great ship to be built as a traditional ocean-going liner and she pointed the way to a future which is now upon us.

Maritime Art

Maritime art has always been in a different category to that of mainstream art, in as much as the work of the marine artist has been created over the centuries primarily as documents of accurate historical value. To satisfy the eye of seamen to whom a picture was of little use if the details were not correct, the marine artist not only needed to convey freshness of atmosphere, he must also show the vessel with absolute accuracy. This being so, paintings down through the ages have been considered as records of the changing shapes of ships. No less in recent times than in the past. Not only do we see the shapes of vessels and their function in detail stretching back almost to pre-history, we can also reap the benefits of that long tradition of artistic accuracy in the observation of paintings which have been created in our own time.

Ships have always been built for practical reasons but, as is the case with most artifacts created for a specific function, beauty cannot help but manifest itself when the object is designed and built sympathetic to the environment in which it is destined to operate. All waterborne vessels have these things in common, each must have buoyancy, each must have a shape which allows for movement in a planned direction, and each must have some means of propulsion. These factors are common to all, whether it be a hollow log on a pre-historic river, or the mighty *QE2* of today.

It is a sobering fact that since the beginning of maritime history only three sources of propulsion have been used at sea: man power, wind power and mechanical power. Each of these dictated the shapes of the ships they were to propel. The days of sail produced the most ethereal of all beauties and also saw the evolution of maritime art which we recognise today as being the most familiar.

Most of the paintings of the sailing ship era were recreations of battle scenes. War was the spur and admiralties were the patrons. They commissioned paintings to commemorate victories at sea. Commerce followed the conquests and as ships became faster, hulls became slimmer and masts taller. Shapes were graceful with swan-like bows and flowing lines, their curves, topped by clouds of sail providing romantic subjects for the artist's brush.

With the coming of steam and iron, ships became independent of the weather and their designs reflected a new mechanical brutality which allowed them to forge through the seas in any chosen direction. Shapes were dramatically changed but owed much to the past. The early steamships were equipped with paddle wheels and a tall funnel with masts and sails to ensure reliability, they are now regarded as charming in appearance, but it was not until the advent of the screw propeller and refinements in engine and fuel power, that the steel built steamship took on the lean and powerful look which is familiar today.

These new ships were not considered worthy of the attention of serious artists at first, the ungainly shapes of the new breed did not inspire beautiful pictures but eventually, the evolution of design, following in the footsteps of advanced technology, produced vessels which became things of great beauty. Especially the passenger liners which were being built to carry the mass of immigrants pouring across the oceans to America and southwards to Australasia. The shipping companies reaped vast profits from those huddled masses, loaded as human cargo in the steerage quarters of the new generation of steamers. But like the cities from which they came, those liners also catered for the more privileged levels of society, carrying them in the prime-cut sections of the ships. In fact, it was from those luxurious first class quarters that the liners obtained their reputation as floating palaces.

Transatlantic liners spearheaded the evolution of all passenger shipping design. They attracted the greatest number of passengers both in steerage and in the sophisticated first class. International competition for this growing trade forced changes in design at a rapid rate. Speed became more important; so too did size and power, it was on the Atlantic that new motive power was developed. Bigger engines meant more fuel, bigger boilers, more funnels and more space, culminating in the appearance just before the First World War of the four funnelled, slim waisted beauties: *Mauretania, France* and *Kaiser Wilhelm De Grosse* appearing as giants of power and safety, a perception shattered only by the *Titanic* disaster in 1912.

Then came the ship beautiful herself: *Aquitania* – to many the most beautiful liner ever built. She was huge, lean lined with four evenly spaced tall funnels, two masts and a snow-white superstructure, square fronted to match her knife edge bow. Her terraced decks swept down aft to finish in the perfection of a curvaceous counterstern of sublime proportions. She was the last of the majestic four-stackers and the most perfect.

After her came yet more power but requiring less boiler-room. Oil fuel had simplified engines and the funnels necessary to take away smoke and gases dwindled to three, two and then only one. This reduction led to larger internal spaces and less clutter on deck. The science of flotation improved, as did safety standards, resulting in internal spaces being sub-divided into lower, more watertight compartments. The advent of aluminium and its welding techniques led to lighter and taller superstructures, while the newly invented stabilizer systems improved sea keeping qualities.

All these influenced the shapes we got to know and each in their own day established a standard of beauty which ended in the 1960s with the conventional looking liner *France* and the unconventional looking *Queen Elizabeth 2*, the last to be built for transporting passengers across the Atlantic.

The changing shape of liners can be followed through these paintings. They are accurate portrayals of a slice of maritime history. Many artists having recorded this beauty which was once part of the vast panorama of the world at sea. Today, when the need for ships seems only to revolve around bulk cargo handling, that beauty seems no longer possible. The shape of practicality now is ugly. Much as I try I cannot train my eye to see harmony and sweetness of line in the box-like shapes of container ships, car transports and oil tankers. Even todays ferries have succumbed to the squared apartment block image which seems to pour scorn on the aesthetic masterpieces of the past.

But perhaps all is not lost, ugliness does not rule supreme. There are new cruise ships which now seem softer. Thankfully, marine architects of today are not only equating efficiency with industrial design, eye appeal is now a factor in selling the idea of holidays at sea as it once was in attracting passengers for ocean crossings. No wonder nostalgia and the age of romance is gaining popularity. How is it that the ability to combine great efficiency, practicality and beauty in the ships of yesterday, seemed to die with them, only to be replaced with a kind of contempt for all they stood for.

Today's marine artists are hard pressed to find scenes of shipping worthy of their talents, the magic seems to have gone. The scenes of yesteryear still pull at the heart strings and inspire painters to paint from imagination and memory rather than from the horrors that now confront them. Soon, if we are not careful, not only will the traditional subjects for painters be unworthy of their art, but the growing pollution of mans aesthetic values might be joined by his pollution of the sea itself, resulting in a universal ugliness never before seen or imagined. Perhaps the beauties of the past as recorded here in these fine paintings may provide some inspiration for both the ship designer and the artist of the future.

Here then is a small review of great ship paintings for you to marvel at, I hope they will rekindle old memories of voyages past or perhaps produce a pang of regret that you arrived too late for the party and missed all the fun.

Paintings in a Book

It has been my endeavour to have these paintings reproduced as closely as possible to the reality of the originals but no matter how technically perfect they may be, the fact is, no book can ever recreate the impact received by the viewer when looking at an original. All the paintings have been reduced to conform with the page size which in itself is misleading. The lighting in a book is constant which is not so when looking at the real thing. Nor is it possible to reproduce the texture of paint on a printed page but what we do have here is a collection of beautiful images representing original works of art and presented in a way which I hope, does them justice.

The creation of this book combine the efforts of many people and hopefully it will be enjoyed as a work of art in itself. Paintings ought to be seen in reality to be fully appreciated and a visit to galleries and museums will reward those who make the effort. So too, would the purchase of paintings enrich the life of those who take the plunge. The cost is outweighed by the pleasure received by owning them and having them as part of your life.

City of New York

This painting was commissioned by the shipbuilders J & G Thomson of Clydebank to commemorate the maiden voyage of the *City of New York*. Here we see the beautiful liner departing from Liverpool on August 1st 1888 on that occasion.

The painting is a hymn to steam with only one small sailing ship representing the past seen sailing off the liner's starboard bow. How graceful the *City of New York* looks with her clipper-ship lines and three tall funnels. Her masts, still rigged fully to carry sail, now only serve as an unnecessary backup to the reliability of steam power.

The river craft, all steamers, still rely on paddles for their motive power, and the scene is bright with the confidence born of the industrial revolution when all things seemed possible in those heady days of Victorian empire and great inventions.

From her foremast the liner flies the American flag, indicating the country to which she is bound. From her main mast she flies the flag of the Inman Line and from her stern can be seen the red duster of Britain. This is an optimistic painting which points the way into the future; not only is this lovely little ship sailing out to meet the ocean for the first time, she also points her bows towards the new century in which will be born the greatest seagoing craft the world will ever see. All of which will, in no small way, owe much of their design and technological miracle to this elegant little liner, one of the most beautiful of them all.

by Raphael Monleon y Torres
Oil on canvas 32" x 59"
Courtesy of Sotheby's

Teutonic

This impressive painting shows the new White Star liner, *Teutonic*, at Spithead on August 4th 1889. She was the centrepiece of a naval review presented in honour of his Imperial Majesty, the Emperor of Germany. He and his Royal Highness, The Prince of Wales had come to inspect the new ship which was the first liner to be built under the direction of the Admiralty and intended for use as an armed merchant cruiser in the event of war. In this painting, her forward gun can be seen on the deck. She flies the Kaisers Imperial Standard from the main mast. The British Royal Yacht, *Victoria and Albert*, can be seen astern. The scene is one of regal grandeur and great excitement. William Wyllie was in the forefront of Britain's marine artists of the Victorian era and this painting certainly reinforces his reputation. The sense of occasion is beautifully portrayed and the painting is undoubtedly one of the artist's best.

by William L. Wyllie
Oil on Canvas 60" x 40"
Reproduced by kind permission of Sotheby's

Orontes

Even though the *Orontes* does not seem to have earned a name for herself in the shipping hall of fame, no doubt in her day she had a personality which endeared her to her passengers and crew. But, apart from her name being entered in the company's fleet archives, there was no reason to remember this ship especially. However, here she is enshrined in paint. It is not known whether or not the artist had been commissioned to paint her or whether the painting is one more river scene typical of the work done by Charles Dixon with the *Orontes* happening to be the centrepiece, but what a wonderfully evocative scene it is.

Here is dockland London at the beginning of the 20th century. It was the largest and liveliest sea port in the world and at that time the Thames was the highway leading to the empire, and virtually choked with traffic. We see it here in 1905 as *Orontes*, only then in service for three years, moves slowly down stream from Tilbury. She sounds her steam whistle in warning as she threads her way through Thames sailing barges, tugs, rowing boats and square riggers towards the sea. This beautiful watercolour almost reeks with smoky dampness and even though *Orontes* is still in the river, the tang of tar and salt air seems to have come upstream with the seagulls to invade the senses. In a few days she will have left the grey, damp, northern waters behind. Ahead lies the sun washed Mediterranean, Suez, the discomforts of the Red Sea, a coaling stop at desolate Aden, and the long voyage south of the equator to Australia. Many months later she will be back at Tilbury where she will be once more part of this incredible scene.

by Charles Dixon
Watercolour 20" x 30"
Courtesy of P&O, London

La Provence

The American artist Antonio Jacobsen became famous by painting portraits of the ships he would see coming into the port of New York. Many of these paintings were commissioned by the ship's captains themselves and found their way eventually into collections in Europe.

His rendering of sea and sky is rather stylised while the vessels themselves always appear stiff and unnatural. Nevertheless, his paintings have a somewhat naive quality and his style is instantly recognisable.

Antonio Jacobsen invariably places his ships so that they present a broad-side view, but in this fine portrait of *La Provence* he has presented his ship in a more realistic way, showing her at full speed in the Atlantic, bound for New York, appearing as frivolous and jaunty as any can-can dancer.

by Antonio Jacobsen
Oil on canvas 30" x 30"
Courtesy of Frank O. Braynard

The Final Farewell, The Lusitania

The final, fateful sailing of the *Lusitania* on May 1st 1915 is here recreated by Ken Marschall in a painting which seems to suggest the loneliness and vulnerability of the only Cunarder which was still in passenger service at that war torn time. Her paint scheme had been altered only months before. She now bore a band of buff around her lower superstructure, just above the black hull, as did many other Cunarders of the period. In the distance across the Hudson, two of *Vaterland*'s three massive funnels are visible at her Hoboken pier, laid up during the hostilities.

Gone are the crowds of well-wishers at the dockside. Only two men on a barge wave farewell as the graceful, four funnelled express liner departs in this, her last, historic voyage.

The true nature of the contents of her cargo holds will probably remain a secret forever. If she were carrying prohibited arms, as claimed by the Germans, then she could have been classified as a military target. But if she were, as had been sworn to by the British, on her lawful business upon the great waters, filled only with general cargo and peaceful civilian passengers, then her sinking can only be described as a heinous war crime and one of the greatest acts of inhuman barbarity in history.

No matter the reasons, the lovely *Lusitania* will be forever linked with tragedy and the death of too many innocent victims. Her name will never more be placed on the bows of another ship. This painting was created in 1990 to mark the 75th anniversary of her sinking, and the artist went to great lengths to ensure the accuracy of every detail. He even interviewed some survivors of the sinking and a number of prints were produced and signed by them to mark the occasion.

by Ken Marschall
Acrylics on board
Courtesy of the artist

Mauretania

The artist names this painting '*Mauretania* arriving in New York early morning 1912'. The composition is an extremely difficult one to paint successfully without creating distortions, but Mr Muller has succeeded brilliantly in giving us a birdseye view.

The promise of today's skyscraper city is beginning to be realised in this historically accurate view. It is in the days of coal fired boilers when every ounce of steam was created from the toil and sweat of hundreds of stokers. The serenity of the ship belies the activities which were necessary to bring her to this point. The *Mauretania*'s escort of tugs keeps pace with her as they prepare to ease her into her pier. A Hudson River paddleboat passes astern of her, cross-harbour ferries bustle on the river and the dying days of sail are represented by a fully rigged ship approaching Manhattan far behind. Some of *Mauretania*'s passengers can be seen on deck and at her bridge front, they watch her approaching New York after another fast Atlantic crossing. No doubt dozens of horse-drawn handsome cabs will be drawn up at the pier awaiting the ship's passengers to transfer them to their hotels, apartments or railway stations for onward journeys across the continent.

The painting is full of life, subtleties and half hidden points of interest. Here is an accurate portrait, not only of the physical properties of a great liner, but it also recreates the Edwardian atmosphere of the era in which she sailed.

by William Muller
Oil on canvas 26" x 40"
Courtesy of the artist

The Morea in Drydock

This finely drawn and precise watercolour is unusual because of its large size but the impact of the image is emphasised by the detail which this medium has allowed the artist to include by using his superb draughtsmanship.

The sense of activity in the picture is especially remarkable, taking into account the relatively static nature of the subject. The *Morea* is shown like a prisoner in the drydock, all ships seen in such a setting look out of place and somewhat bizarre, appearing uncomfortable and out of their element. But life goes on in and around them. The noise is deafening as the shipyard workers repair, replace and refurbish the wear and tear of previous voyages.

Those drydocks are in themselves miraculous feats of engineering. They are designed to pump tens of millions of gallons of water into and out of their vast areas within a few hours. The immense strength and power of their hydraulic systems is incredible. Their gates are capable of opening and then damming the sea outside. The theory is simple. A huge, open-ended bath is filled with water enabling the biggest ships to be floated into it. The gates at one end are closed to enable the sea to be pumped out again which leaves the vessel isolated and dry in its dock.

After the underbody of the hull is examined, repaired, cleaned and painted, the process is reversed and the dock is filled gradually again and the gates reopened to allow the ship to be towed out to resume her life afloat.

The true immensity of a ship's bulk can only be fully appreciated when seen from the floor of a drydock and the experience is stunning, especially if it is one of the great liners. The *Morea* was one of the lucky ships of the M Class built for P&O. She entered service in 1908 and sailed into and out of the First World War without drama and then on into the post-war era. She served her company with distinction being known as the most beautiful of the sisters. She finally went to the breakers in Japan in 1930 and no doubt much of her metal was recycled into weapons used against her creators in the war between Japan and Britain a decade later.

by Bernard F. Gribble
Watercolour, 31" x 40"
Courtesy of P&O London

Malwa

Between 1903 and 1911 the great P&O Line built ten sister ships for the Australian mail service. They sailed from Britain through Suez to India and were for their time quite exceptional. Although each was similar to the next, the class was improved upon as each vessel entered service.

They ranged in size from 9,505 tons of the *Moldavia*, built in 1903, to 12,358 tons of the *Medina*, built in 1911. Of those ten ships only four would survive the First World War and sail into the 1930s. As in any family, each one developed its own personality resulting in stories of heroism, fame or obscurity, whether their lives were short or long.

The *Macedonia* had a career which spanned a full 27 years whereas the youngest twins, *Maloja* and *Medina*, sailed for less than six.

The paintings here which represent this class of great liners, show them in the course of their careers. The painting of the *Morea* in drydock depicts the tender loving care showered on ships to keep them in tip-top condition.

The *Malwa* is shown at Kronstadt on a pleasure cruise at a time when the world was at peace and in the days when the sailors of the Tsar could visit the liner as she lay at anchor amongst the Russian fleet. The elegant *Medina* is shown in two paintings. The first showing her at her most glorious, her fabulous maiden voyage departure as a royal yacht carrying her sovereign and his queen to their Durbar in India. The second painting depicts her as a passenger liner five years later, rushing unknowingly to her appointment with a German u-boat and destruction.

These paintings encapsulate the history of those early 20th century British ships in a way not possible by photography. The colour, drama and the character of the age, are beautifully recreated and each picture is an interpretation of an event seen uniquely through the imagination and skill of its artist.

by William Wyllie
Oil on canvas 66" x 36"
Courtesy of P&O, London

George Washington

At the beginning of the 20th century transatlantic liners entering New York would sail up the Hudson and dock at either the Manhattan or the Hobokan side of the river. It was not until the 1930s that Manhattan would become the major borough for ocean liner docking.

In this spirited water colour of the *George Washington* leaving Hoboken we see the ship as she begins to turn under her own power to sail down the Hudson bound for Bremerhaven. Across the river the buildings of Manhattan are faintly visible through the mist. The picture is dated approximately 1910 before New York has become the skyscraper city we now know. The smokiness of the coal burning era casts a pall upon the scene. Tugs, ferries and a railroad transporter share the busy river with her as she manoeuvres at the start of her homeward voyage.

The traditional style of the ship with her twin ochre funnels and four masts seems to represent a backward look to the days of the sailing ship, remarkably disguising the fact that within the confines of her hull are extraordinary interiors which represent a great leap forward into the realms of futuristic shipping decor.

by Walter Zeeden
Watercolour on paper
Courtesy of German Shipsmuseum, Bremerhaven

31

Olympic or Titanic

It is a time honoured tradition which still sometimes applies, that whenever a shipping company contemplates the building of a new ship, an artist is commissioned to paint the vessel as she will appear in service. These portraits are done from preliminary drawings and shipyard plans and in many ways serve a similar function to that of the admiralty models built as illustrations of ships-to-come in the old days of Samuel Pepys. Seldom did these artists' renderings become exact replicas of the real thing. The finished vessels usually having additions or changes in details of the construction which could vary from the original plans.

Nevertheless, a painting of an intended ship placed in its element, the sea, and given life through artistry, could be a strikingly accurate portrayal of what was eventually to become reality. In the case of sister ships, such as the White Star 'Big Three', the first two were planned as twins and any portrait painted before their completion would have had them looking identical. In reality, however, the *Titanic* differed slightly from her older sister *Olympic* when she was finally completed, but this portrait cannot be definitely assigned to either one of the sisters in particular. The date that Fred Pansing places on his canvas of 1911 suggests this to be of the *Titanic*, but by this time, the *Olympic* had been sailing for a few months and this picture looks remarkably like her. The *Titanic* was intended to be identical, but just before completion, her promenade deck was partially glassed in which would have made her instantly recogniseable. Nevertheless this is a fine example of an early 20th century steam ship painting. It is interesting to compare this one with the romantic portrait of the *Olympic* painted by William Muller 75 years later, both paintings create a sense of reality, even though both were painted without the benefit of actually having seen the vessels at sea. The Pansing picture imparts the aura of Edwardian formality to perfection. It is a painting without sentiment and creates little affection, whereas the Muller painting recreates the atmosphere of the ship and its surroundings in a somewhat softer way, resulting in a painting which demands affection. Such is the difference in style between one artist and another.

by Fred Pansing
Oil on canvas 34" x 44"
Reproduced with kind permission of Sotheby's

Olympic

The four funnelled White Star liner *Olympic* is seen here in 1930 leaving New York on a calm evening and bound for Europe. The Fall River Line steamer *Commonwealth* is rounding the tip of Manhattan astern of her while tugs and the Statue of Liberty are left behind as the great ship gathers speed and heads for the open sea.

This calm and atmospheric painting seems to express the elegance and dignity of that very special, and spectacular, liner. She was the only survivor of an incredible trio. Of her sisters, one was never to be remembered and the other will never be forgotten. They were designed and created to run a luxury transatlantic service before the First World War. They were, at over 45,000 tons, the biggest ships in the world when built, but were never intended to compete for the speed prizes being chased by other ships at the time. Great size and unsurpassed luxury was their intended claim to fame but the fates decreed otherwise.

Olympic was the first, entering service in 1911. Her sister, *Titanic*, while on her maiden voyage to New York a year later, kissed the cheek of an iceberg which became the kiss of death for her. The third sister, *Britannic*, was born into a war. She entered service as a hospital ship and met her fate in the blue waters of the Aegean where an enemy mine lay in wait for her.

Olympic carried the torch for her ill-fated sisters for 24 years and was to be a successful and well loved ship all her life. This painting seems to express the hidden legacy of her family history, with its touch of solitude and hints of what might have been, here perfectly caught by the sensitive touch of a master.

by William Muller
Oil on canvas 18" x 20"
Courtesy of the artist

Empress of Asia

It has been the lot of many ships of this century to have been destined to sail in two world wars. One of those ships was the beautiful Canadian Pacific liner *Empress of Asia*, her name representing the nature of her calling. She was a true daughter of Britain returning to the land of her birth only in times of war.

This painting is a typical portrait of a ship at sea incorporating all the little symbols designed to represent a sense of place and function. Here we see the *Empress of Asia* at speed in the China Seas the great bat wing sails of the Chinese junks representing the waters in which she sails. At her main mast she flies the chequered flag of the Canadian Pacific Railway Company, at her stern is the blue ensign of the Royal Naval Reserve proclaiming to the world that her master and at least six of her officers are part of Britain's Royal Naval Reserve Force. From her foremast she flies the rising sun of Japan, her next country of destination, and the smoke pouring from her three working funnels, atest to the fact that in her boiler room her complement of Chinese stokers, in sharp contrast to the luxuries enjoyed by her passengers in the top decks, are shovelling thousands of tons of coal into her furnaces providing the power for her to steam on her transpacific voyages.

Built as one of a pair, she and her sister, the *Empress of Russia*, were primarily designed as links in the chain which bound the British Empire together. The Canadian Pacific Railway Company provided a unique service, ships from Liverpool to Canada, transcontinental trains from the Atlantic to the Pacific coasts, and again beautiful ships linking Vancouver with the British crown colony of Hong Kong and the ports in between. Both ships were identical, apart from their wheelhouses, whereas the *Asia* was fitted with portholes the *Russia* was fitted with square windows.

The ships, with their three tall funnels over a length of nearly 600 feet, appeared larger than they actually were at just under 17,000 tons. The palatial accommodation each ship provided for their 284 passengers travelling in first class and the 100 in second class, was in sharp contrast to that provided for the 800 Asiatics carried in steerage. Their cargo was reminiscent of that which was carried by the sailing clipper ships, tea and silk being the most important and typical of the route.

The *Empress of Asia* and her sister sailed into two world wars. The *Empress of Russia* surviving until 1945 only to be totally destroyed by fire while fitting out for her post-war life at the shipyards in England. The *Empress of Asia*, however, was not lucky enough to survive the war. She was attacked by 27 Japanese aircraft and sank in flames off the coast of Singapore on February 5th 1942.

by Norman Wilkinson
Oil on canvas 20" x 30"
Courtesy of Communications Partnership PLC, London

Aquitania

The roaring twenties was a period of madness. A great war had been fought which had changed everything. The old order was gone, nothing was secure and the watch-word was fun. Ahead lay the great depression and another more destructive war. The ocean liners were now employed more with travel for pleasure. The American immigration laws had been changed and the flow of people from Europe had become a trickle. Prohibition was in force and thirsty Americans crowded European ships for a few days of unbridled alcoholic pleasure. Midnight sailings became popular, originally planned so that the arrival time in Cherbourg was at a more acceptable hour but the opportunities a night sailing presented for *bon voyage* parties could not be ignored. It then became traditional to board early in the evening for a night of dining and dancing before the ship sailed. Although the *Aquitania* was an Edwardian she was not staid and she threw herself into the age of the flapper and the charleston with the best of them.

In this gorgeous painting the ship is seen backing out of Cunard's Pier 54 at night. A tug pushes at her bows, others nuzzle her flanks and another tows her stern. She is ablaze with lights, crowds line her decks, dressed in formal wear. They wave to friends on the dockside, many of whom have probably just disembarked after *bon voyage* parties on board.

The great ship will be turned into the river and slowly leave New York behind. Ahead lies six wonderful days to Europe. Meanwhile the parties will continue until dawn. This was the norm in those eastward crossings in all classes, the third class too being filled now with the new tourists, mostly students bound for a few weeks in London or Paris.

The painting expresses the light-hearted sense of pleasure which those night sailings always seemed to possess, one more aspect of the delights associated with steamship travel, especially in the 1920s.

William Muller not only recreates the scene, he has magically imbued his canvas with a sense of presence, all that is necessary here are the sounds of the cheers and the noises of departure. The picture is bursting with a vibrant sense of life which makes us feel part of this exciting experience.

by William Muller
Oil on canvas 24" x 38"
Courtesy of the artist

The Berengaria Sailing from Southampton Bound for New York

This monumental looking painting is typical of the composition favoured by liner artists when creating a painting for possible use by the shipping companies as postcards or advertising material.

The liner is made to look even bigger than she is by placing her alongside small craft which become dwarfed by the titan. The three-quarters-on bow view is usually the most flattering especially when the ship can be described as handsome rather than beautiful. Some of the biggest ships in the world were designed to be as graceful as yachts but not the *Berengaria*. She and her sisters were built to create a sense of awe and, even though their appearance was thrilling as the largest ships in the world, they could not be described as great beauties.

In this painting, Charles Dixon has given the ship a radiance derived from colour and form, softened by the butterfly appearance of the accompanying yachts. The warship brings gravitas to the occasion and the composition of each unit in relation to the next draws the eye repeatedly back to the commanding presence of the *Berengaria* herself.

Pictures such as this have been described in derogatory terms as being 'chocolate boxy' but this is a very fine painting and could only be on the top of a chocolate box because its subject was synonymous with the height of luxury. What better sight than this to whet the appetite for all things exciting and elegant, a crossing aboard the *Berengaria* promised all that and more.

by Charles Dixon
Watercolour on paper 22½" x 37½"
Reproduced by kind permission of Sotheby's

Empress of Canada

In this painting the artist has disregarded an unwritten taboo, which is not to paint a ship sailing away, it is probably a rule coupled with that of not painting a storm scene which was coined more for commercial reasons than for any other, the thinking being that storms and departures were not happy subjects. But there is no sadness in this joyful picture of the beautiful *Empress of Canada*, ploughing through rough seas, the painting is lively and optimistic and full of mid-ocean light and space as could only be seen on board during a transatlantic crossing.

The ship was originally the Canadian Pacific liner *Duchess of Richmond*, built in 1928 and after a career which included trooping during the Second World War, was upgraded to first class status and rebuilt as an *Empress*, making her maiden voyage as such in 1947. She, and only one of her three sisters survived the war, and they sailed with distinction until coronation year 1953 at which time the *Empress of Canada* was overwhelmed by fire as she lay in her Liverpool dock. She was completely gutted and capsized, prematurely ending her life. Her sister, the *Empress of France* survived until the end of 1960 when she sailed to the breakers, so ending the story of a quartet of ships which, in their day, were important links between Britain and Canada, sailing as Duchesses as part of a company known for its style and elegance around the world.

by Norman Wilkinson
Oil on canvas 20" x 30"
Courtesy of Communications Partnership PLC, London

Viceroy of India

This lovely water colour is typical of the work done by Jack Spurling for the P&O and BI shipping companies. The painting was completed in 1928, a year before the *Viceroy of India* actually entered service.

The other steamship shown in the background is the *Manela*, 8,300 gross tons. This ship, owned by the British India Steam Navigation Company, was built by Barclay Curle and Company Limited, Glasgow, and launched in April 1921. She was propelled by twin screws and powered by steam turbines. She carried 130 passengers between England and India, via Suez, and was scrapped in 1946.

The artist has placed both ships having sailed from Tilbury and pictured heading out of the Thames towards the sea. The sailing ship in the background is the training ship *Exmouth*, later to be named the *Worcester*. She was one of the last of the old sailing wooden walls of England. Far in the distance can be seen the smoking chimneys of factories and steamships while the docks still appear to be crowded with the towering masts of the remaining sailing ship fleets still in operation on the world's oceans in the 1920s.

by Jack Spurling
Watercolour
Courtesy of P&O, London

45

Europa

Even the most powerful and largest of liners could, in the right setting, present a picture of calmness and indeed it appears so in this painting of the *Europa*, which shows the liner towards voyages end in a late evening. The great bulk of the ship serenely steams past a pleasure yacht, becalmed in the river, waiting for a breeze to bring her to the open sea. Crew members aboard the *Europa* wave greetings to the lone yachtsman from the well deck and in the background lies the red painted Wessel pilot boat.

The *Europa* has probably just picked up her pilot to guide her into the port of Bremerhaven after her crossing from New York and the glow of the setting sun warmly bathes the ship in a golden light. Even though she is moving slowly she creates the impression of enormous pent up power.

This is a subdued painting of a subject which could be overwhelming but the artist has softened the image with his clever use of colour and composition. The counterpoint of the vulnerable sail boat brings to the painting a human dimension which only adds to the majesty of the event.

by Walter Zeeden
Oil on canvas 40" x 30"
Courtesy of the German Ships Museum, Bremerhaven

Britannic

This painting commemorates a scene once familiar to Liverpool. *Britannic* looks much as she did when first I saw her. The artist has provided clues to show what is happening and when. He has chronicled a moment which dates the action as between June 1930, the time of her maiden voyage, and January 1934 when the White Star Line merged with Cunard. From that date on, the house flags were combined and flown by all the fleet. The *Britannic* here flies only the White Star burgee and is shown in the Mersey heading downstream under tow. She doesn't fly any foreign flag which means she is not heading out to sea but has disembarked her passengers at the Princes landing stage and is now proceeding to her dock, probably Huskisson where her cargo and mail will be unloaded and the turnaround completed in preparation for her next voyage.

As she moves slowly down the river, she dominates her surroundings. The Harland and Wolff profile perfectly balanced on her 700 foot length. She was, at 27,000 tons, one of the worlds biggest motor ships and a perfect example of an ocean aristocrat of the 1930s.

by Derrick Smoothy
Oil on canvas 20" x 30"
Author's collection

Rex

Included here are paintings of both the *Rex* and the *Conte di Savoia* not only because of the interest in the ships themselves but because they were found, quite by chance, hanging side by side on the walls of a gallery in New York.

They were both painted in the 1980s, by artists who painted the ships some thousands of miles apart, quite by coincidence. The paintings become a pair in much the same way as the ships themselves, they too, coming from different creators, found themselves as running mates on the Atlantic.

This painting of the *Rex* shows her as she enters New York harbour on a morning in 1936, passing historic Ellis Island, where countless immigrants, many of them Italians, first stepped on to United States soil.

The ship appears to be exhaling vast amounts of smoke after the exertions of her long voyage from Italy and the artist has brilliantly recreated the atmosphere of lightheartedness which surrounded this Latin beauty.

These paintings represent the exquisite artistry of two men who used colour and texture in different ways, the high quality ensuring their compatibility each to the other. These artists are among those few who must undoubtedly be numbered amongst the great marine masters of this century. The painters who specialise in the majesty inherent in the great liners are as much masters of their art today as those almost deified artists who created the massive sea pieces in the days of sail.

by William Muller
Oil on canvas 24" x 36"
Courtesy of the artist

Conte di Savoia

This painting, by Stephen Card, represents a *tour de force* in ocean liner portraiture. The ship is seen as she leaves the Atlantic flying her company and national flags, symbols of pride, while passing the British colony of Gibraltar. The sea has changed from the Atlantic to the aqua-marine of the sun kissed waters of the Mediterranean.

The power and elegance of this exquisite vessel is made palpably obvious in this painting. You can almost feel the heat of the morning sun and feel the breeze across the decks. It is a painting of great subtlety. Only a mariner can be aware of the nuances involved in such a scene. Not only do we have a sailors eye view of a maritime event, we are here presented with a work by a painter who is a master of his craft. This picture was painted some 50 years after the event. It was done as a tribute by the artist to a ship of distinction which did not live long enough to receive the acclaim which was her due.

by Stephen J. Card
Oil on canvas 20" x 30"
D. Powers collection

The Monarch of Bermuda Meeting the Queen of Bermuda for the First Time On a Morning in March 1933

It is not often that sister ships operating on the same route are seen together in port. Passing each other at sea is usually the only time they are seen in close proximity to each other but occasionally, either through an anomaly in the timetable or when both are seen in the same harbour together, as shown here, due to the positioning voyage of one of them which is the subject for this painting.

Here we see the lovely *Monarch of Bermuda* as she is about to dock in New York after one of her regular voyages from Hamilton. She arrives at her pier at the same moment as her new sister, the *Queen of Bermuda*, completed her delivery voyage from her builders in Britain. Both ships are virtually identical and many people watching the scene assumed that the cleanest looking ship was the newest. But in fact it was the other way around. The *Monarch* had been repainted in honour of the start of the two ship service and was pristine and gleaming.

The brand new *Queen* arriving was a little bedraggled and in need of new paint because of the battering she had received during her transatlantic crossing. The *Monarch of Bermuda* had waited in the lower bay so that she could lead the new *Queen* into Manhattan, and both ships were escorted by a flotilla of tugs into the city. The composition here is unusual for a modern painting taking its inspiration from ship portraits of the 18th century, when it was common practice to show the same vessel from different angles, thus giving an accurate and comprehensive view of the subject.

In this case, however, the subject is two similar but separate ships manoeuvring with the aid of their tugs to adjacent piers. This gives us the opportunity of comparing the perfection of their lines to advantage and offered the artist a golden opportunity to paint a twin portrait, and also a maritime event which was important for the island of Bermuda in the 1930s, opening up, as it did, the potential for mass tourism and economic growth for the Island.

by Stephen Card
Oil on canvas 20" x 30"
Courtesy of H.H. Outerbridge collection

Washington

This dramatic painting is technically a war picture, but as the United States had not yet entered into hostilities against Nazi Germany, it is a picture painted on the fulcrum of time, on the knife edge between an uneasy peace and a fullscale war.

As a neutral, America should have been able to sail the seas without fear of attack on her ships but this was not always the case and, to proclaim their neutrality, her liners went to sea with their national flags emblazoned on their flanks as can be seen here illuminated by the search lights glow on the hull of the United States Line ship SS *Washington*.

This painting depicts the rescue of American sailors from a United States oil tanker which had been torpedoed by an enemy u-boat and sunk without warning, within sight of land. Here we see the beautiful liner hove-to in a calm sea on a star-lit night, picking up the survivors from lifeboats. The *Washington*'s funnels are floodlit and she is blatantly showing lights from her portholes and open decks. No doubt the u-boat is in the vicinity and, even though the American liner is advertising her presence and her neutrality so openly, it must have been a time of extreme tension for all on board, the ship being such a juicy and easy target for an enemy with little time for the niceties of diplomatic rules.

This impressive picture which portrays the tension of the moment so perfectly, is one of the prized possessions in the American Merchant Marine Museum at Kings Point, New York, where it hangs in a place of honour.

by Howard Barclay French
Oil on canvas 50" x 36"
Courtesy of Frank O. Braynard

Normandie

Two liners, above all others, battled to become the best of their age. *Normandie* of France and *Queen Mary* of Great Britain were evenly matched for their rivalry. Both were more or less of the same size, both were capable of record breaking, both were over 1,000 feet long and both were the finest their countries could produce. They competed for the same passengers in the same market and both ships were wonderful. The *Queen Mary* was a traditional looking ship a natural descendant of the previous generation. Her style was solid if not stolid and her so called modern interiors were a riot of expensive high quality bric-a-brac resulting in a massive cosiness which endeared her to her high class clientele. Above all she was the epitome of everything that was associated with aristocratic Britishness and the result was superb.

Normandie was a very different creation altogether. From the first it was decided that she would be a co-ordinated entity designed from keel to masthead to become a symphony of art deco in steel. She was not only modern, she was futuristic and represented a great leap from traditional thinking. The final result was a liner which was an harmonious combination of all aspects of French artistry and engineering skills.

Her design was the brainchild of a brilliant young Russian emigrant named Vladimir Yourkevitch. He was a marine architect of outstanding ability and he dreamed of producing a revolutionary ship which would be the biggest, fastest and most beautiful ever seen. *Normandie*'s underwater design was as revolutionary as was her superstructure. She had a bulbous forefoot which gave added buoyancy and permitted the massive hull to slip through the seas with less resistance than would have been the case on a conventional hull. Her bows were swan shaped, greatly emphasised by the innovative way the hull had been painted. Her foredeck was enclosed by a whaleback construction which presented a smooth surface. Her bridge front and superstructure were streamline as were her three massive pear shaped funnels. Her aft sections were a series of curved terraces which swept down in tiers to end in an elegant spoon stern reminiscent of a bustle.

All in all *Normandie* was a voluptuous, highly feminine, fashionable and very French ship. To successfully express those attributes on canvas is no easy task. So complex was the design of the liner that most paintings of her failed to do her justice, but not this one.

William Muller has allowed his brush to flow and his imagination to flourish. Stateliness, pride, excitement and drama are all miraculously brought to life. This ship towers over her flotilla of tugs. The city itself seems to shrink in her presence as her enormous bulk glides up the Hudson into Manhattan. The scene comes to life and you can feel the excitement experienced by those on the ferry as they crowd the rails to gaze at the suppressed power emanating from the liner. It is the finest painting of that fabled ship the author has ever seen and it is a sensitive rendering showing to perfection the atmosphere of those heady days of transatlantic supership travel.

by William Muller
Oil on canvas 22" x 32"
Courtesy of the artist

Strathmore

Of all contemporary images recorded, none were more evocative of a period than the great pictures of ocean liners painted by Kenneth Shoesmith. He had an uncanny talent for placing on a flat surface the things we all see but vaguely remember. Travel is an activity which heightens our sense of awareness, all our senses seem to be sharpened and we float in an atmosphere charged with emotion. These are the feelings of pleasurable anticipation which this artist has been able to recall.

Perhaps his talent to paint the presence of great ships was due to his ability to grasp those feelings common to us all and in so doing he forces us to recreate them as if we were present at the scene once more. This greatly talented and mostly self taught artist seldom painted easel pictures. His great reputation lay in his ability to create the most beautiful posters for shipping companies ever seen.

He worked mostly for the Royal Mail Line, the company he sailed with when he was an officer in the Merchant Navy. However, his talent as an artist came to the fore and he spent the rest of his life painting. His career as a poster artist was only part of his great talent. Many of his paintings were exhibited in royal artistic venues, and he was commissioned to paint murals aboard the *Queen Mary*, which to him was the high point in his career.

However, it was with his first love, the paintings of great liners in exotic ports, that he excelled and in this painting of the P&O liner *Strathmore* he shows to perfection his ability to recreate the sights, sounds, bustle and even the heat and smell associated with the arrival of a ship, in faraway places.

Here we see the beautiful P&O liner *Strathmore*, bound for Australia, slowly entering Suez. She is surrounded by bum boats, vendors, and the sails of Arab dhows. The blinding whiteness of the ship and of the buildings along the shoreline, with the sapphire blue of the water, all speak of heat and exotic places.

This is a watercolour, heightened by body colour but it gives the strong impression of being an oil. Kenneth Shoesmith has a reputation among modern marine artists as one of the giants, even though his name is not well known to a wider audience. His influence has been enormous on those who paint passenger liners and this example of his talent confirms his position as a leader of 20th century marine art.

by Kenneth Shoesmith
Watercolour on board 21" x 30"
Courtesy of Ulster Museum, Belfast

Queen Mary – A Reign Begins

The tween days are days of quiet contemplation when nothing spectacular seems to happen. The arrival at Long Beach of the *Queen Mary* in 1967 was such a day. Sandwiched between the ending of one life and the beginning of another. So too was the day represented here in this painting by Charles Pears of the *Queen Mary* arriving in Southampton for the first time.

This is a tranquil picture, clear and full of subtle symbolisms. The artist has chosen to show the new ship without a name, perhaps the painting hasn't been finished yet. But in all other respects the scene is exactly as it was on that day, Friday 27th March 1936 at 2.15pm.

The *Queen Mary* is seen being manoeuvred to the entrance of the huge King George V graving dock, especially built to accommodate her and her future sister. She passes the White Star liner *Majestic* dressed overall to honour her. The *Majestic* lies idle, her career over as she waits for a buyer. She was too, at one time, the biggest ship in the world. Built by the Germans as the *Bismark* in 1914 but never to sail under their flag, she was awarded to Britain as part of war reparations and eventually sold to the White Star Line. Here, *Queen Mary* represents the future, *Majestic* represents the past. The painting is not dominated by the ships but by the men waiting to greet her. These men are the dock workers, dressed in their baggy clothes and cloth caps, they represent all the men who, with their sweat, pride and love, built the great liners and gave them vitality. Here they are waiting to guide the *Queen Mary* into her dock to complete the work before she finally sails, filled with the rich, the famous and the ordinary, at the start of a career that was to last for the next thirty-one years.

by Charles Pears
Oil on canvas 65" x 50"
Courtesy of National Maritime Museum, Greenwich

The Final Farewell

A ship as famous as the *Queen Mary* not only attracted the attention of writers, she was also the subject for many artists.

In this painting, by Derrick Smoothy, the great vessel is seen leaving New York for the last time on September 22nd 1967. It is a picture representing the end of an era. Here the ship sails from Manhattan escorted by three Moran tugs. They are straining to keep up with her as she picks up speed. She had departed from the familiar Cunard pier at noon, to the sounds of horns and the cheers of a large crowd gathered there to bid her farewell.

From her main mast she flies her enormous paying off pennant. This red white and blue ribbon was 310 feet long – ten feet for every year of service. She is dressed overall and smoke streams from her enormous Cunard orange red funnels. The skyscrapers of Manhattan are receding in the background as the ship points her bows eastwards for the last time.

by Derrick Smoothy
Oil on canvas 36" x 24"
Courtesy of the Simon Kendall collection

Amra

This large painting, probably intended to commemorate the maiden voyage of the *Amra*, shows her in the Irawaddy River as she approaches the docks at Rangoon. A golden spire of a Burmese temple in the background sets the scene as the ship, herself small at only 8,314 tons, is shown towering over all she surveys like a giant.

Perhaps a slightly odd painting as the impression of great size and power is disconcerting and out of proportion to the actual size of the vessel. We can only assume the artist has deliberately emphasised the importance of the ship depicting her as a symbol of power. The puny native craft emphasise the dominance of the British steamer in their midst.

by Norman Wilkinson
Oil on canvas 60" x 36"
Courtesy of P&O, London

Nieuw Amsterdam Arriving in New York

European ships sailing to America usually set course for New York, a harbour which was a constant hive of activity and during the heyday of passenger ship travel was the most popular setting used by artists for their paintings. The combination of great liners and great buildings so intimately entwined offered a glamorous scene not equalled anywhere else on earth. The famous transatlantic liners shown there could have been painted leaving or arriving in any one of their home ports, but the impact of the picture would not have been nearly as dramatic. Southampton, Le Harve, Rotterdam, Bremerhaven, Oslo or Genoa, did not present the same aura of excitement to the observer hence the plethora of paintings set within the confines of Manhattan. Each picture so very different from the next but all bearing an instantly recognisable atmosphere.

This painting of the Dutch beauty *Nieuw Amsterdam*, arriving at her Hoboken pier, is a good example of the artistic thinking of the time. For many years the ships of the Holland America line did not dock in New York proper but did so on the New Jersey side of the river, thus presenting the opportunity of getting a panoramic view of the skyscrapers and other ships in the harbour.

The painting shows an early morning arrival, the tide is high and the daily parade of incoming liners is under way. The fleet of Moran tugs were always to be seen scurrying back and forth within the harbour, assisting the great ships into or out of their piers. The time of arrival was usually in the morning and those of sailing would be in the afternoon or evening.

The *Nieuw Amsterdam* in her new grey livery presents a vision of suppressed power as she is turned across the Hudson to be manoeuvred into her dock. The towers of Manhattan are spread out behind her and, almost as if it were a separate painting in miniature, the artist shows the German liner *Berlin* approaching her pier with the Empire State building in the background. The date of this arrival scene is sometime in the mid 1950s.

The *Berlin*, being the first passenger ship to re-open the North-German-Lloyd transatlantic service after the war, only came into service in 1955. She was a ship of 19,000 tons and was the former *Gripsholm* of the Swedish American line built in 1925. The Germans bought her and refurbished her to re-open their traditional Bremerhaven to New York service. Her maiden voyage to New York symbolised the burying of many hatchets and was further proof of the miraculous changes which had developed on the international scene since the ending of the war.

by Stephen Card
Oil on canvas 30" x 20"
Courtesy of the Heritage House Gallery, Bermuda

Mauretania (1939)

All great ships entering spectacular harbours present scenes of drama but somehow nothing quite compares with the beauty and glamour of a liner sailing into the city of New York. This pent-up tension emanating from the skyscrapers and piers filled with famous liners seem to create an atmosphere out of which dreams would be made.

This exciting painting seems to portray these feelings perfectly. It expresses the impression of awe and of wonderment which always seem to inhabit the world of great ships thus creating an atmosphere uniquely their own. So much so that no painting was better suited to become the jacket of this book.

The painting brings together technical skills of both the artist and the mariner. Stephen Card, a sensitive and accomplished painter, is also a working sailor. Being a ship's captain and former Harbour Master of Bermuda, he approaches each painting with an eye for perfection which is obvious in all his work.

In this painting the beautiful new *Mauretania* enters New York harbour at the end of her maiden voyage. Documented history states that she berthed at pier 90 on June 24th 1939 at 9.12 a.m. on a sunny morning. From this information the artist, using charts of the harbour as reference, worked out the position of the sun as it would have been when the ship approached the Battery. From that information he was able to recreate the shadings and shadows falling on the scene with accuracy.

In the written account of her rival in New York it was stated that she was greeted by the new liner *Panama*, outbound for Christobal, and here we see her as she is about to pass the incoming new liner starboard to starboard. *Mauretania* is dressed overall in celebration of her arrival and is already escorted by the Moran tugs detailed to guide her into her pier.

We have been made part of the scene, as the artist intended. The painting epitomises all that is best in modern marine narrative art, no wonder the finest maritime artists seem to be men of the sea for it is their life that they commit to canvas so expressively and accurately. It is thanks to them that we can relive those golden moments of a bygone age frozen forever through the magic of their art.

by Stephen Card
Oil on canvas 30" x 20"
Courtesy of the Heritage House Gallery, Bermuda

America

Occasionally we are reminded of music when looking at a painting, seldom though with modern marines. They are not usually lyrical but this wonderful picture is an exception and as we gaze upon it can almost hear the lush strains of George Gershwin's Rhapsody in Blue. Both seem to have the same feel of languor and sophistication found in exclusive New York supper clubs.

Skyscrapers and ocean liners were the most potent symbols of the twentieth century and here they are together perfectly merged. The razzmatazz and art deco magic of Manhattan throbs in the background as the SS *America* slowly steams out of the glittering rain washed city. The ship seems to sizzle with suppressed yankee vitality as she moves powerfully towards the ocean. She is a vision of a glamorous reality, with just a hint of Broadway, all caught with a glacial clarity in this beautifully atmospheric painting which combines the static power of a city-scape with the elegant fluid movement of a marine. The unusual setting and theatrical lighting is uniquely 20th century. The picture is a tribute to the etheral beauty of the port of New York and of the liners which were once so much a part of its life.

by Stephen J. Card
Oil on canvas 30" x 20"
The author's collection

Queen Elizabeth

This lovely painting was commissioned by Cunard as a tribute to their greatest liner. The *Queen Elizabeth* finally brought the dream of a weekly transatlantic service to a reality for the company. She and her running mate, the fabled *Queen Mary* were the jewels in the crown of Britain's merchant marine. They became the most famous ships in the world and when they were retired the seas seemed empty without them. But a new *Queen* was built to replace them and was ambiguously named *Queen Elizabeth 2* in honour of both her reigning sovereign and the great ship which preceded her.

It is fitting that this fine painting should have been created to hang in a place of honour aboard that ship. The picture shows the *Queen Elizabeth* leaving New York in 1952 followed by the last of the White Star liners *Britannic*, both ships bound for England. In those days there were dozens of ships sailing weekly between New York and Europe, today only one liner is left to carry on the traditions of the past, she is affectionately known as *QE2* and is the last of the great Cunard *Queens* to call New York her second home.

by Stephen Card
Oil on board 24" x 36"
Courtesy of The Cunard Line

Media

This sparkling painting seems to glow with the freshness of a spring day. The lovely Cunarder *Media* is shown as she steams on a south-westerly course, outbound from Liverpool for New York. She is passing the south stack lighthouse off Holy Island, Anglesea, North Wales. Her cargo derricks and rigging have been stowed securely as she reaches her full speed and prepares to go deep sea at last. Her ocean voyage will take a week, during which time 250 first class passengers will be pampered with all the comforts and pleasures synonymous with crossing by Cunard.

The artist has, with his usual brilliance and passion for detail, brought the ship back to life on this canvas. Even going so far as to have the liner flying the blue instead of the red ensign. Knowing that the *Media* was Captain Treasure-Jones first Cunard passenger ship command, and knowing that he was a captain in the Royal Naval Volunteer Reserve, Stephen Card assumed, rightly, that he would choose to sail his ship under the blue ensign, and there it is proudly streaming in the wind. The picture was painted from an account of a voyage undertaken by the author at which time Captain Treasure-Jones was in command.

by Stephen Card
Oil on board 22" x 34"
The author's collection

The Orcades at the Coronation Review

Only three ocean liners were present at the fabulous Spithead naval review held to honour Queen Elizabeth II after her coronation in June 1953. They were the *Strathnaver* of the P&O Line, the *Pretoria Castle* of the Union Castle Line and the *Orcades* of the Orient Line. Each ship representing a company whose history was interwoven with that of the empire itself.

The new Queen was now head of a commonwealth and Queen of many lands but no longer was there an Empress of India. The empire itself was being broken up and reforming into a number of self governing nations. Nevertheless, in 1953, the coronation ceremony and its maritime counterpart, the naval review, did present a vast panorama of colour and pageantry with warships representing millions of subjects living under the British crown. The might of Britain's imperial Navy was still impressive, the world had not yet taken to the skies and the number of ships still sailing the seas was colossal.

The coronation review of 1953 was the last time such a vast fleet would ever be seen together. It was spread out in formal lines stretching for miles between Portsmouth and the Isle of Wight and consisted of 208 warships belonging to the Royal Navies of Britain and her colonies, 52 other vessels representing the merchant services, the coastguards and the fishing fleets, and a fleet of visiting warships belonging to foreign powers which numbered 16 and included battleships, aircraft carriers and heavy cruisers. The total number of ships reviewed by her majesty that day was 280 and it was through this incredible sea of grey that the brightly coloured liners moved, for on that day, filled with static, homage paying ships, the only vessels which sailed was the Royal Navy frigate HMS *Surprise* from which the Queen was to review her fleet, and the three great liners from which her guests would also view the spectacle.

In this painting, the *Orcades* is seen steaming slowly through the long lines of warships. When the review was finished the Queen's ship anchored in the middle of the fleet and the three liners anchored at the head of the contingent of merchant ships. That night her majesty, with the Duke of Edinburgh, boarded the battleship HMS *Vanguard* for dinner. At 10.30 the order went out to light up the fleet and with the turning on of thousands of lights, which traced the shapes of each ship, the sky was simultaneously filled with fireworks display, the like of which had not been seen over the skies of England since before the war.

The Queen and her party returned to HMS *Surprise* just before midnight, there to sleep protected by her navies.

She disembarked the next morning at 9.20 to return to London. Hundreds of thousands of people had lined the shorelines to see the spectacle, not realising it was to be the last time such a vast collection of ships would be seen ever again.

by Howard Jarvis
Oil on Canvas 41" x 30"
Courtesy of P&O, London

Edinburgh Castle

This painting is a splendid example of the work of one of the most famous and prolific marine artists of the 1930s and 1940s. Norman Wilkinson's paintings were commissioned by most of the great British shipping companies of the day and in this picture he has perfectly captured the power and grace of a new liner undergoing her speed trials.

Here we see the *Edinburgh Castle* in 1948 at speed on a breezy November day off the Isle of Arran in the Firth of Clyde. It was here that the 'measured mile' was situated and where most ships determined their actual speed and ran their sea trials. These had to be satisfactorily completed in accordance with the terms of the building contract before the builders could hand them over to their owners. Therefore, in this painting the *Edinburgh Castle* is still the responsibility of Harland and Wolff's shipyards. Only after the completion of these trials would the ship be handed over to the Union Castle Line, ready to enter the service for which she was built.

by Norman Wilkinson
Oil on canvas, 30" x 40"
Courtesy of Caledonia Investments PLC

Himalaya Leaving Tilbury

This large and cooly atmospheric painting shows *Himalaya* leaving Tilbury on October 10th 1969. She was the last of the P&O ships to sail from the familiar landing stage on the Thames, from that date onwards Southampton was to be the company's home port.

This painting creates a mood of sadness as the ship, dressed in bunting, attempts to impart a sense of occasion to the damp, cold autumn day. She is escorted from her berth by tugs but it is not a day of celebration for the port, for this sailing represents the decline in the fortunes of Tilbury which had seen comings and goings of great liners for almost a hundred years. The grey sky is reflected sombrely in the great waters while the industrial drabness of Gravesend broods forlornly in the background, seemingly unaware of the bleak symbolism of the occasion.

This is a painting in the true sense, not merely a portrait of a ship. It is impressionistic in its feeling and creates a great sense of tranquillity and ponderous movement.

by W.E. Thorpe
Oil on canvas 54" x 42"
Courtesy of P&O, London

Chusan at Night

It is not usual for a fully signed painting to be classed as anonymous but in this case it seems to be so, even P&O, from whose collection this picture comes, has no record of where the artist has come from or what his biography might be. A search for his name in many places was to no avail, but the lack of biography in no way lessens the impact and quality of this very fine nocturnal scene.

The picture was painted before *Chusan* acquired her new funnel top in 1952 and shows her as envisaged by her designers. Her traditional silhouette beautifully etched against the night sky. The painting was probably to commemorate the ship's maiden voyage. The title of the work is simply 'Chusan At Night' and probably is not meant to represent her at any specific port. Nevertheless, the painting shows her at anchor lying off a large town under a star studded sky. She floats on a mirror calm sea with her brilliant array of lights reflecting off its surface.

This sight was one which was familiar to thousands of people, either shore bound or privileged to sail, when great ships called at exotic warm water ports around the world. They appeared briefly as majestic visions only to disappear again within a few hours.

The ethereal atmosphere is beautifully recaptured in this highly competent maritime piece which shows it to be the work of a highly trained and skilled marine artist.

by Edward Beckett
Oil on canvas 30" x 40"
Courtesy of P&O, London

United States at Sea

Even today, if you ask anyone what the liner *United States* was famous for, the answer would immediately be she was the fastest liner in the world. So it is appropriate that the painting of that beautiful ocean greyhound should show her as she would have appeared at the height of her glory at sea.

The *United States* is seen sweeping in from the east at high speed through rough seas and at the moment of passing the Ambrose lightship. It is from that point that all transatlantic crossings were measured. In this spirited painting, William Muller has managed to convey a sense of speed coupled with enormous power and beauty. The composition, colour and deft brush work here create an impressionistic painting. The little lightship, obviously is labouring in the rough seas, while the great liner, all buoyant thousand feet of her, forges through them seemingly without effort.

The painting is a lovely study of contrasts – wind, waves, space, colour, clouds and ships – modern maritime art at its best.

by William Muller
Oil on canvas 28" x 40"
Courtesy of the artist

Braemar Castle

The *Braemar Castle* was the last of a trio built in 1952 for the round Africa service of the Union Castle Line. She was also the last ship to be built in the company's post war rebuilding programme. An elegant ship with fine proportions, she was a smaller edition of the company's beautiful mail ships of the period.

The *Braemar Castle* carried passengers and cargo on voyages which were practical, exotic and perfect for seagoing holidays. She carried 552 cabin class passengers in solid comfort without superfluous fripperies and at 17,029 tons was small enough to enter most ports around the continent.

In this painting the ship is seen leaving Mombasa in Kenya. Since sailing from London she has called at Rotterdam, Las Palmas, Ascension, St Helena, Cape Town, Port Elizabeth, Durban, Lourenco Marques, Beira, Dar-es-Salaam, Zanzibar, and Tanga. We see her as she sails for Aden, Suez, Port Said, Genoa, Marseilles, Gibraltar and then back to London. During the course of this two month continental circumnavigation, the ship will have picked up and dropped off passengers and cargo ranging from motor cars, appliances and goods manufactured in Europe, to the poetic cargoes of Africa which included gold, fruit, copper and perhaps diamonds.

Those voyages around Africa were very popular and relatively inexpensive and combined a cruise-like atmosphere enhanced by the flavour of actually being aboard a liner undertaking a regular voyage. But these maritime odysseys were not destined to last throughout the sixties. Their viability came under attack from the advances in air travel, the rise in fuel costs and finally the hammer blow of the closure of the Suez Canal during the Arab Israeli war in June 1967. With the dying of that unique service also ended a great travel experience never to be resurrected.

This large painting perfectly recreates the atmosphere which greeted passengers in any of the African ports. A combination of harbour noises accompanying the movements of ships and dhows, palm trees and vibrant colours shimmering in the heat, all wrapped in a pervading African perfume of coffee and spices and of damp vegetation.

by John Stobart
Oil on canvas 31½" x 48½"
Courtesy of Caledonia Investment PLC

Orsova at Aden

Aden was one of the traditional refuelling stops on the long route from Britain to India and Australia, the heat there was intense and nothing relieved the aridity of its dry mountainous scenery. To passengers and crew alike Aden was a hell-hole to be endured only for as long as it took to load coal and later oil. In this painting by Charles Pears the artist has found beauty in the combination of colour and shapes presented by the vision of the lovely corn-yellow *Orsova* resting on a blue sea with the sun striking the mountains in the background. The stillness and heat are wonderfully suggested and we feel as if we could swelter with those aboard the ship.

Here, *Orsova* is in her original Orient Line colours. In 1966 the company became part of P&O at which time all the ships conformed to P&O livery and lost their distinctive and authorative yellow hulls. This painting was commissioned early in the ship's career and shows her as she was intended to look, her colours complimenting her oddity and making her a beauty.

by Charles Pears
Oil on canvas 40" x 28"
Courtesy of P&O, London

Uganda

Sad paintings are considered to be those which show a ship sailing away. This one certainly conveys melancholy. The once beautiful, gleaming liner is seen here, dirty and forlorn, heading towards the setting sun and oblivion.

The *Uganda* had died in reality at anchor in the far reaches of an English river earlier that day. Only her remains are sailing to the breakers under the name of *Triton*, her soul remains in the memories of those who knew her.

This fine little painting by Stuart Beck is a tribute to all ships which sail on their last voyages to their valhalla, empty, dirty, rust stained and proud.

by Stuart Beck
Oil on board 12½" x 7"
The author's collection

Southern Cross and the Lady Jocylin

This painting is an example of the artist's flight of fancy and represents a mythical coming together of two milestone events in the history of the Shaw Savill and Albion Shipping Company. It is not unusual for artists to fantasise on the meeting at sea of two distinct but separate eras of a company's marine history. Here we have a portrait of the beautiful sailing ship *Lady Jocylin*, which seems to be sailing into the past while the beautiful new steamship *Southern Cross* sails past her and on into the future.

The Furness Withy Shipping Company was, and still is, a combination of companies under whose umbrella sailed great shipping companies of the past, the Shaw Savill and Albion Line being only one great cog in that wheel of enterprise.

The painting, in the opinion of the author, was done before the *Southern Cross* was actually built because the ship in this painting, though similar in many ways and undoubtedly intended to represent the *Southern Cross*, has undulations and curves which are exaggerations of the lines eventually incorporated in the finished ship, the reality being no less beautiful than this artist's vision. Nevertheless, it does show how graceful and novel her design would be.

The picture was commissioned by the company for their own collection to mark the centenary of their first sailing, with the *Lady Jocelyn* and is the only contemporary painting of the *Southern Cross* which could be unearthed for this book. The painting has an additional interest in as much as it was painted by an Australian artist who has chosen to sail these ships in waters familiar to himself. The great seas surrounding Australasia, illuminated by the brightness of sub-tropical light, complement to perfection the new livery which had been chosen by the company for this, their newest liner, the painting vibrates with colour, the power of the steamship contrasting with the silent graceful beauty of the billowing sails worn by her ancestor seems to express the differences between sail and steam beautifully.

by John Allcott
Oil on canvas 20" x 30"
Courtesy of Furness Withy Group

Windsor Castle

John Stobart painted two pictures of the lovely *Windsor Castle* for the Union Castle Line, one of which is a very large and formal painting of the ship arriving in Cape Town. The other, chosen to be reproduced here, is more a loosely painted oil sketch and has a freshness and sense of occasion which is missing in great formal commissions.

In this picture the ship is seen leaving the place of her birth on a dull English day. The scenery of the shipyards is far removed from the colour and tropical glamour which will be her environment for the future. Here, the curves and soft colours of this great liner contrasts with the brutality of the industrial scene she leaves behind. Out of that crucible of steel and fire, she sails into her future, a thing of beauty, wrought by man to bring joy to all who will see her.

This is a simple picture with understated meanings, its informality only serving to enhance the majesty of the occasion.

by John Stobart
Oil on canvas 24" x 20"
Courtesy of Caledonia Investments PLC

Canberra

This painting of *Canberra* shows her in her later years as she imperiously arrives for a visit to Istanbul on one of her Mediterranean cruises.

Externally, the ship is little changed from the day she sailed on her maiden voyage in 1961. She now carries a plaque on her bridge-front as a memorial to her participation in the Falklands War, and forward, port and starboard, she has the P&O logo on her superstructure, placed there in 1987 to commemorate the 150th anniversary of the foundation of the company. It was in that year that this painting was created, and it symbolises the global routes that this wonderful old liner has sailed during her lifetime.

Here she is, in that narrow stretch of water which separates Europe from Asia. The domes and minarets of the exotic city make a romantic backdrop to the bustle of harbour activity. Traditional steam ferries flit between the two continents as *Canberra* prepares to anchor in the Bosphorus with her bows pointing towards Russia.

Soon her passengers will be swarming ashore to sample the Turkish delights awaiting them and from every vantage point in the city the great ship will be seen and admired, especially as night falls when she will be floodlit to proclaim her presence as the last British liner, still sailing, which was built during the hey day of ocean travel.

The artist has, with a lightness of touch, recreated this scene without resorting to photographic realism. The painting is full of life, showing the personality of the ship, beautifully portrayed through the talents of an experienced marine artist, as Mr. Smoothy undoubtedly is.

by Derrick Smoothy
Oil on canvas 20" x 30"
Courtesy of the Simon Kendall collection

QE2

The maiden voyage of a new liner is always an event of great importance and in the days before steamship travel became obsolete the port of New York would welcome a ship as no other city could.

That first entry into Manhattan was always a splendid occasion with fire boats spraying water fountains, tugs and harbour craft dressed overall and screeching a welcome, aircraft swooping overhead and sometimes even dropping flowers onto the new ship.

The traditional welcome was part of New York's folk lore but as the number of ships decreased so too did the enthusiasm of the welcome. But all was not quite finished when the *QE2* finally arrived at the port on her maiden voyage in May 1969, to an old-fashioned New York greeting.

It was a noisy, flamboyant, joyous affair. Not quite the hysteria which greeted her predecessor the *Queen Mary* in 1936, or the silence which accompanied the *Queen Elizabeth* as she secretly entered the harbour after her first wartime dash across the Atlantic in 1940.

Strangely, it was not the day of high drama which prompted William Muller to paint the ship on the occasion of that voyage, but he chose rather to paint her as she left the harbour at the start of her homeward voyage when there were no special celebrations.

The ship is seen as a long, sleek liner with a curved swan's bow and spoon shaped stern. Her single funnel and mast structure, rather puny in comparison to her status, wears no obvious Cunard livery to connect her with her ancestors. A nod has been directed to the past with the name of the company placed upon her superstructure and with one boat and the funnel scoop only being painted in the traditional red.

The *QE2* is seen sailing out of the port with the symbols of that great city prominently placed. A Staten Island ferry passes the Statue of Liberty, the Manhattan skyline now much changed, recedes into the mists and one pugnacious tug seems to be bidding her farewell. This is a quiet and elegant painting and is an important view of the liner as she originally was.

This painting of the *QE2* as she first appeared has been chosen as being more in keeping with the age in which she was created. The ship at that time being designed to deliberately break with the traditional image then being held of passenger ships of the day. It was an attempt to stimulate interest in the growing market of cruising holidays when all that was wonderful in the past was being derided as old fashioned and unwanted.

Thankfully that has now been discounted and the seafaring traditions of yesterday are once more appreciated with the *QE2* herself being transformed, and sailing fully robed and crowned as a Cunard *Queen* at last.

by William Muller
Oil on canvas 24" x 36"
Reproduced by courtesy of Henry O. Smith III

QE2

The shape and purpose of the ocean liner has changed dramatically since the days when the Inman liner *City of New York* sailed out of Liverpool in August 1888 bound for New York and into the 20th century.

Now, one hundred years later, we are at the threshold of another new century and liners no longer fill any practical role. To be sure, bigger and more luxurious passenger ships are being built than have ever been built before but they are destined for the leisure not the transportation system. Only one great liner remains to enter the 21st century, she is the reborn *QE2*. Perhaps not the newest ship sailing in the 1990s but she is the last of the great liners as we define them. A ship still employed regularly to cross the ocean going from A to B and filled with passengers, sadly now only a part time activity for her, but a valid one nevertheless, and for many who don't fly she is still the only way to cross.

The thread of continuity which binds her with the ships of the past and to those new cruise ships which sail into the future, gives the *QE2* a very special place in maritime history. She is a very different vessel to the one which entered New York for the first time in June 1969. Then, she was a new-look *Queen* trying to forget her ties with the past. Today, she has taken on the mantle and the traditions of the great Cunarders of yesterday. Even though virtually rebuilt, and no longer a steamship, she is the worthy successor of those great and noble vessels.

The *QE2* is a noble ship herself and now, resplendent in the traditional Cunard livery, her massive hull sweetly shaped to take the worst of Atlantic storms, she looks familiar to those who knew the great liners of the past. This is the familiarity of shapes developed over centuries to ride the waves and not to fight them. The curves and rhythms wrought from steel and designed to endure incredible stress through decades of ocean voyages, are the lines of a transatlantic liner. And with her massive new funnel, heightened superstructure, hers is a shape which connects the past with the future.

In this new portrait by Stephen Card, commissioned by Cunard as a brochure cover for the 1991 season, the *QE2* is seen leaving Palma during a Mediterranean cruise. But the great Atlantic beckons, and her line voyages from Southampton to New York will continue to serve a purpose, valid still in these frantic days of overcrowded flights to overcrowded destinations.

The *Queen Elizabeth 2* is an exciting ship. She is indeed, not only a product of the 20th century, but is the only ship of her generation destined to point her bows towards a new century.

by Stephen Card
Oils on board 23" x 17"
Courtesy of the Cunard Line

Liners as Royal Yachts

In the days of the great imperial dynasties in Europe, especially those with a maritime history, it was a mark of splendour for the sovereign to travel overseas aboard his own yacht. These vessels grew in stature until finally they emerged as ships possessing proportions equal to any but the largest liners of their day. The most impressive of these royal palaces afloat were those of Russia, Germany and Great Britain. They were named *Standart Hohenzollern* and *Victoria and Albert*. Tsars, Kaisers and Kings would sail triumphantly to each others realms, there to be greeted with great pomp and naval reviews, designed to impress each other with the might of their fleets. Less often a monarch would sail to his lands and dominions across the world to show himself to his subject peoples.

Of them all, none shone as brightly as the monarchy of the United Kingdom. It was especially so in the 19th century when she was the centre of the largest maritime empire in the world. Great Britain ruled the seas with a fleet of ships both naval and merchant, created to unite and protect an empire scattered over every ocean on the planet. Africa, India, Asia, Australasia, Polynesia, America and the Caribbean, all had their British colonies and dominions within their sphere.

The apogee of this vast empire came during the reign of Queen Victoria, at the latter end of the 19th century. She was by then an old lady and the question of her sailing to her overseas possessions wasn't even considered. She loved her yachts but the longest voyage undertaken by her was to the continent of Europe and, on occasion, Ireland. It was left to her son, King Edward VII, to arrange overdue royal visits. He did not travel overseas himself but sent his heir, the Duke of York with the Duchess, in his place.

When the time came to implement these great regal voyages it was decided that the royal yacht was too old and too unstable to be entrusted to trans-oceanic passages. Therefore, the first of a few very special liners were chosen to be chartered from their owners and refurbished to regal standard. To each was granted the highest honour of becoming a temporary royal yacht, fit to carry the sovereign or his family.

Between the years 1901 and 1953, five reigning kings and queens ruled the empire and four great ocean liners were thus honoured.

A few other liners sailed on voyages carrying members of the royal family but they were never described as yachts, even though they flew the royal standard for the duration of those voyages. This section is dedicated only to the four special ships and to the paintings completed while they were in the exclusive service of their sovereign. Included also are the two lovely royal yachts themselves. It was between the ending of one and the commencing of the other, that a need for substitutes was necessary. It was that unusual situation which created those unique and romantic marine Cinderellas.

The Royal Yacht Victoria and Albert III 1899-1955

The Royal Yacht *Victoria and Albert*, shown in this painting, was the third ship to bear that famous name and was by far the most splendid. She was built to replace the existing yacht which was thought to be unworthy of the might which the monarchy now represented. The century was drawing to a close and the Queen herself was nearing the end of her life when her new yacht was built. Rumours of its instability convinced her never to board it, fabulous though it was.

The reign of Edward VII, coupled with a need for naval shows of strength, created the setting for many maritime occasions in which the *Victoria and Albert* played her regal part. She was a truly Edwardian symbol but was never to venture on the epic voyages which was henceforth to be part of royal life. Sumptuously equipped she was the most magnificent of all the European floating palaces, a beautiful, three masted, twin funnelled vessel embellished with gilded scroll work, she was an impressive sight when, with flags flying and dressed overall, she made her entrance into countless harbours around the coasts of the United Kingdom and those across the Channel but as impressive as she was, she proved unsuitable for trans-oceanic voyages. Therefore, the practice of chartering ocean liners for use as temporary royal yachts began. It is for this reason that this particular painting of the *Victoria and Albert*, shown entering Belfast on a state occasion, is included. Here she is seen passing the gaunt, skeletal cranes of Harland and Wolff's shipyard which act as a counterpoint to the splendid events taking place in their shadows.

by Kenneth Shoesmith
Watercolour on board 18" x 30"
Courtesy of the Ulster Museum

HMS Ophir Sailing from Portsmouth

This very spirited painting is typical of marine art developed from the great naval scenes in the days of sail. The artist has filled his canvas with movement, the sea is alive with boats and tugs, escorting this temporary royal yacht out of Portsmouth Harbour on March 16th 1901. She is bound for a circumnavigation of the globe, carrying the Duke and Duchess of York on their first tour of the Empire.

This event took place virtually at the start of the Edwardian era, the flags and bunting fly to celebrate the departure of the heir to the throne from British waters and the sense of pride and excitement generated by the start of the new reign of King Edward VII can be felt.

As the *Ophir* sails out of the port she is seen passing HMS *Victory*, Nelson's ship and still the flagship of the British Royal Navy. This great sailing battleship, afloat then, and seen here dressed overall has her yards manned by her crew in celebration of the event. This painting seems to emit the freshness of wind and salt water and is a beautiful example of traditional maritime art. It is a testament to the feeling prevalent at that time, which was for Great Britain, the pinnacle of her great imperial days.

by Murray Paddy
Oil on canvas 20" x 30"
Courtesy of P&O, London

HMS Balmoral Castle

This beautifully uncluttered painting shows the temporary Royal Yacht steaming from Portsmouth on October 11th 1910. The shadows and clouds of a grey English autumnal day seem to blend with the white ship whose twin yellow funnels match that of the tug which tows it giving the only gleam of colour to the picture.

HMS *Victory* is to the right of the canvas, not dressed overall and the few observers in their rowing boats seem oblivious to the Royal departure. This was an event worthy of recording but not, it seems, generating much excitement.

Nevertheless, it makes for a dignified and lovely marine painting and shows Norman Wilkinson at his lyrical best.

by Norman Wilkinson
Oil on canvas 27" x 16"
Courtesy of Caledonia Investments PLC

HMS Medina

as a Royal Yacht sailing from Portsmouth bound for India

This is one of the best known paintings of a liner in royal yacht livery and is one that is filled with the glory expected of such a scene.

Here we have the ship sailing from England with the King Emperor aboard, bound for the great durbar, the colour, the harbour activity and the composition on the panoramic canvas all perfectly chronicle a great day in British history with artistry worthy of the old masters.

by William Wyllie
Oil on canvas 89" x 52"
Courtesy of P&O, London

Gothic

as a Royal Yacht

This spirited portrait of *Gothic* in the pacific, shows her as she steams away from the Island of Tonga under the watchful eye of the cruiser *Black Prince*.

This Royal New Zealand Navy ship escorted the Queen throughout her New Zealand tour and only relinquished that honour when relieved on approaching Australian waters, at which time units of the Royal Australian Navy took up the escort duty. They included the aircraft carrier *Vengeance*, two destroyers and a cruiser. As the Queen progressed around the world, each of Her Majesty's navies in turn took up the baton of protection until finally, aboard her own yacht *Britannia*, and under the protection of the Royal Navy, she finished her tour in the familiar waters of the Thames at the pool of London the centre of her own capital.

by Charles Pears
Oil on canvas 20" x 30"
by gracious permission of HM The Queen

113

Her Majesty's Yacht Britannia

at Tower Pier 1954

Artistic traditions of the 18th century are incorporated in this beautifully composed painting. Though the subject is rooted in the mid 20th century, the overall feeling the picture recreates is one of historic continuity.

Here we see a maritime royal homecoming – Her Majesty, Queen Elizabeth II, arriving back in her capital after an epic voyage around the world. The Queen undertook her tour of the Commonwealth less than a year after her coronation and the hopes of the new reign are symbolised by the regal elegance of the new Royal Yacht *Britannia* bearing her majesty for the first time into the heart of her realm, escorted by ships of the Royal Navy.

Leslie Wilcox was commissioned to paint this splendid occasion and he has succeeded in bringing the scene to life with an eye for detail which makes for a compelling picture. The crowds of people, each one a miniature portrait, and the view of the city at the water's edge with the Tower of London and the open bascules of Tower Bridge beyond, seem to exude excitement as the lovely ship, dressed overall in her flags of royal symbolism, makes her stately progress into the pool of London. The focus for the painting is the view of the tiny figures of the Queen and her family greeting the crowds from the top of the ship's bridge. That little detail, expresses the human element of this state occasion and gives it the warmth of a personal dimension which otherwise would have been lacking. This delightful painting now hangs in the place of honour aboard *Britannia* herself and it is with the gracious permission of Her Majesty that this reproduction is included here.

by Leslie Wilcox
Oil on canvas 28" x 52"
By Gracious Permission of Her Majesty the Queen

Liners in War Paint

It is a sad reflection on civilisation that the genius of mans creativity which is capable of producing life enhancing works of art, is also responsible for creating the horrors of war. This partnership of creation and destruction touches every corner of human endeavour and is as much a part of the history of ships as it is of the history of man.

Some great liners, supposedly built for purposes exclusively peaceful, were subjected by all belligerents to the brutality of being used as weapons in times of war, ill suited as they were for the job. They were victims more often than victors in battle. Their exploits were quietly performed and, due to their great size and inherent lack of protection, were always vulnerable to destruction.

Warships, built to induce fear, wore the colours of conflict from the beginning of their lives. Merchant ships, on the other hand, especially passenger liners, were, in times of hostility, shorn of their glitter and repainted in an attempt to conceal their identity. Some weird and wonderful colour schemes were devised to confuse the enemy, especially during the First World War when, for the first time in history, mankind was confronted with the savagery of all out war.

Politeness and honour became things of the past and instead came perfidy, stealth and mass destruction. Civilians were now as involved as armies. Ships which plied their peaceful trade on the surface of the seas were subject to annihilation from below and from the air above. These new dangers prompted thoughts about the possibilities of disguising them by the simple use of paint. In Britain many artists were called on to solve the problem, among whom was the famous marine artist Norman Wilkinson. It was he who devised a new method of camouflage in 1915. This was the brilliant idea of using multi-colour designs which were intended to confuse an enemy. The end result was startling. Innovators of the art world, who were working on new movements in painting such as abstraction, were quick to see the possibilities of adapting these styles for subterfuge. The result of these was to transform the huge liners into the largest moving murals ever created. The sight of a great ship at sea completely covered by zig-zag lines and shadings of multi-coloured dazzle paint must have been bizarre and magnificent. Pablo Picasso considered these war time experiments a by-product of cubism.

However, the effectiveness of this extreme paint work in deterring an attack was doubtful and by the outbreak of the Second World War it was decided by the admiralty not to repeat the experiment. Plain grey was to be the battledress worn by most ships in the future when the bright colours of peace were once more covered over. Even the greatest liner of all time, born into a world on the brink of conflict, sailed on her maiden voyage in secrecy, unfinished and under veils of grey, to New York.

The *Queen Elizabeth* was to be almost six years old before donning her coronation robes of Cunard splendour. She and her consorts were to sail those hostile seas appearing as spectres, doing so with such grandeur as to make the savagery around them seem unworthy of their participation. Many great liners were destined never to sail again in peacetime and few came through unscathed. Their crews, only familiar with the brotherhood of life at sea in peace, quickly had to learn about the grim realities of war. The beautiful ships, once famous and now sailing incognito, carried tens of thousands of troops to the battlefields but for too many of them there would be no ticket home again.

Many fine paintings were completed during those appalling wars, expressing the dignity and vulnerability of the ships to perfection. No book showing the art of the liner would be complete without them and this section is but a sample of the great work done during those terrible years.

Dazzle in Drydock

The strange cubist shapes of dazzle camouflage are seen here in close-up, the idea of Norman Wilkinson during the First World War, it was put into practice by the Royal Navy and also the United States. The intention was to confuse an enemy submarine as to the true direction a ship was sailing. This weird paintwork produced some remarkable visual results but the practical results were harder to determine and the practice was dropped in the Second World War.

by John Everett
Oil on board 20" x 24"
Courtesy of National Maritime Museum, London

Medina with War Ships

There is no title to this painting but it is believed to depict an event which perhaps prompted the artist to record what was to be the liner's last sighting at sea before her own destruction.

Medina was the last of P&O's great series of M Class ships built before the First World War. She made her maiden voyage as a royal yacht carrying King George V and Queen Mary to their coronation as Emperor and Empress of India in 1912. After that exalted voyage, she returned to her true vocation as a mail ship on the Australia route, sailing via India.

She was not destined for a long life, even though during the war she never came out of her peacetime livery and passenger service. Her last voyage from India ended in disaster, almost at her own doorstep. She had made her usual mail call at Plymouth, disembarking some passengers before sailing on the last coast-wise leg to Tilbury on 28th April 1917. As she forged up the channel she passed a flotilla of British warships heading south. The time was logged for that meeting as 5.30pm.

It is believed this meeting is the subject of Arthur Burgess's painting. It is a picture full of power, life and purpose, showing the liner heading for home, seemingly secure within the sights of the Royal Navy. But her fate lay waiting a mere half an hour later. *Medina* was then attacked and sunk by a torpedo from the German submarine U31 and by 7.15 that evening had disappeared beneath the waves. The destroyers, HMS *Spitfire* and HMS *Laurel*, possibly those depicted in the painting, returned to help the stricken ship but to no avail. Her passengers and crew were taken off by them and other boats in the area without further loss of life, sadly the fourth engineer and four firemen were killed by the explosion as they toiled in the bowels of the ship.

Amongst her passengers for her voyage from India was Lord Carmichael, returning to England from his governorship of Bengal. He had on board with him his personal belongings including works of art, oriental artifacts and manuscripts, collected during his years as an administrator of the raj. All these went down with the ship.

An interesting footnote to the story is that seventy-one years later, some of those possessions were raised and, with other souvenirs of a famous liner, were sold at auction in England on May 26th 1988. Surprisingly, little was recorded of this sale which represented the final chapter in the life of a renowned ship which at one time was at the very heart of great imperial events.

by Arthur Burgess
Oil on canvas 28" x 22"
Courtesy of P&O, London

Leviathan

This unusual painting shows the power the sea has over all things great or small. Seldom does an artist take the opportunity of showing a great passenger liner in mid-ocean battling through such immense waves. If such a sight were presented to prospective passengers, none would ever set foot aboard a ship again. But, of course, ships did, and do, encounter similar conditions, even though, perhaps, this is exaggerated somewhat.

Frederick Waugh specialised in stormy ocean pictures and he has let his imagination run wild with this one. Here we see one of the world's biggest ships, almost miniaturised by the huge scale and power of the seas it is encountering. So violent and wild are they that we almost lose the destroyer heaving in the foreground, and practically hidden by the giant waves.

The painting is an allegory of the insignificance of man and his creations when faced with nature at its most violent. Here we are shown how puny he really is. We dwarf ourselves with the enormous things we build but they, in turn, are dwarfed by the immensity of nature.

The *Leviathan* is shown in dazzle paint during the war when she was a troopship. Her dangers are not only the storms she is battling but in calmer waters she will be in danger from enemy submarines too, hence the escort of a destroyer. But for now the sea is the enemy of friend and foe alike.

The painting was presented to Captain Harold Cunningham, master of the *Leviathan* when he retired in the early 1930s. His two daughters presented it to the American Merchant Marine Museum in 1989, where it hangs today in the *Leviathan* gallery as a memorial to one of the world's most remarkable liners.

by Frederick Judd Waugh
Oil on canvas 50" x 36"
Courtesy of the American Merchant Marine Museum, Kings Point, New York

121

Jervis Bay

This large panoramic picture is a perfect example of modern, narrative, marine art, painted within the traditional concepts of the past.

Originally, the basic idea behind any naval painting was its ability to depict power and heroism. They were intended as historical, visual records, created with a strong bias towards propaganda, and usually commissioned by the King or by the admiralty, very much as government photography and television reporting is commissioned today in times of war. Those traditions were developed from the Dutch maritime artists of the 17th century and progressed through to the great British naval paintings of the 18th and 19th centuries. Those battle set pieces created by Willem van de Velde, Peter Monamy and Nicholas Pocock, were the forerunners of the marine painters of the modern era.

Montague Dawson, being in direct descent to the masters of the past, has, in this great work, shown us the pride, bravery and patriotism which were present during the saga of the *Jervis Bay*'s action in 1940. His artistic license has resulted in a painting which conveys, as no other medium can, the sweep of distance and the atmosphere and coldness of that vast ocean. The approaching menace of the enemy and the fearful vulnerability of the fleeing convoy too, is miraculously created. But, above all, it shows the pugnacious and purposeful attitude of the frail *Jervis Bay* herself.

This is not a painting showing national power but it is a painting which shows the national pride and purpose which was so sorely needed at that time. As such, it is a highly successful work of art, both technically and emotionally, and must surely rank as one of the finest naval paintings to come out of the Second World War.

by Montague Dawson
Oil on canvas 77" x 41"
Courtesy of the Furness Withy Group

Rawalpindi

How vulnerable *Rawalpindi* looks in this painting by Norman Wilkinson. The tall, elegant shape of an ocean liner looks completely out of place in such a setting. She leans to a turn, smoke pouring from her funnel, her guns fire in defiance as the *Scharnhorst*, coming up behind, and the *Gneisenau* ahead, close the range. They are pounding her into oblivion.

The painting, however, differs from the official account in as much as the ships are seen clearly with the wind blowing. All flags are flying crisply and the heavy smoke is being whipped across the scene like a funeral pyre. The sea is rough, not quite the run for a fog bank or the grim shapes of the battle cruisers emerging from mists as recounted in the story. This is a narrative painting and the artist has taken artistic license and permitted himself to show the action in a highly dramatised form. Here is only a suggestion of greyness and mistiness. But there is also a crispness. You can almost hear the crack and roar of the gun fire.

The clarity of the scene, as imagined by the artist, tells us more of the heroism involved than if it were told through the softness of mists and the painting is better because of it.

by Norman Wilkinson
Oil on canvas 60" x 36"
Courtesy of P&O, London

Rangitata

In this painting the *Rangitata* is seen in her grey war paint escorted by tugs while entering port. She was converted to a troop transport in 1940 with her sisters *Rangitiki* and *Rangitane* and they could carry 2,600 troops.

The *Rangitiki* had a lucky escape when the convoy she was part of was attacked in mid Atlantic by the German pocket battleship *Admiral Sheer* on November 5th 1940. It was only through the extraordinary heroism of their escort, the armed merchantmen *Jervis Bay*, that the convoy was able to scatter and disperse, *Rangitiki* being one of the lucky ships to escape.

The third sister was not so lucky, she was intercepted off the New Zealand coast by the German auxiliary cruisers *Orion* and *Komet* on November 27th 1940. The *Rangitane* was shelled and badly damaged then sunk by torpedoes. 299 survivors were taken aboard the enemy ships, and 16 men were killed in the attack.

This painting, in its tones of greys and browns, expresses the lonely and unfussed comings and goings of great liners during the dangerous and sad days of war. They were the backbone of Britain's fight for survival, bringing in the food and supplies to keep the nation from dying, as well as carrying the thousands of troops to the theatres of war around the world.

by Arthur James Burgess
Oil on canvas 36" x 30"
Courtesy of the National Maritime Museum, Greenwich

Home From War

The incredible chain of events which led to *Canberra* suddenly becoming part of Britain's war machine in 1982 is best chronicled by Neil McCart in his book P&O's Canberra published in 1989 by Kingfisher. He explains the run up to events and the dangerous mission itself in great detail. Suffice it to say here that, after the Argentine Military Junta annexed the British colony of the Falkland Islands in April 1982, claiming Argentine sovereignty through means of a full scale invasion and occupation of the islands, Britain decided that the tweaking of the lion's tail could not be ignored and so set in motion plans to retake her possession of 150 years.

This was an option which Argentina had not counted on. They, being convinced that Britain's days of military intervention in imperial affairs was over, had planned the entire operation assuming that a severe rap on the knuckles, diplomatically and economically, would be all that Britain would, or could, inflict upon them. But they did not count on British pride. Losing her empire through nationalistic self-determination was one thing, but a full scale invasion of a British possession by a foreign dictatorship was quite another and too much to bear.

Therefore, when demands to the aggressor to go back from whence they came fell on deaf ears, it was decided to mount a full scale military operation to regain possession of the islands. This necessitated the forming of a task force to sail from Britain. The speed with which it was executed amazed everyone. *Canberra* was notified towards the end of her 1982 world cruise that she was going to be requisitioned by the admiralty and when she arrived in Southampton at 7.30 on the morning of April 7th, a large contingent of workmen swarmed aboard her to prepare her for war. Virtually all the plans had been finished before *Canberra* arrived in England and troops were in Southampton already prepared to sail.

In a little over two days the ship had been fitted with landing pads for helicopters, interior modifications had been carried out and, on April 9th, filled to capacity with troops, she sailed from England bound for the uncertainties in the South Atlantic. Her voyage south was interrupted by fuel stops at Freetown in Sierra Leone and at Ascension Island where she lay for sixteen days hoping for a diplomatic solution to the conflict. That was not to be and, on May 6th, *Canberra* sailed, in convoy with eighteen other ships, to do battle in the Falklands, carrying her troops of 40 and 42 Commando, Royal Marines and the Third Batallion of the Parachute Regiment.

The great ship, now nicknamed *The great white whale* by her non-paying passengers, anchored in San Carlos water on 21st May and immediately started disembarking her troops. A couple of hours later she came under attack by enemy planes. She, and other vessels of the task force, were repeatedly under fire until mid afternoon. She left her anchorage undamaged before midnight and sailed for safer waters off Port Stanley. From there she proceeded to South Georgia for a rendezvous with Cunard's *QE2* and embarked troops from that ship for San Carlos once more.

After a few weeks of fierce fighting and constant air attack, the Argentine invasion forces surrendered finally and thousands of prisoners were repatriated to Argentina. *Canberra*, after being guaranteed safe conduct, sailed with over 5,000 prisoners aboard, for Puerto Mandrin, arriving there on June 19th. Her last task was to return to Port Stanley to embark part of the victorious army for the happy voyage home.

She arrived back in Southampton on July 11th to a tumultuous reception and, in this painting, Roger Desoutter shows her as she enters her home port escorted by an armada of small boats. She is rust stained and war weary, her crew and complement of fighting men crowd every vantage point on her decks to watch this great pageant unfolding before them. The conversion of *Canberra*'s upper decks for use as helicopter pads can be seen above the broad windows of the Crows Nest bar forward and also amidships. The satellite navigation dome, fitted as part of the electronic fitments for war, can be seen at the base of her mast. The atmosphere of pent-up emotion can clearly be felt in this evocative and highly charged emotional picture.

The composition of this painting is very similar to that which Derrick Smoothy chose, showing *Canberra*, swan-like and sparkling, again entering a cruise port some six years later. Hopefully, she will go down in history as the last passenger liner to be requisitioned in the midst of a peaceful life, to sail on a voyage to war no matter how victorious it should turn out to be.

by Roger Desoutter
Oil on canvas 33" x 24"
Courtesy of P&O, London

Liners as Artistic Inspiration

The key word in all art forms is communication. That is the focus for the interaction between artist and appreciator, without which art cannot live, for it has no purpose. It is a communication between people that has no barriers, no boundaries in time, place or language. This is the measure of the true value of a work of art.

Many artists do not restrict themselves to the recreation of recognisable objects, their work having little to do with the narrative or portraiture. These artists have the ability to express thought, feeling and inner vision, using only colour and shape. They are categorised by the methods in which they paint, names are found to describe their styles, such as impressionism, cubism, vorticism or abstract expressionism. These styles represent the way artists interpret life as it changes. Traditional or futuristic, they can express the world around us in symbolic terms and great is the beauty they create.

Not only established marine artists painted ships. Others also found the subject fascinating. The inevitable excitement and drama which always accompanied the movements of those beautiful monsters was filled with colour and shapes which demanded artistic attention. A ship may only be the sum total of its parts but those parts in themselves are also things of beauty. Funnels, masts, ventilators and curved bows were made for interesting pictures. Launchings, dockings, sailings and ports were the stuff of dreams and these too inspired artists to paint. A few of these pictures are included here, to illustrate the endless artistic possibilities inherent in that lost world of the ocean liner.

Most of the artists who painted the pictures reproduced in this book are unknown outside a small circle of marine art connoisseurs. The pictures are scattered throughout the world and have never before been seen together. Hopefully this publication helps to bring their beauty to a wider audience, who can, at last enjoy this wonderful and neglected art form.

Dunottar Castle

In this tiny oil, which was painted at the same time as a larger one called 'The Departure', we see the excitement and hub-bub surrounding the passenger ships of the early 20th century. The subject was most probably picked because of the news value of the day – the *Dunottar Castle* being the first ship of the Castle Line to carry mails from Southampton to Cape Town in 1891. She was also the first ship in the company to have two funnels.

This is not a ships portrait, but is an artist's interpretation of an exciting event, most skilfully done and typical of the strong style and boldness found in Frank Brangwyn's work.

He was not a marine artist as such, but found his inspiration among the docks, shipyards and industrial sites which, in the early 20th century, were places of high excitement and dramatic events.

by Sir Frank Brangwyn
Oil on canvas 7" x 10"
Courtesy of Caledonia Investments PLC

The Mauretania in the Mersey

Frank Copnall was primarily a portrait painter and as such exhibited in the Royal Academy many times. This picture is a fine example of British impressionism, a style of painting originally created by the great Claude Monet in France at the latter part of the 19th century.

The *Mauretania* was delivered to the Cunard Line in Liverpool on November 7th 1907 and her first appearance in that port was an occasion of great importance. She was the second ship of a phenomenal pair. Her sister, the *Lusitania*, having been in service for the previous three months, had already established herself as the fastest and biggest liner in the world and in this painting we see her twin promising to be even faster and more magnificent.

To a local artist like Frank Copnall, the scene must have been almost irresistible. You can feel his excitement in the quick brush strokes and his lightness of touch. The mistiness of an autumn day is brightened by the crimson of those four towering funnels and the entire painting expresses majesty and pride. It is a lovely example of a painter taking pleasure in his subject.

This is a lovely painting, expressing the essence of a fabulous liner effortlessly imposing her personality on her surroundings.

by Frank Copnall
Oil on canvas 21" x 31"
Courtesy of The National Maritime Museum, London

The Titanic Fitting Out

This almost black painting by Charles Dixon has been included because it is believed to be the only contemporary picture of the *Titanic* painted from life. It seems prophetic that the scene was painted at night, illuminated only faintly by electric light. This was how the ship probably looked as she lay dead in the water, slowly filling by the bows after her collision with an iceberg.

Here we see the *Titanic* being fitted out at the Harland and Wolff shipyard in Belfast in March 1912. Men are working around the clock to get her ready for her maiden voyage. The liner is a hive of activity. Furniture, carpets, kitchens and carvings are all being placed in their pre-designed positions to make her the most magnificent ship in the world, tragically, all to become wreckage a few weeks later.

The painting is very dark and is filled with menace. Charles Dixon usually painted scenes of atmospheric smokiness, his watercolours sometimes being of a sparkling brightness. This is a unique interpretation of a ship preparing for what was supposed to be her joyous entry into service, but in retrospect no optimism is expressed here, only the loneliness of a sad prophecy.

by Charles Dixon
Watercolour on paper 18" x 12"
Courtesy of the Ulster Transport Museum

Titanic

The Sea Hath Spoken

The following is a description of the painting by the artist himself.

It shows the port side of the ship, the first funnel, and early activity at about 1.50 am on April 15th 1912.

Boat 6, containing Mrs J.J. (Molly) Brown, Mrs Meyer (daughter of the founder of Saks Fifth Avenue), Major Arthur Peuchen, and lookout Frederick Fleet who first sighted the iceberg, … is in the foreground.

Boat 4 can be seen hanging against the side of the ship, being filled from A Deck by 2nd Officer Lightoller. Boat 4 was the last lifeboat (excluding collapsibles) to leave the port side of the ship, at about 1.55 am. The boat contains Mrs Astor, Mrs Carter, Mrs Clark, Mrs Ryerson, Mrs Thayer, Mrs Widener, among others. No lifeboat held a more influential circle of women.

The *Titanic* is listing to port at this time, the fore-castle just about to become awash. It was shortly after this that the ship began to sink much more rapidly and in fact the occupants in Boat 4 were quite concerned that they get away from the ship as quickly as possible, so quickly was the vessel now plunging under. Wireless operators Jack Phillips and Harold Bride are working frantically to alert nearby shipping of the disaster. The four antenna lead wires can be seen rising to the aerial overhead. Just abaft that is the protective housing over the forward first-class staircase and dome, aglow with light. A few minutes before, the last of eight distress rockets was fired high into the air from the bridge. At water level, the two sets of tall rectangular windows are the main first-class entry doors in the side of the ship, just forward of the reception room on D Deck, which is now beginning to flood.

Engelhardt collapsible boat D has just been manoeuvred into launch position at the forward end of the port Boat Deck. It will be the very last boat lowered by falls at 2.05 am. In a few moments, the soon-to-be famous Navratil children would be placed in this collapsible by their father and other notables such as Mrs Henry B. Harris and Hugh Woolner. The boat would be filled with the assistance of Lightoller, as was Boat 4.

Many portholes to the first-class staterooms on C Deck can be seen to be open, a result of curious passengers leaning out of them to see why the ship had stopped shortly after the collision with the ice. Indeed, these open ports remain so today, photographed by Dr Robert Ballard and his team in 1986 after his discovery of the wreck.

by Ken Marschall
Acrylics on canvas 18" x 24"
Commissioned by Dennis Kromm

Blue Funnel in Shanghai

Of all the exotic ports in the world to which she could sail, a ship bound for Shanghai carried with her a special aura of adventure. In those romantic days, not too many years ago, when China was as remote as a fantasy. No place on earth could have been more foreign or strange to European eyes and the name Shanghai conjured up visions of silks, jades, colours and smells. Exotic and mysterious were the words used to describe that far off international conclave on the coast of China. Books and movies were set there and the imagination could soar at the prospect of the intrigues taking place on its famous Bund and infamous docks.

Kenneth Shoesmith, with the vivid imagination of an artist and the practical experience of a seaman, has combined those qualities into this painting, which literally bursts upon the senses with the power of a visual explosion. All the preconceived notions we may have about Shanghai in the inter-war years are here to see for ourselves. The artist brings us to his sailors port, the great steamer is almost lost in the excitement and hub-bub of oriental sights and sounds. The heat can almost be felt, the sounds heard and the odours smelled and we expect to be jostled in the crush of activity.

The painting is very much a recreation of an art deco world and even though it was painted as an easel picture, it has much of the quality the artist used for his large decorative piece commissioned for the drawing room aboard the *Queen Mary* in 1935 which thankfully is still in place aboard the ship today.

The international port of Shanghai was administered by the great powers and China herself held no sway there. All the great maritime nations traded with that city and the goods of China poured from its docks into freighters bound for all points of the compass. Great passenger liners from Europe were familiar sights as they sailed the Yangtze and into its narrower tributary the Whang Pu there to tie up at the wharfs of the sophisticated city. These great ships, filled with administrators, traders, tourists and missionaries, were for years part of the skyline of Shanghai. To the sailor it was one of the world's fabled ports, known for its waterfront bars, girls and fist fights. Ships of the British merchant navy were always in port – Britain had the biggest fleet in the world and her sphere of influence was the globe itself.

One of the most important shipping companies was that of Alfred Holt, sailing out of Liverpool and known as the Blue Funnel Line. Their ships were distinctive, not only because of the colour of the funnel but because of the silhouette of the ships themselves. But this rusting freighter, sporting its blue funnel, hardly seems a likely representation of the pristine yacht-like vessels of the Blue Funnel Line.

This ship is the antithesis of the glamorous liner. She is the *Ixion* built in 1912, probably carrying 600 steerage passengers and represents the other side of the coin in the days of ocean travel. The inclusion of this painting in a book devoted to passenger liners, breaks with a self-imposed discipline. However, the world of passengers on cargo ships could be one of quiet glamour and was always filled with interest. To sail into Shanghai aboard a freighter must have been one of life's great joys.

In this painting, the ship seems anonymous but the scene is not and as a painting filled with the atmosphere and beauty of a bygone era, it demanded to be included here on merit alone.

by Kenneth Shoesmith
Oil on canvas 36" x 55"
Courtesy of the Ulster Museum, Belfast

Coaling

To fuel a steamship at the beginning of this century was not only an operation which required great logistical skill, it was also a long, slow and laborious job requiring the muscle power of hundreds of unfortunate men. Until the use of oil as a fuel was established, the effort involved to propel a steamship from A to B was truly awesome. Within, and surrounding, the sleek, elegant lines of those beautiful vessels, toiled a veritable anthill of labourers working under a system not far removed from that of slavery.

The ships on the transatlantic run would take on their fuel at each terminal port, there loading their bunkers with thousands of tons of coal brought to the ship's side by trains comprising hundreds of coal wagons and augmented by coal barges secured alongside the ship as it lay in its dock.

On the colonial routes, requiring the ships to anchor in harbour, the coaling was done from coal lighters or barges which would be manoeuvred to the ship's side. There, thousands of tons of fuel in bags would be hoisted onto the backs of 'coolies' who would climb gangways to empty the coal into chutes let into the sides of the ships, leading directly into the bunkers. At the same time more thousands of tons of clinker, ash and coke, from the coal already burned on the voyage, would have to be unloaded from the ship and again put into lighters and disposed of. These processes would take many hours and continue sometimes into the night illuminated by floodlights.

The many coaling stations on P&O's route from England to India included Gibraltar, Malta and Aden. These ports being supplied with the fuel by fleets of colliers chartered by the company. A ship's efficiency was dependent on the quality of coal used aboard and the mind reels with the thought of the filth, toil and many tragedies which accompanied the voyage of a liner across the oceans of the world in those days.

From coal miners and loaders to the stokers, this was literally the black side of the bright picture usually painted of the glamorous days of the early steamship. The grime beneath the glamour was seldom mentioned in the chronicles of the day.

This watercolour by William Wyllie is but a glimpse of the kind of activity which would surround a P&O ship coaling in one of the intermediate ports between Britain and India or Australia. There is much straining, clamouring, climbing and hauling. The ship's officers had to be very aware of how the coal was being bunkered so that the trim of the ship was not adversely affected. At the same time the stewards, working in cabin and saloon, were fighting a losing battle against coal dust which always managed to seep into nooks and crannies, creating extra work in maintaining the ship's pristine interiors.

It was because of this dirt associated with coaling that P&O ships were, in the early days, painted black, even though it was the worst colour for keeping a ship cool in the oven like conditions of the tropics. It was only with the wide use of oil fuel that white became a practical proposition for steamship companies, bringing the swan-like image we know today into the exotic ports around the globe.

by William Wyllie
Watercolour on paper 15" x 20"
Courtesy of P&O, London

Conway and Mauretania

The *Conway* was one of the last wooden sailing battleships to survive. She was moored for many years in the Mersey after becoming a merchant navy training ship. Kenneth Shoesmith had also been a student, finally graduating as a junior officer, his spare time was spent painting the passing parade of ships entering or leaving Liverpool.

In this wonderful painting, which depicts the passions of Shoesmith's life, his admiration for the ships of the Royal Navy past and present, dominate the composition. But the elegance and beauty found in great passenger liners adds to the painting in such a way as to give it the colour it needs for completion.

Here too is a perfect portrait of the first *Mauretania* arriving in port, escorted by tugs and providing a counterpoint to the grey steel battleship brooding in the corner.

It is a picture symbolising the maritime history of Britain. Military might and commercial might bound by past glories, with the cadets providing a glimpse into the future.

by Kenneth Shoesmith
Watercolour on board 30" x 47"
Courtesy of Ulster Museum

Cruising

In the 1930s cruising had become so popular with the travelling public that many of the shipping companies converted older units of their fleet into full time cruise ships.

One of the most successful of those was the Royal Mail liner *Atlantis*. She had originally been built in 1913 as the *Andes*, sailing on their Southampton to South America service, but in 1930 she was withdrawn and converted for full time cruising. When finally she emerged from her Liverpool shipbuilders, she had become a swan of a ship. Converted from coal to oil fuel, she was painted white, her passenger capacity reduced from the former 1,350, to 450 first class only. She carried the name *Atlantis* upon her bows and, as such, spent the last decade of peace roaming the world on luxury pleasure cruises.

Her home port was Southampton and from there she sailed to every sea on earth. The most popular cruises were those which lasted from one to three weeks, sailing to the Mediterranean and north to the Scandinavian fjords.

In this painting the *Atlantis* is seen at anchor in the Geiranger fjord, looking like a jewel set on the icy waters and dwarfed by the mountains. Kenneth Shoesmith was the artist who revolutionised shipping commercial art. He had been a first officer in the Royal Mail Line before retiring from the sea to devote his life to painting. His seaborne experiences gave him a unique insight into the world of ships and this practical involvement, coupled with his undoubted brilliance as an artist, earned him a reputation as the best poster artist of his era, and the admiration of his peers.

This little painting is not typical of Shoesmith's work but shows his ability to recreate the essence of a scene. In this gem of a picture he does not make his ship the dominant force. He allows her to be dominated by the might of Norway's mountain scenery. The little town with its famous bridge can just be seen in the background. Small boats of the fishermen and the tenders from the *Atlantis* herself ferrying passengers back and forth hardly ruffle the quietness of the day. This is cruising as painted by Kenneth Shoesmith and what he paints is what is remembered by those who have enjoyed the experience.

by Kenneth Shoesmith
Watercolour on paper 20" x 15"
Courtesy of G. Swaine collection

Leviathan

Artists who work in watercolour and tempera create a sense of moment. There is nothing ponderous about the medium, it is, as the name implies, a method of painting which is fluid and somewhat ethereal. There is little room for mistakes. What the painter sees and feels is put down on the paper and there it stays. Even in the auction houses, watercolours and drawings are separated from 'real' paintings which are classified as oils, but many collectors and connoisseurs prefer the lighter touch of a painting in watercolour or those in tempera.

So it is with the great French marine artist Albert Brenet. His best work is done with a sureness and immediacy which is always fresh looking and, even though he could paint large pictures, they always appear intimate.

This lovely view of the *Leviathan* in her United States Lines colours, arriving in Le Havre and escorted by tugs, is a fine example of his work. He tells us the story as much by what he has left out of the picture as with what he actually shows. Our imagination tells us the rest, that there is much more of the ship to be seen and that there are tugs to follow. But what he has put down suggests the great size and power of the liner, even more than if it were completed.

by Albert Brenet
Tempera on paper 30" x 15½"
Courtesy of Frank O. Braynard

On Board the Columbus at Sea

An ocean liner is lonely looking when it is removed from the cosiness of its harbour, its immense size shrinks. Its shapes and curves blend into an image of vulnerability when seen against the vastness of sea and sky and at last the whole can be seen for what it really is. But within that graceful ship, separated from the hostile elements only by a shell of thin steel, lives a community, a civilisation in microcosm.

It takes imagination to truly appreciate the complexity of activities taking place aboard that manmade floating satellite. It is a vessel honeycombed with great rooms and lofty dining saloons, with grand staircases, carpeted and sweeping upwards to streets of decks, lined with cabins, staterooms and suites and everywhere people, talking, walking, eating, reading, dancing and loving, all activities associated with a small town, transferred to the ocean, and moving at speed between continents.

From the open decks can be seen the sweep of endless skies, the ocean stretching around, seemingly forever.

Here, in this exciting painting, Claus Bergen has swooped down on the decks of the German liner *Columbus* in mid Atlantic in the 1920s. He has brought us with him but we are apart from the activities going on, and, as observers, feel as if we could step aboard and join in the games of shuffle board or take a seat, cover ourselves with a blanket and call for a steward to bring tea on a tray.

This is the top deck facing forward. Ahead lies America. The day is fine but breezy and the sea has a slight swell. The on-rushing inevitability of the liner is shown by the white foam from waves pushed aside by the powerful bows. Here, time itself has been crystallised, stamped by the fashions worn and the distinctive traditional shapes of funnels, lifeboats, davits and ventilators. It is a painting filled with the atmosphere of its time and is a great example of a marine artist's talent for bringing us into his world, allowing us to live for a moment within the confines of his canvas.

by Claus Bergen
Courtesy of Gemeinde Lenggries

Duchess of Bedford

This painting portrays a moment when past and future meet prophetically. It is more than merely a scene of a yacht and a liner, sail and steam seen once more together. Strangely the true significance of the picture was unknown to the artist when he painted it. Fate and coincidence were to work together before its prophetic nature would be recognised.

Here we have the beautiful J class racing yacht *Britannia*, passing across the bows of the Canadian Pacific liner *Duchess of Bedford* as she steams towards Southampton. At the helm of the *Britannia* is her owner the King. He, who was crowned Emperor of India in Delhi in 1911 and representing here the might of the British Empire.

The elegant cabin class liner coming in from the Atlantic unknowingly represents the future demise of that empire, for in the years ahead she will be renamed the *Empress of India*, a name she would never bear at sea. As she was preparing for her first voyage in 1948 after a refit to first class status, India declared herself a republic, thus heralding the end of Britain's imperial power. The unfinished ship was hurriedly renamed the *Empress of France* to avoid diplomatic embarrassment, little being said of this potentially sensitive name change. However, in this painting, for one brief moment both the Emperor and the future Empress serenely pass each other without recognising themselves in the mirror of tomorrows history.

by Norman Wilkinson
Oil on canvas 8" x 9"
Courtesy of Communications Partnership PLC, London

Men of Iron

William Connor was an artist enthralled by the people of Ulster. His paintings were seldom brightly coloured. The women with shawls over their heads were prominent in most of his work. So too were the mean streets of Belfast filled with their horses and carts reflected in the rain washed pavements. The countryside of Northern Ireland also supplied a never ending source of subjects for his brush, but always brooding over the province and the primary source of its income, were the shipyards of Harland and Wolff.

Few places in the city did not overlook the gaunt shapes of cranes and gantries towering over the harbour and the great ships being built there. The early years of the 20th century were the great years for British shipbuilding. Fabled liners grew and finally sailed to the far corners of the globe. At times of national emergency the grey shapes of warships too were to be seen at the edge of Belfast Lough but crucial to all the giant happenings there were the men who toiled to produce those vessels.

The term 'Belfast built' usually meant the best in the world and those rough mannered men were proud of the ships they created. This pride is really the subject of this powerful oil painting of a ship waiting to be launched. She is dominated by the figures of men who helped to build her. From her fore peak flies the union flag of Great Britain, bringing to the painting its only flash of colour and emphasising that powerful emotion which motivated those workers. The intensity of feeling generated by the emotionally charged political union with Great Britain, dominated every aspect of life for those Ulster-men of iron who, with their bare hands, built those great and beautiful vessels and sent them down to the sea.

by William Connor
Oil on canvas 30" x 50"
Courtesy of Ulster Transport Museum

The Departure

The artist has taken the moment of departure as his subject for this evocative and splendid painting. This is a picture that demands close scrutiny to derive the greatest pleasure and satisfaction from. It is only now that the size of the ship as seen next to the pier with her tugs can be appreciated. Even though only a section of the liner is shown it only adds to the drama of the event.

Here we see the North German Lloyd liner *Columbus* moving away from her New York berth. She has, only a few moments before, cast off her lines. Unseen tugs at her stern are pulling her out while others push her flanks away from the dockside. Passengers crowd her decks waving to friends and family who have rushed to the ends of the pier for final farewells. Many aboard are sailing happily for holidays in Europe but others are leaving forever and the slow measured events of departure prolong the poignant moments of goodbye, the faces of loved ones beginning to blur with the increasing distance.

There is constant noise as people yell, tugs hoot and seas boil from the turmoil of thrashing screws while the great ship herself adds to the cacophony with blasts from her horns. Background sounds of New York's traffic blend with the muted noises coming from the river and nostrils quiver with the smell of salt air, sludgy water and smoke. This is a sight and an experience from the past, now alas, largely forgotten. Even the view of the city with the afternoon sun illuminating the tall elegant skyscrapers, is today seldom seen from the deck of a ship. But it is all here in this nostalgic painting.

It makes no difference knowing that this is the *Columbus* sailing. The atmosphere would have been just as compelling no matter which ship was the subject for the picture which seems to miraculously freeze an instant in time which comes to life the moment we look at it.

by Claus Bergen
Reproduced by kind permission of the German Ship Museum, Bremerhaven

Bremen

Here we see the express steamer *Bremen* leaving Bremerhaven. The picture is dated 1929 and the style is wonderfully reminiscent of its era. The influence of art deco being very clearly felt.

This is a painting designed to impart a sense of power and enormous size. The ship was huge at over 50,000 tons and stretched for more than 900 feet but the artist has insisted on making her even bigger by reducing the scale of the tugs and exaggerating the streamlining of her superstructure and funnels. This is not a poster design but its modernity does suggest the importance of creating a powerful image rather than a mere accurate portrayal of the ship itself.

Commercial art was very much part of the artistic style between the wars, and the line between salon painting and that used for advertising became blurred. Each very much influencing the other.

Nevertheless, in this picture the artist has expertly brought the anticipation of a sea voyage onto his canvas and we can feel the excitement generated by the great ship's departure. A scene such as this was once commonplace in all the great ports of the world, it is only now, when such activities are all but forgotten, that a painting like this comes into its own, serving to bring alive again travel experiences which were in those days an everyday occurrence.

As time goes by, the idea of voyaging by ocean liner seems more fantastic and improbable. These contemporary paintings only go to prove that the fantasy was, in fact, reality.

by Hans Bohrdt
Oil on canvas 40" x 50"
Courtesy of German Ships Museum, Bremerhaven

Manhattan

This is a painting which precisely depicts the activity surrounding a great liners arrival in port. Albert Brenet has, without excessive detail, managed to portray the atmosphere of disembarkation with quiet certitude. White coated porters carry luggage off the ship and into the customs halls. The gangways are in place and passengers stream ashore after their transatlantic voyage. For them it has been a week wrapped in an atmosphere of discrete luxury, enjoying the best of American hospitality where no doubt, between the dining and the dancing, cocktail parties were loud with the chatter of tongues loosened by the great new drink invented aboard the ship and which today is her only memorial. The 'Manhattan' is ordered and drunk all over the world without a thought being given to the lovely liner whose name that glamorous cocktail bears.

But this voyage is not quite over yet. She will sail again in a few hours bound for Bremerhaven, at that time her terminal port, before once more sailing for home. It is believed that this painting was completed only months after the ship entered service, and is seen her with her funnels having been heightened to reduce the smuts from falling on her decks. They were altered in the first few months of her life thus giving her the look of an aristocrat.

by Albert Brenet
Tempera on paper 20½" x 23"
Courtesy of Frank O. Braynard

Queen Mary

American artists living in New York were never far from the activities of the port. Its waterfront was always filled with maritime movement, especially in the 1930s, when the greatest ships ever built would sail into and out of the city and, even though those ships lay only temporarily within the shadows of the skyscrapers, they were at one time an integral part of the cityscape.

It was during this decade that Reginald Marsh did most of his best work and became very much a New York chronicler. His paintings were discovered and appreciated by the founders of the Whitney Museum early in his career and that secured his reputation in America.

Reginald Marsh's subjects ranged from the Bowery to Coney Island, city litter, taxi dance halls and burlesque all found expressions through his brush. In 1937 he was commissioned to paint murals for the Rotunda in the New York custom house. For this he chose to show the entry of a liner into New York harbour. The mural included ships, tugs and even a glamorous movie star to add a little cheesecake to the scene.

He always carried with him a card giving him access to study the ships in port whenever he wished and it was obviously on such a visit that he painted this fine watercolour study of the *Queen Mary*. It is a quick and powerful impression of one of the greatest symbols of that decade as seen by a fine contemporary artist.

by Reginald Marsh
Watercolour on paper 14" x 20"
Courtesy of the Forbes Magazine Collection, New York

Paquebot Paris

For Demuth's generation transatlantic liners were fascinating. They were a world in themselves with their own special shapes. He enjoyed the giant smoke stacks and ventilators upon the boat deck, the whole ship was a monster of power and speed.

Charles Demuth was an American artist and he lived for many years in Paris. He was conscious of the new things that were happening in French art but mainly he saw his American friends there and lived a good life. This was not a question of work, for he could always paint in America. The important thing was to absorb what was in the air. The Americans learned from walking along the Seine staring over at Notre Dame and looking at bookstalls. It was a whole way of life which lasted until the crash of 1929.

Paris was the best part of being American but to get their you had to go by sea. This painting combines the artist's great love for the bits and pieces of ships and his great love for French style and art. The SS *Paris* at the time being the greatest example of French artistry afloat.

Charles Demuth was not a marine artist. He was typical of the new wave of American artists who were being highly influenced by the new art movements in Europe. The ship merely acted as an inspiration and is a perfect example of how the age of the ocean liner was one of the visually dominating influences to be seen in the early 20th century.

Apart from its title, there is no way that one would know that this painting is of the *Paris*. She was a liner with three funnels, Demuth has chosen only to show two. Their overall shape and French line colours seem to be correct but this painting is typical of Demuth's precisionist style, reminiscent of cubism. Nevertheless, it could not have been painted anywhere else than from the deck of a 'twenties ocean liner.

This exciting painting hangs in the Columbus Gallery of Fine Arts, Columbus, Ohio.

by Charles Demuth
Oil on canvas 25" x 20"
Courtesy of the Columbus Museum of Art, Ohio

On Board the Queen Mary

The French artist Raoul Dufy was born in 1877 and saw great changes in the development of artistic style during his life. In his formative years, he was greatly influenced by Monet's impressionism and later he turned to painting in the broad colours of the fauvists, until cubism became the overriding spur to his work through his friendship with Cezanne and Braque. However, it was only after developing his own style after years spent designing textiles and ceramics in the 1920s, that the public started to value him. His personal mode of expression consisted of curlicues, commas and little brush strokes resulting in a free composition, brought together in light, clear and sparkling colours.

This picture is an example of his style and is typical of his work. He loved the sea and in this watercolour done while aboard the *Queen Mary* in 1936, Raoul Dufy shows his affection and knowledge of marine structure with the minimum of effort.

The painting is at once an atmospheric and physical statement full of light and breeziness with a strong feeling for the bulk of the ship upon which it is painted. It is a superb maritime painting by a mainstream artist in love with the tang of the sea and the shape of its ships.

by Raoul Dufy
Watercolour on paper 19½" x 24½"
Courtesy of the Forbes Magazine Collection, New York

Deck Scene aboard the Arcadia

It is seldom that a ship in its entirety is seen by her passengers. Their impression of her is usually formed by odd glimpses of separate parts, the funnel or funnels being the most easily recognisable feature. Often they became the symbol of that particular vessel. And so it was with the P&O liner *Arcadia*.

She was a lovely traditional looking ship built in 1954 as part of the post-war rebuilding programme. Whereas the *Himalaya* and the smaller *Chusan* were similar to each other in profile, the newer twins, *Arcadia* and *Iberia*, identical in most respects, differed in their funnel tops. The *Arcadia* wore a black dome similar to a brimless bowler hat and the *Iberia* looked as if she was always waiting for hers to be fitted.

They were impressive looking ships but proved unequal in service. For some inexplicable reason the *Iberia* never received the same degree of affection from her passengers and owners as did the *Arcadia* and did not quite measure up. She had only sailed for 18 years when she was sent to the Taiwanese breakers in 1972.

The *Arcadia* remained in service for a further six years, during which time she operated as a one class cruise ship making friends wherever she went. Her career took her around the world many times and when she arrived for her appointment with the Chinese cutters torch in 1979 she left behind a career in which she had carried 430,000 passengers over 2,650,000 miles, all on peaceful, pleasure voyages.

The painting here representing this delightful ship is one which shows her distinctive funnel dominating her broad sun-drenched sports deck. The artist has painted the picture from a vantage point on the ship's bridge and with the glimpse of a striped canvas deckchair brings back memories of lazy days afloat.

It is a painting in watercolour which tells a traditional story, nostalgically enhanced by views of ships paraphernalia fast disappearing from the seas of today.

by Claude Muncaster
Watercolour on paper 12" x 20"
Courtesy of P&O, London

The Arrival

Although nothing is complete in this painting, it tells the story of exciting events using only fragments, colour and instantly recognisable shapes.

Here we have on canvas the fleeting impressions we all get when confronted with too many things to look at. The feeling of movement is there as too is the atmosphere of a busy sea port. Nevinson's special style remained throughout his life but his dedication originally to a futurist movement and to the English school of vorticists established him as an artist of the first order. In this painting he has found the essence of the era of sea travel and placed it onto a flat surface and we can understand what he is saying. It is an easy painting to read but must have been difficult to paint. His control of colour and shape brings order out of chaos and we experience a panoramic view distilled into a rectangle through the mastery of an artist with vision.

by Christopher Nevinson
Oil on canvas
Courtesy of The Tate Gallery, London

Liner Histories

City of New York

There were so many great and important liners which spanned the turn of the 19th and 20th centuries that to choose one typical of the time proved to be more difficult than imagined. This book is about great liners and their paintings of the 20th century but time and especially manmade measurements of time do not fall neatly into a rigid pattern. Edges blur and any ship which was built in 1888 and survived until the 1920s is, in the author's mind, very much a ship of the 20th century. Apart from these considerations, the painting here of the *City of New York*, and the beauty of the vessel herself, was sufficient to earn her the place as leader of this artistic shipping cavalcade.

The *City of New York* was the first transatlantic express liner to be over 10,000 tons. She was also the first to be fitted with twin screws. Her mechanical reliability was to be proven in a world of caution. So much so that when built her masts and spars were fitted to carry auxiliary sails, just in case of breakdown. But these proved completely unnecessary and they were disposed of after a few years and she was left completely to rely on her engines, rather like a learner swimmer dispensing of his water wings and going solo.

But the *City of New York* did retain the tell-tale signs of her evolution from the days of sail. She had three tall masts, a full clipper bow, complete with figurehead and the slim hull lines of a past age. Her counterstern was worthy of the *Cutty Sark* itself and her three tall funnels firmly placed her in the steamship era. But this combination of old and new were so finely incorporated in her design that the result was sublime. She and her sister ship, the *City of Paris*, were as beautiful as any ships ever could be. Some say they were the most beautiful liners ever built.

Those lovely 'City' liners were built for the Inman Line, a British company which had been sold into American ownership in 1886. But from the time of their maiden voyage in 1888 to February 1893, both ships sailed under British registry. This was due to a United States law prohibiting any foreign-built ships from sailing under the American flag. Eventually the owners of the Inman Line did a deal with congress, changing the name of the company to the American Line and promising to build two other ships in American yards. They also procured a United States mail contract and changed the names of the two existing ships simply to the *New York* and the *Paris*.

After these agreements had been made, congress passed a law permitting the sisters to be registered in the United States and thereafter they flew the stars and stripes. They had been Blue Ribband holders as the fastest liners in the world while under the British flag. America had to wait for half a century to finally wrest that coveted speed prize from the Europeans.

The *New York* was filled with innovation. Her first class passenger accommodation was superb and many years before her time. She had hot running water and her fourteen luxury suites included private bathrooms and lavatories. Her kitchens were isolated and enclosed in steel to eradicate cooking odours. Her public rooms were spectacular – wide, spacious and tall, gleaming with stained glass windows and carved woods. Her great dining hall was 50 feet long and rose to a height of 25 feet, covered by a vaulted ceiling of stained glass worthy of a cathedral in its magnificence.

The *New York*'s days as a three funnel beauty lasted only until 1903 when she was rebuilt emerging with only two. The *Paris* had been altered two years previously.

The *New York* had two wars to fight during her life. In the Spanish American war of 1888 she was an auxiliary cruiser and in the First World War, from 1917, she became a troopship, after which she sailed again for her company, before being sold to a Polish line in 1921. The end came in 1923 when she was broken up in Genoa. Her career had lasted for 35 years, during which time she had yielded her place as the biggest, fastest and most incredible liner many times over, and she left the seas to giants such as the *Imperator*, the *Aquitania* and the *Olympic*, all owing much to her for their style, luxury and position in the evolutionary saga of 20th century shipping.

Teutonic

The *City of New York* and the *Teutonic* had been built within a year of each other, both winning the Blue Ribband as fastest ship on the Atlantic. So intense was their rivalry that on one occasion each had sailed from Liverpool within an hour of the other and for days had raced across the ocean within sight of each other, but on that occasion the *Teutonic* was the faster and tied up at her Manhattan berth less than four hours before the *City of New York*. The year of that unique transoceanic race was 1890.

The *Teutonic* was built in 1888 by Harland and Wolff in Belfast for the White Star Line. She was the first liner to be designed as an armed merchant cruiser and built with a government subsidy. It was a precedent which resulted in the building of some of the world's biggest and fastest liners. The *Teutonic*'s intended role as possible warship was proudly proclaimed by Britain. So much so, that the Kaiser of Germany insisted on visiting the ship and from that visit he decided that Britain's naval power had to be matched by Germany, thus starting the great arms race which inevitably led to the First World War. But that conflict was only a glint in the Kaiser's eye when he stepped aboard the new *Teutonic* at the naval review off Spithead on August 4th 1889 and was dazzled by the power and design of the new liner. Not only could she be a powerful weapon of war, but the ship was then the most luxurious liner afloat and destined to be the fastest. It was the start of the great race for the Blue Ribband between Germany and Britain and, although the race was to be run eventually by ships of the Cunard Line representing Great Britain and not by the White Star, the *Teutonic* remains a milestone in the international history of great express liners.

That visit to Spithead and the naval review was in fact *Teutonic's* maiden voyage even though it was an affair of state. A few days later she returned to Liverpool for the start of her commercial life, sailing from that port to New York on August 7th and the start of a career that was to span the next 31 years, during which time she would sail as speed queen in peace and as an armed merchant cruiser in war, after which she was demoted to being a troop ship before finally going to German ship breakers in 1921.

Orontes

Orontes was the first ship to be built in the twentieth century for the Orient Steam Navigation Company, otherwise known as the Orient Line. She was, in her day, typical of the many liners which linked Great Britain with her colonies. Not large by today's standards, she was, at under 10,000 tons, an attractive ship with a tall funnel and two pole masts. She was the first in the fleet to be propelled by quadruple expansion engines giving her a service speed of 16 knots.

The *Orontes* was built in 1902 by Fairfields of Glasgow and she carried 640 passengers, half of which were carried in a third class fitted to the usual standards then prevailing for the immigrant trade. Her first and second classes were comfortable but not deluxe.

The voyage to Australia, via Suez, was long and hot and, in those pre-airconditioned days, the passage through the Red Sea must have been a floating hell for all on board. In 1916 she was requisitioned as a troop transport by the admiralty, returning to Orient Line service in October 1919. Her last voyage was in February 1921 when she was laid up until being sold as an exhibition ship in 1922 and renamed the *British Trade*. This enterprise obviously never got off the ground as a few months later she was re-sold to her old company and renamed *Orontes* once more. But she never sailed again and was broken up in 1926.

La Provence

The French liner *La Provence* was the third of a trio of sisters. She was built as a larger development of *La Lorraine* and *La Savoie*, the first of which sailed in the first year of the 20th century, having been laid down and launched in the last year of the 19th century.

La Provence was a true daughter of the Belle Epoque and was the largest French liner of her day. But, at only 13,753 tons was considerably smaller than the prides of the fleets of Great Britain and Germany. However, what this ship lacked in size and speed she made up for in style and luxury. She was the trail blazer for the future of the French Line in developing their philosophy of providing moderately sized ships, filled with innovations and new decorative fashions.

These were eventually developed into the world renowned liners the *France*, the *Paris*, the *Ile de France* which led to the brightest star ever set afloat, the incredible *Normandie* which broke all world records for size, speed, luxury and chic at the time. But it was with

the little turn of the century *La Provence* that it all started. She it was who provided, for the first time, the ambience of gilt and white decorated rooms, creating an airiness and lightness of atmosphere which broke with the heavy decor usually found aboard other ships of the day.

She dined her first class passengers at tables set for intimate groups, sitting on swivel chairs upholstered in fine fabrics, rather than at the endless rows of bench like tables which were more in keeping with an army mess hall.

La Provence sailed her elegant way between Le Havre and New York from 1906 to 1914 at which time she was pressed into service for the French navy as an auxiliary cruiser and renamed *La Provence II*. On February 26th 1916 she met tragedy and was torpedoed in the Mediterranean by the German U-boat U35. Nine hundred and thirty troops and crew died in the horror of her sinking.

Mauretania and Lusitania

No life story of the great *Mauretania* can be told without linking it to her near twin the *Lusitania*. Both, for many years, ruled the North Atlantic together as monarchs. Their achievements and place in maritime history is forever assured but for very different reasons.

Both were ships acclaimed in their time as technological miracles and as far reaching in concept at the beginning of this century as Concorde has been at the end of it. They were mighty ships, larger than anything then afloat and faster than anyone thought could be possible. They were designed solely for peaceful commerce, or so it was said, and built to a standard of beauty which brought the steamship into a class of elegance, formerly attributed only to the clipper ships of old. Both won the celebrated Blue Ribband as fastest in the world, each from the other, but *Mauretania* had the edge and retained the record for over 20 years. Their development and propulsion was highly controversial and, through their adoption of the new power system of steam turbines, they paved the way for a future generation of high powered fast liners.

The British government indirectly supplied the finance for the building of both liners through schemes such as mail contracts, loans and other financial smoke screens. They specified to Cunard the parameters within which the ships would be built with an eye to their eventual conversion, if necessary, as ships of war. No doubt at the time naval intelligence was well aware of the happenings in the Kaisers Germany and, though not officially acknowledged, Britain was preparing for an inevitable conflict. The two great Cunarders were to be part of that preparation.

Meanwhile, at the shipyards, their progress during construction was followed avidly with mounting excitement, whipped up by the company's publicity department and, when those beautiful ships finally came into service, the requirements of war and peace had resulted in two of the most spectacular vessels ever to be set afloat. They were almost identical, both of nearly 32,000 tons, slim bodied and graceful, measuring over 780 feet from their knife edged stems to their graceful counter sterns. Their crowning glory were four tall, evenly spaced funnels, painted in Cunard crimson orange banded and topped with black. Their hulls were black with white upper works and they presented a vision of power and majesty never before seen on earth. Their personalities were quite different – *Mauretania* being English and *Lusitania* Scottish.

The interiors of both were equally as splendid with all the luxury and quality associated with the finest country houses. The workmanship was incredible. Wood panelling carved in-situ, plasterwork ceilings, leaded and stained glass domes over vast social halls, grand sweeping staircases with ornamental metalwork supplemented by elevators, previously only seen in the greatest hotels. The interior designs of these ships continued a trend found in all the luxury liners of the age with opulence and craftsmanship equal to that formerly reserved for cathedrals and royal palaces. The amazing fact was that, whereas the great buildings of the world were created to stand for all time, ships were simply part of a throw-away economy. They would become obsolete having a life span of only three decades or so after which they would be demolished and disposed of piecemeal as almost worthless.

It has been said that the fashion for period style and furnishing was an attempt to separate the ship from the sea because passengers did not wish to be reminded that they were afloat. It would have been virtually impossible for any passenger to believe he was anywhere but on a ship and rather than hide the fact, those interiors only served as an incredible counterpoint to the endless vistas of sea and sky outside. It must have seemed miraculous to be cocooned in the familiarity of such plush and lush furnishings, surrounded by vast but slightly miniaturised versions of the Ritz or Marlborough House.

Though the passenger accommodations were spacious, especially in first class, they existed within the finite confines of a hull and as such had an Alice in Wonderland feeling of being a little smaller than life. If the scene from windows or deck did not convince you that you were at sea, then the sea itself certainly would. The sensation of domes, pillars, staircases and elevators changing position from level to leaning, soon changed your mind and you became well aware that this was a ship afloat. The frisson caused by feelings of apprehension, coupled with land based familiarity, only served to make the whole ambience of sailing a delicious experience.

Spectacular changes were to develop from the day the world first said hello to the *Mauretania* until the day the *Queen Mary* said goodbye almost sixty years later, both ships being directly linked to each other. True, one had four funnels and the other only three; but when the *Mauretania* sailed into New York for the first time in 1907 she was met by a fleet of horse-drawn handsome cabs to convey her passengers to the city; and when the *Queen Mary* sailed into Long Beach after her last voyage, man was about to walk on the moon, such was the rate of human progress. Liners, however, remained essentially unchanged.

Those future scientific changes were beyond imaginings when the *Lusitania* and *Mauretania* started their careers. The *Mauretania* was destined to live into old age, during which time she built a reputation for herself which resulted in love, then adoration, and finally veneration from her passengers. She was a ship with a soul, so it was said by her many captains through the years. President Franklin Roosevelt presented a model of her to the Smithsonian Museum in Washington as a tribute to his favourite ship and, when she finally went to the shipbreakers, her builders presented a five ton model of her to Winchester Cathedral as a votive offering and memorial to her achievements.

All this adulation was a far cry from the fate which overtook her sister. Today the name *Lusitania* does not conjure thoughts of elegance and romantic voyages, all that is forgotten when mention is made of her. Controversy, intrigue and tragedy are her epitaphs. She went into history as a victim of war. There is no doubt that the *Lusitania* was torpedoed without warning off the Irish coast, with an appalling loss of innocent life on May 7th 1915, but it has latterly been suggested that she was not the innocent victim as claimed. No doubt there was a measure of subterfuge involved.

It was claimed that the *Lusitania* sailed on purely peaceful voyages between New York and Liverpool after 1914, on a truncated passenger service still run by the Cunard Line, inspite of the dangers of war. She was still dressed in her company livery and no attempt was made to disguise her. Her sailing schedules were public property and, although Germany declared the waters around Britain as a war zone, she had not yet resorted to unrestricted submarine war-fare. To save fuel, the *Lusitania* sailed leisurely, not attempting to keep to her usual speed. It was stated policy that any vessels carrying cargoes of arms or strategic war supplies to the beligerents would be declared legitimate targets by both sides. *Lusitania* sailed with passengers and general cargo and it was in this guise that she was attacked and sunk. Many neutral Americans on board were killed. It was this atrocity that helped to propel that nation into declaring war on Germany.

After the subsequent official enquiries had made their pronouncements important questions were still unanswered. Was the *Lusitania* as blameless as stated? Was she carrying ammunition and arms, as had been suggested? Was she, in fact, a blockade runner with the full knowledge of the British admiralty? If so, there is no doubt that it was with the knowledge of the German high command too. If that was so, then it was greatly possible that the attack had been pre-planned before she even sailed from New York. The evidence seems to suggest that this was so.

One small, spine chilling clue emerged later. This was that a medallion, minted by the Germans to honour the sinking, was circulated so soon after the appalling event as to make it appear that it was struck prior to the ship having sailed from New York. Whether or not the mystery surrounding this appalling act will ever be completely clarified, the fact is that the end of the *Lusitania* was violent. Never again was the name to be given to another ship. Not so with the *Mauretania*. Her name was again placed on the bows of another Cunarder and carried proudly to the end of her days which was to coincide with the virtual ending of the era of steamship travel.

George Washington

The German liner *George Washington* sailed under the flag of the father-land for only five of her incredible forty two years of life.

She was a remarkable ship in her day and, even though unexciting to look at, her exterior masked an interior which was to become a bench mark in liner decor.

The age of the super liner was about to dawn when she was first built and the size of ships would grow quickly from the 25,000 tons of the *George Washington* in 1908, to the 35,000 tons of the *Mauretania*, 45,000 tons of the *Olympic* and then 52,000 tons of the *Imperator* launched in 1912.

With these great leaps in size came changes in interior design. German ships by tradition were floating examples of teutonic grandeur. This usually manifested itself in over-stuffed and heavy furnishings, with dark and over-carved wood panelling, interspersed with studded leather and wrought iron.

It was left to the French to invent the ocean liner style which influenced the ships of the inter-war years, however, seemingly quite by chance and without fanfare, the North German Lloyd built a ship which was in fact the first to be designed with soft and subdued interiors. The *George Washington* was a vessel whose decor was finished in the most elegant of tastes. She was a ship created with a combination of American classicism mixed with the sensuality of art nouveau. Her motifs were derived from scenes associated with her namesake. George Washington's home of Mount Vernon featured in murals aboard as did paintings of the capital and the White House.

These clever touches represented a compliment from the ship's builders to her intended passengers and the Americans loved it. So much so that, when eventually they obtained possession of the ship, due to the fortunes of war, she continued to sail even under the American stars and stripes, with her original name. This was an honour not accorded to many other vanquished ships which when transferred to the victorious nations continued their lives under different names and subsequently with different personalities.

The *George Washington* was berthed in New York when war broke out in 1914 and there she was interned. She was used as a troop transport until 1921 when she was taken over by the newly formed United States Lines. She sailed as one of their first class liners until 1931 when she was withdrawn from service and laid up until 1940 when once more she was taken over as a troopship to fight yet another war against her original builders.

She was finally scrapped after a major fire aboard in 1951 at the grand old age of 42. Few chronicles pay justice to her importance as the first liner to break the mould of traditional thinking in liner interiors. She was a one off, very beautiful, elegant, and sailed under her two flags with distinction.

Olympic

The wonderful White Star Line is best remembered for its great North Atlantic liners but it was in the fantastic gold rush days in far off Australia that the line was really born. Beautiful ships from the final days of sail were the forerunners of the giant steamships which were to make the company a household name in the early days of this century.

The original company was named after the swallow tailed burgee of red with a white star which flew at the mastheads of all the ships, sail or steam, which the line owned. The full name was to be Oceanic Steam Navigation Company Limited when the steamship company was created on the foundations of the old.

Traditions die hard and from the rigours of sail came the beginnings of the great steamship era and with them the series of liners which presaged the building of three sister ships planned to be the envy of the shipping world.

Olympic was the first of the trio and the only vessel to survive an expected life span. She made her maiden voyage from Southampton to New York in June 1911. Her entry into service marked a new era of grand luxury at sea. She, and her intended consorts, were to offer passengers a crossing lasting a week without the excessive fuss and vibration usually part of an express sailing. The record breaking was left to others and the White Star Line was to rely on vast size and superlative service to entice passengers away from the five-day boats of the other shipping companies. A voyage with White Star was seen as a gentle, elegant interlude by those people who valued quality and wished to be given the extra time in which to enjoy it.

Olympic was beautiful and, at 45,000 tons, was the biggest ship of her day. She had four evenly spaced tall funnels painted in the buff with black top livery of the company. In contrast to other four funnelled liners, her upper decks were remarkably uncluttered because of the discretion of her ventilating system. Her name, and the names of her sisters, were especially chosen to emphasise their grandeur.

On the day of her launch, on October 20th 1910, she left behind on the adjoining building berth of Harland and Wolff's Belfast shipyard, a half completed sister ship. This second giant was to be named *Titanic*, a third sister, provisionally named *Gigantic*, was to follow. With these three massive ships, the White Star Line planned to maintain their primary services between Southampton and New York. The secondary service operated by the company had its home port in Liverpool and was already being served by four ships renowned as being the finest passenger liners then sailing on any ocean.

Olympic was 100 feet longer than the Cunard fliers *Mauretania* and *Lusitania*, the then largest ships in the world. Her extra size provided accommodation of unrivalled extent and magnificence. Her first class dining saloon was immense and by far the largest afloat. Decorated in Jacobean style it was based on the 17th century interiors of Hatfield House.

This splendid room was 114 feet long and, with a breadth of 92 feet, used the full width of the hull. It could seat 532 diners at a single sitting. The other great first class public rooms were equally as impressive, with a main lounge modelled on a room from the palace of Rothesay, the smoking room was a haven of Georgian elegance. The swimming pool was 30 foot long and the Turkish baths were recreations of the mystical east.

Harland and Wolff employed almost 4,000 men to complete the fitting out of *Olympic* alone and, on the day she left Belfast completed, her sister *Titanic* was launched. She too was designed to be fabulous and, with the third awe inspiring ship waiting in the wings, the company would have been literally on the crest of a wave. But all that was not to be. The *Titanic* replaced the dream with a nightmare. The days of arrogantly tempting fate with unassailable sounding names, was quickly reversed and with the sinking of *Titanic* the company was left with the prospect of two instead of three great ships to operate their tight schedule to New York.

The third liner of the trio, *Gigantic*, was now to be named *Britannic*, a monumental climb down from the giddy heights of invulnerability. Even this truncated service was not to be. War came to Europe and, whereas the *Titanic* symbolised the ending of certainty in man's dominance of nature, her sinking also symbolised the ending of long held attitudes both socially and politically. Nothing was ever the same again anywhere.

The *Britannic* sailed from her builders, not in the proud colours of the White Star Line, but in the white uniform of a hospital ship, emblazoned with red crosses. She was barely a year old when she too was sunk - thankfully not with a ship full of injured but the mine which exploded under her belly killed too many of her complement.

The sole surviving giant was the first-born *Olympic*. The *Titanic* disaster ripped the heart out of the company; with the destruction of *Britannic* the company was never to fully recover its strength. The building of the *Olympic* was the high point in the White Star's history and when she finally went to the ship breakers at the age of 24, she brought with her the soul of the company.

With the dawning of the decade of the 1930s came a new dream. A giant ship of 60,000 tons was to be built and her keel was actually laid. She was to have been named *Oceanic* and would be White Star's answer to Cunard's *Queen Mary*. But the economic crash finished her as it almost finished the new Cunarder. Two 27,000 ton motor ships were built instead – *Britannic* and *Georgic*. With these the company clung to its individuality, if not its independence, and when the White Star Line was swallowed by Cunard in 1934, those two extraordinary ships were to become the last flag bearers of the company up to the outbreak of the Second World War.

At the end of the conflict there only remained the *Britannic*. That lovely old ship appeared as an oddity amidst the Cunard fleet with their tall crimson funnels contrasting sharply against the squareness of *Britannic*'s motorship looks and short buff funnels. She sailed her traditional route as a White Star orphan to the end, a proud reminder of the once glorious days when *Olympic* was the new flagship of a fleet which seemed to be destined to become the greatest in the world.

Aquitania

The *Aquitania* was, when built, the big sister in a fleet that constituted twins and quartets. She was half as big again as the *Mauretania* and *Lusitania* and, at 45,000 tons, represented a large step forward for Cunard. She was designed and built as a one off, no sister ship ever having been planned to accompany her. She was, in the author's opinion, and in the opinion of many others, the most beautiful four funnelled liner ever built and was known throughout most of her life as the 'Ship Beautiful'.

The *Aquitania* was built in time to make only a few voyages before the outbreak of the First World War. Then she was employed as a troopship, a hospital ship and a troopship once more, before being reconditioned and converted to oil burning before re-entering transatlantic service. If ever a ship's design could be called sublime then *Aquitania* must surely be the one to be so called. She was as graceful as a clipper and every inch of her 901 feet length was in perfect proportion.

Externally she resembled her two faster sisters and was similar to the White Star triplets, only one of which, the *Olympic*, lived to sail with her. Their similarities in size and design drew comparisons, but *Aquitania* was by far the prettier. It is difficult to know why this was so because the *Olympic* too was very lovely, the rake of masts, the size of funnels, the shape of superstructures and the curves of sterns, all added up to very different looking ships, and to put the cherry on the top was the colour of the *Aquitania*'s funnels. The indescribable orange/red of Cunard banded with black was the crowning glory to all Cunarders which put them in a class apart, four such crimson towers certainly made *Aquitania* an incredible sight.

She never looked massive or overpowering like the later generation of ships, but was always yacht like in her elegance. Her interiors were spectacular. A series of grand saloons, accurate to every period they copied, Jacobian, Louis Quinze, Georgian, Carolean. Not for her the single theme decor of the future. It was all unashamedly reproduction down to the door knobs. Deeply carved wood abounded everywhere, moulded stucco and plasterwork ceilings, domes and leaded glass, marble fireplaces and grand staircases, miles of teak deck, mullioned windows and fan lights, potted plants and palms, furniture and artworks, all assembled with the lightness of touch typical of Britain's Edwardian era.

The *Aquitania* was the distilled essence of her era's luxury both inside and out. She never seemed to be affected by changing fashion, she sailed with the best for over 30 years, always independently, always an individual. She joined the greatest ships ever built as they sailed the Atlantic. *Lusitania, Paris, Imperator, Normandie* and *Rex*. They all came and went during her lifetime. She sailed unscathed through two world wars, only to sail again, this time tired and demoted as an immigrant ship in the post-war period.

The *Aquitania* finally went to the ship breakers in 1950. She was the last four funnelled liner in the world. She was incredibly beautiful even then, and her passing was mourned by thousands of people whose lives she had touched during those historic decades.

Berengaria

Without fully realising the precedent they were creating, the *Berengaria* was to become the first of Cunard's queens; she was named after the wife of Richard the Lionheart.

The *Berengaria*, then named *Imperator*, was the first of a giant trio of liners designed and built in Germany before the First World War. Their concept was brilliant being the brainchild of the Kaiser's friend Albert Ballin who was the Director General of Hamburg America Line. It was his dream to create the biggest and most luxurious ships in the world which would represent Germany's new found might and maritime supremacy. So luxurious was the

Imperator that her marble lined private bathrooms and heavy furnishings made her quite unstable at first, requiring much of what had been installed in the shipyards to be removed after her first voyages to restore her to an even keel.

The lesson was learned and the two ships which followed, the *Vaterland* and the *Bismarck*, were built with greater regard to sea worthiness. However, all three were incredible examples of the latest thinking in marine engineering and architecture.

The keel of the *Imperator* was laid in June 1910 at the Vulkan Werft shipyard at Hamburg on the River Elbe. Her launching was more in the nature of a grand state military occasion, with Kaiser Wilhelm II performing the ceremony. The launching platform was aglitter with spiked military helmets, the Kaiser himself, resplendent in white, had his helmet emblazoned with a gilded imperial eagle. This great show of bombast reflected the Kaiser's keen interest in martial affairs and was typical of his theatrical sense of power, which especially came to the fore when in competition with Great Britain. The *Vaterland* and her sisters were the products of brilliant minds and incorporated many firsts in marine architecture.

Up to that time it was common practice for funnel uptakes aboard liners to thrust right through the centre of a ship's hull, taking the smoke and gases from the engines to the funnels. But in the case of these new giants this trunking was divided up the ship's sides, only meeting at the base of the funnels. This innovation resulted in huge expanses of the ship's interiors being available to create vast open spaces in which to place the great public rooms aboard. This technological advance was copied for later continental ships and was especially used to great effect on the French liner *Normandie* many years later.

But the British never did take advantage of its possibilities and all their home built liners struggled to obtain uncluttered spaciousness which was virtually impossible with huge funnel uptakes blocking every vista on board.

Nevertheless, when the Cunard Steamship Company received the *Berengaria* as reparations for the loss of their *Lusitania* at the end of the First World War, they took full advantage of her enormous spaces to recreate an interior worthy of the greatest English country houses.

The *Berengaria* made her maiden voyage for Cunard in April 1921 but at the end of that year she joined the *Mauretania* on the Tyne to be converted from coal to oil fuel. Her upper promenade deck was partially glassed in and with her three giant funnels now painted in Cunard orange red with black trimmings, she presented a magnificent sight. She carried 972 first, 630 second, 606 third and 515 tourist class passengers and, with the *Aquitania* and *Mauretania*, made up Cunard's big three express ships for their prestigious run from Southampton to New York.

The *Berengaria* proved to be very popular with her passengers and developed a reputation for being flamboyantly glamorous, filled as she was with the glittering stars of the newly invented Hollywood movie industry.

On March 3rd 1938 she was badly damaged by a fire whilst in New York. Her last transatlantic voyage was made without passengers when she returned home for possible repairs, but her days were done, and she was sold for demolition eight months later. Her career spanned 26 years in which time she had served under the rule of the Kaiser of Germany and the reign of three British kings.

She was powerful and magnificent and, even though a little down at heel towards the end, looked every inch an imperial sovereign as she sailed for the last time to the shipbreakers at Jarrow.

The White Empresses of Canadian Pacific

Most of the world's great steamship companies had their beginnings firmly rooted in the traditions of the sea stretching back to the age of sail but not the great Canadian Pacific which eventually grew to become one of the world's most prestigious steamship companies. It had its roots firmly embedded in the railways of Canada.

Canada, that vast country north of the United States, stretching from the shores of the Atlantic to the Pacific was part of the British Empire and was administered as such from the halls of power in London. Whereas the nations of the empire situated east of Suez or south to Australasia and Africa were well served by companies flying the red ensign and belonging to the P&O, Orient, British India and the Union Castle Lines, the routes westward before the building of the Panama Canal, were blocked by the land masses of the American continent. It was here that the Canadian Pacific Railway Company evolved the grandiose scene of joining Britain with Hong Kong through links of transport by sea and land and then sea again.

After the completion of the trans-continental railroad from Montreal to Vancouver, it was a natural step to continue westward to the Orient. Connections between Europe and Canada were already well established by ships of British companies sailing from Glasgow and Liverpool. But Canada, being so vast and underpopulated, was in need of settlers, especially to populate the lands west of the great lakes. The Dominion government, as an inducement to the company to build the trans-continental railroads, gave them large tracts of land along the intended routes. Those lands the company eventually sold to the settlers they were carrying. Therefore, each part of the Canadian Pacific Company prospered and eventually grew to become one of the commercial wonders of the world, owning railways, ferries, liners, tankers, tugs and hotels, and on into the age of the airliner. But all that was in the future when their first chartered steamships sailed across the Pacific in 1887.

But it was with the great ships of the 20th century that the company earned its reputation for international glamour, especially those vessels which gloried in the name of *Empress*. They were, in their day, among the most attractive vessels in the world, those which created the style first sailing on the Pacific between Vancouver and Japan and then on to Hong Kong.

In 1891 the company built three sister ships. They were the *Empress of China*, the *Empress of India* and the *Empress of Japan*. They were of only 6,000 tons each but their style created an image of beauty which was to become synonymous with the name Canadian Pacific. Those first three ships with their clipper bows and figureheads seemed to be the ocean liners salute to the beauty of the sailing ships which they were replacing. Never again would steamships possess such ethereal grace – the necessities of the future would eventually replace the softer curves of the past with the newer beauty dictated by great size and power – but always the white *Empresses* were to be distinguished by their elegance.

The North Atlantic service was first served by the company itself when it bought the Beaver Line with its fleet of passenger ships whose names were prefixed with the word 'mont', such as the Montrose and the Montreal. The first of the company's *Empresses* to be built for the Atlantic service was in 1904 when the *Empress of Britain* was ordered from Fairfield's yards. She, and her sister ship the *Empress of Ireland*, were of 14,000 tons and represented a great step forward in the company's bid for transatlantic passengers. But with them came the first great tragedy to befall the company.

On May 29th 1914, the *Empress of Ireland* was rammed in fog by a Norwegian collier the SS *Storstad* while still in the St Lawrence River. She sank in less than fifteen minutes within four miles of the riverbank. One thousand people lost their lives and only 400 survived the disaster.

The company was to lose many ships in the great wars which followed but were never to lose as many people as were lost on that peaceful fog-bound river, that terrible night in May.

The *Empresses* represented by the paintings here span the years from just before the First World War in 1913 to the post war period of the 1950s.

Viceroy of India

In 1929 the 19,648 ton passenger steamer *Viceroy of India* was hailed as the ship of the year. She differed from all other P&O liners in that she was the first on the route to be a truly luxurious liner with interiors equal to any on the transatlantic run. She was built as a one off and had no sister ship.

The new levels of opulence to be found aboard reflected the demand for pampered luxury now expected by the travelling public even in the midst of the depression. The *Viceroy's* accommodation, especially that created for first class passengers, was gorgeous. Her smoking room was a reproduction of a medieval castle's great hall complete with hammer beams, huge fireplace, cross swords and baronial arms. The furniture and upholstery were all in period and the impression received whilst sitting in that room, with the scenes of India outside the windows, must have been fantastic.

The ship had a dining room pillared in marble, while her music room was graciously palladian in style. Her splendid indoor swimming pool was the first fitted into a P&O liner. This was decorated with columns of marble which supported a stuccoed ceiling. The walls surrounding the large tiled pool itself were resplendent with a frieze copied from the Roman baths of Pompeii.

Ventilation was on the Punka Louvre system which was installed throughout the vessel and ensured cool conditions in the cabins and public rooms whilst in the tropics.

Her motive power was by turbo electric drive, a relatively untried novelty at the time. Steam turbines, developing 17,000 horse power through electric motors, enabled the ship to average 19 knots, smoother and quieter than ever before.

Her propelling machinery was so quiet that Lord Inchcape said after her maiden voyage: 'she probably has no equal afloat, in fair weather she will slip through the sea still and silent so that, except for visual evidence, the curls at her bow and the wake away astern, men will deem her motionless. From stem to stern, from keel to truck, the *Viceroy of India* is a big steam yacht, smart to a degree for which many yacht owners sigh in vain. True to her character in this and all other respects, she is, in June, to become a yacht bearing happy people on a succession of cruises to the Mediterranean.' Those words, couched in the phrases of a bygone era, were to be proven correct.

Soon after her launching the *Viceroy of India* broke the London to Bombay record with a time of sixteen days, one hour and forty-two minutes. She was to become immensely popular as the flagship of the fleet, both on her normal runs to Bombay and on her equally popular cruising career. It was originally proposed to name her *Taj Mahal* but that idea was changed while she was on the stocks and she was given the imperious name of *Viceroy of India*, as a tribute to the representative in India of the King Emperor himself.

The ship was to act as a ship of mercy for many people in the course of her career. In September 1935 she rescued 241 passengers from the stricken White Star liner *Doric*, after a collision off the coast of Portugal and a further 279 passengers were rescued from the damaged *Ceramic* in 1940 off the coast of South Africa.

The *Viceroy* was converted for trooping in November of 1940 and met her end from a chance encounter with a German U-boat on 11th November 1942 at which time she was torpedoed and sunk with the loss of four lives. The *Viceroy of India* was a bench mark in the history of P&O, no other ship of the company before or since has quite measured up to her unique combination of style, elegance and vice-regal bearing. She was literally the most imperious of all the ships created to sail on that, the most imperial of all the world's steamship routes.

Bremen and Europa

Some of the most famous ocean liners ever to be set upon the seas were undoubtedly those created by the designers and builders of Germany. Those ships started life as grand and noble ambassadors representing, as they did, the artistic inventive and cultural achievements won by generations of German men and women of vision. However, these great qualities were to be overshadowed by others less desirable and few, if any, of the greatest German liners built in the 20th century would end their days under the flags or names with which they entered service.

If ocean liners were built as symbols of peace and international cooperation, then too we must take the symbolism of their eventual fate as meaning the failure of those hopes and a devaluation of the finer intentions of their creators.

The list of great German liners, especially those built for the transatlantic service, reads like a lesson in 20th century history. The most unforgettable and typically Germanic of those were the three great sisters of the early years, the *Imperator*, the *Vaterland* and the *Bismark*. Those ships started life upon the pedestal of grandiose pride. Their existence in the world of the maritime powers was intended to be unassailable but pride is not as durable as steel and even if the reasons for their building was eventually destroyed, those ships themselves managed to survive. The blame in this change in status lies with vainglorious military ambition, a fault not only in the exclusive domain of Germany. Other nations, from time to time, attempt to dominate and strut, and all eventually fail.

The ships themselves are blameless, and their very existence attest to this. Most are, or were, victims of circumstance. After the great war the *Imperator* became Cunard's *Berengaria*, the unfinished *Bismark* was ceded to the White Star Line and renamed *Majestic* and the *Vaterland*, already in American hands, sailed on as flagship for the United States Lines being rebuilt and emerging as the *Leviathan*.

Their change in nationality, triggering a change in personality, only served to prove that they themselves still retained their true reason for being, and that was the drawing together of the strings which bind people in the club of common humanity. Few, if any, lessons were learned by the experiences and horrors of the First World War. Man's inhumanity to man still flourished but even more virulently with the lead up to the Second World War. Between these wars came a new shipping renaissance with new building and new technology leading to even bigger and better ships. These again became vessels used for power politics. The *Queens* of Great Britain, the *Normandie* of France, and the two great Italian contenders, all followed in the wake of the great German duo of the late 1920s.

The *Bremen* and the *Europa* made Germany once more pre-eminent on the Atlantic. These two ships, launched a day apart, were identical and were intended to sweep all before them. Both won the coveted Blue Ribband and started again the headlong rush for shipping supremacy on the Atlantic. They became the symbols of a resurgent nation and until they hoisted the repugnant swastika to their mastheads, were internationally acclaimed as masterpieces. But they, like much of their age, was corrupted by the anti-human Nazi philosophy and were destined for destruction.

When the dust finally cleared on a devastated Europe, the *Bremen* had gone the way of many of her contemporaries, but the *Europa*, or what was left of her, was handed over to France as a sort of consolation prize. She was to be rebuilt and massively injected with gallic charm and when this reborn ship of hope, which was grafted to the body of an enemy set sail again, she had emblazoned upon her bows the name *Liberté*. This great ship sailed into a new age of peace and of massive changes. Not only was the age of great liners coming to a natural end but also the steam had seemed to run out of the arrogant posturings in Europe, cooperation was now the watchword.

The ocean liners were merely the tools of man and their use, as was their fate, was inextricably bound to the activities of those who created them whether that be for good or for ill.

Britannic (1930)

When ocean liners are spoken of, a few famous names are remembered. Those are the ships in the hall of fame, there, either because of a great tragedy or because their existence was something of a triumph. Who has not heard of *Titanic*, *Lusitania* or *Andria Doria*?

Why does the mention of *Normandie*, *Queen Mary* or *Ile de France* bring to mind visions of grandeur and glamour?

Many other names would be recognised too. Most of them belonging to the super-ships of the Atlantic. However, in their day there were legions of other liners, known and loved but never destined to become megastars. One such vessel was the *Britannic*. She lived her life without fuss and few people now remember her. Nevertheless, she was a ship around which important events revolved and she deserves a niche in maritime history.

Britannic was the last of the great White Star liners to sail under that company's colours. She was unique both in her propulsion and in her design. Her silhouette was radical for a transatlantic liner and many thought her less than beautiful. She was conceived and built to the high standards associated with her owners, based on comfort over speed and she proved highly successful throughout her long career being always popular.

She was your author's favourite. I write this while sitting on a chair from her first class dining room, a treasured keepsake rescued from the breakers yard and acquired many years after my first ever voyage which was aboard that glorious ship, and I recall it vividly. Its impact was so great that everything surrounding the experience remains like a time capsule in my mind. My memories are probably little different from those of thousands of people who travelled by sea after the war and I record my personal reminiscence here.

Those post-war years became the golden age for ocean travel – like a great burst of light from a guttering candle before being extinguished forever. I made my crossing, sailing from Liverpool on May 4th 1951 bound for Cobh and New York. The *Britannic* was not my choice, she was chosen for me rather in the manner of a Victorian marriage. Even as much as six years after the ending of the Second World War, Britain was still in the grip of post-war austerity and shipping companies were overwhelmed with requests for bookings, especially to New York. The liners were filled to capacity, which meant applying for a berth months in advance, the company allocating cabins at their convenience. I am speaking of the economy traveller and the class was tourist.

It all seems like a dream when I look back through the years. Everything was so different. Few people such as I travelled then, it just wasn't the thing. Attitudes were rooted in the past, the war had acted like a brake, stopping the world for half a decade and, when it was over, life resumed as if still in the thirties. This resulted in a strange juxtaposition of old and new social and economic conditions. Transportation operated much as before. People travelled by steam train and ship, trams ran in the cities, cars were the exception rather than the rule and airlines had not yet changed the lives of everyone. The war had speeded up technological advance to an astonishing degree but that had not yet burst upon the everyday scene. It was all waiting in the wings. In the early 'fifties the Korean War was in full swing and the H-bomb had just been tested.

The King of England opened the festival of Britain on the day I embarked for New York. The country was only just waking, as if from a nightmare. Sailing westward to the glitter and abundance of America was like a dream coming true and the joy of going on a fabled ship only added to the bursting feeling of excitement. I left my Belfast home for Liverpool aboard the lovely miniature liner *Ulster Monarch*. She was a vessel of 3,000 tons sailing under the flag of the Ulster Imperial Line. We entered the Mersey before dawn. The passing panorama of docks and ships lining the river all the way to Liverpool was fascinating. At one point in the distance I recognised the tall masts and twin squat funnels of *Britannic*. No more of her could I see then, her bulk was obscured by warehouses, but that first glimpse made the whole adventure come to life and I knew then that it was a reality. Perhaps the passage of time colours memory but the emotions felt still seem delectable almost forty years later.

Instructions sent by Cunard about embarkation requested that passengers present themselves at the Princes landing stage no later than 11am. The ship was due to sail at 3pm, I was there at 8.30 with suitcases and steamer trunks, hours too early and virtually alone.

The Princes landing stage has gone now. It was a curious contraption, more a thing than a place and synonymous with liner travel for thousands of passengers sailing from Liverpool. It was a vast floating complex of stages, huts and moving gangways, all attached to the land by a series of articulated bridges. Embarkation and customs halls were raised above the broad wooden stages, looking like elongated cricket pavilions. Windows overlooked the river and rows of wooden benches were the only seating. There was certainly nothing there to compare with the facilities offered by the ocean terminal then newly built in Southampton.

I don't remember seeing any first class passengers at the time. Most of the largest ships were still divided into three classes then, first, cabin and tourist. Before the war *Britannic* had originally been a three class ship, her top class then called cabin, and her other two being tourist and third. Liners were caught in a class trap. Shipping companies trying to out-do each other with descriptive names for the various economic divisions dividing their vessels. Sanity was restored in the post-war era, the giants carrying passengers in first, cabin and tourist while the intermediate liners, like *Britannic*, were reduced to first and tourist. The degrees of comfort which the lower class now offered was almost as splendid as the first class of twenty years before. A few ships in the 'fifties were sailing as immigrant carriers where standards were much lower than those found in tourist class, but not as basic as the old steerage of pre-1914 days.

I waited alone in that vast hall, my senses filled with the sights and sounds coming from the busy river, and time flew. Gradually the place took on the aura of anticipation with the arrival of uniformed officials representing the face of authority or the assistance of Cunard. The hall filled rapidly, boat trains arrived at the riverside station with passengers from London. The place echoed with the hub-bub of noise and excitable conversation. Accents of all kinds were sounding like an orchestra tuning up. Liverpool porters were lugging cases and trunks, Cunard shore staff shuffled papers and loud speakers issued information. There were tickets to be shown, passports to be stamped, exchange controls complied with and customs examination. All part of the ritual required to leave the United Kingdom in those highly regimented post-war days.

Each new official request was a step nearer to the great moment for me, but as yet there was no ship, only grey mist and a choppy river. Suddenly the atmosphere seemed to change. People started gravitating towards the windows, the sound of a tug hooting and a whistle blowing was heard and, very faintly at first through the mist, one, then another tug appeared straining with lines taut against an unseen burden, and finally she came into view.

She made her entrance as dramatically as any prima donna would onto the stage of an opera house. *Britannic*! Proud, huge, majestic and elegant. A beautiful vision of gleaming black hull, with white upper works, portholes and windows receding into the distance. Towering, slightly raked masts, and two massive squat black topped buff funnels proclaimed her as a White Star liner.

As she approached the landing stage her shape was overcome by her bulk which seemed to fill the windows, until only a section of a black wall of riveted steel plates was visible. Doors were opened in her hull and the moving walkways were lined up on their rails to give access between the landing stage and the ship. Eventually, I stepped aboard, to be enfolded in a cocoon of polished wood, deep carpets, crisp linen and gentle, perfect service.

It was the start of eight days of delight suspended between two worlds. I cannot now distinguish any one day from the next. I am only aware that everything seemed different, even the sounds were romantic and new. Bells, sirens, creaking joinery, the buzz of excited conversation and the hiss of the ocean in the distance. Light seemed brighter. The odours of salt-air mixed with oil, polish, perfumes and cigars, can only be smelled aboard a ship at sea. These ingredients of perception, wrapped in an atmosphere of exclusive excitement bring joy to those who ever experience it.

Those same sensations were present to a greater or lesser degree on every liner no matter on which ocean they sailed. Rough seas and sickness, part of the shared experience, horrible as they may be at the time, were soon forgotten, chased from the memory by drama and the overwhelming joy of being aboard and going somewhere special. I believe that to be the characteristic ingredient which separates those days of the passenger liners from today's cruise ships. The ship was the only practical means of getting from shore to shore. Your shipmates were all the more interesting because of it too. There was a shared feeling of adventure and anticipation tinged with excitement and pathos. It was a voyage in the true sense and not simply a pleasure trip to the sun.

The ending of voyages come across you gradually in many subtle ways. The spell cast by the ship and its environment is gently relaxed. Sea birds suddenly become land birds. Information about disembarking is found under your cabin door. The farewell dinner has been eaten, and forgotten suitcases are once more opened and begin to bulge. Sleep on that last night has been fitful, your cabin no longer seems as familiar. Your personality, too, has changed, with the town clothes you now wear to go ashore. Your shipmates appear as strangers somehow, awkward and anxious to leave. On the horizon a smudge has hardened into firmness, later to be confirmed as land.

Arriving in New York by sea is one of lifes most incredible experiences, especially if it is for the first time as it was for me. As the *Britannic* sailed slowly towards Manhattan the full enormity of my adventure was thrust upon my awareness. There it all was at last, a hundred American movies coming to life before my eyes. The Statue of Liberty, the skyline, the automobiles rushing by on freeways, looking like mobile liquorice allsorts in their pastel colours and white-walled tyres. Skyscrapers appeared bearing names almost as famous as the liners themselves which nuzzled the docks, creating a fringe of ships around the city.

My voyage was over, never to be forgotten.

Rex and Conte di Savoia

The 1930s was a decade which saw the birth of an exclusive group of super-liners built for the transatlantic service, they were known as ships of state. France, Italy, Germany and Britain each produced at least one, and most built a pair of these maritime masterpieces. Cost was no barrier, they were created as floating embassies and filled with the best of their nations art and workmanship. But of the eight greatest built between 1928 and 1939, namely *Normandie*, *Empress of Britain*, *Queen Mary*, *Queen Elizabeth*, *Rex*, *Conte di Savoia*, *Europa* and *Bremen*, only three survived the great conflict. The other five were either burned, bombed or sunk into oblivion like huge expensive toys; they were victims of an international game called war. The mind reels at the senseless waste of it all, but for a few short years those wonderful ships existed and their magnificence is still the stuff of dreams.

The least likely of those to have been created were the two Italian divas *Rex* and *Conte di Savoia*, they were not conceived as sisters but fate and Mussolini pushed them together. The *Rex* became the ship to capture the Blue Ribband for Italy, while the *Conte di Savoia*, the slightly smaller and slower of the two, was the one endowed with the greater beauty. She was elegant and, in a world devoted to art deco modernity, strutted her stage with a flamboyance usually associated with a bygone era. Her interiors were in the best traditions of Latin theatricality. At just under 50,000 tons, she was built to cram as many as four classes of passengers into her hull. A fact which departed from the sense of vastness usually seen in the three class ships of the day.

However, the concept of super-ships sailing from the mid Mediterranean ports to New York was, in the 1930s, a foretaste of the cruise ships which sail today. The southern, warm water voyages were popular but they never reached the high fashion acceptance of the cognoscenti which the direct routes from New York to the channel ports commanded.

The *Conte di Savoia* was splendid. Her wide open decks descending in terraces where open air swimming pools were laid out like Mediterranean lidos, complete with cabanas and coloured umbrellas. Her broad glass enclosed promenade decks were sheltered walkways, their windows stretching from deck to deck resulting in a windless corridor of light in which to sit – quite unlike anything else then sailing on the Atlantic – the views being uninterrupted by steel bulkheads usually found aboard the ships built for northern climes. The *Count* was never built for speed, unlike the *King*, in fact, they were built for different companies, each possessing very different philosophies.

Mussolini decreed that all Italian shipping lines were to be amalgamated into one with a single national identity, all the more to extol the virtues of his style of fascism and power. Like himself, his two greatest ships were not destined to sail into old age. Both liners were bombed and sunk in their home waters by the RAF in 1943 and 1944, thus bringing to an end the megalomaniacal attempt to give Italy seaborne supremacy.

Monarch of Bermuda and Queen of Bermuda

The New York to Bermuda service was, by the 1930s, very profitable, thanks to Furness Withy and Co. It was they who opened the island to tourism and, by so doing, created a dual success. The company built hotels and a golf club to cater for Americans, primarily New Yorkers and, to transport them, they developed an offshoot of their company, called the Furness Bermuda Line.

In the first two decades of the century there were few visitors to the island but, as its popularity increased, the company chartered a number of ships to operate an emerging trade. This proved so popular that Furness designed and built their first ship especially for the route. She was the *Bermuda*, a twin funnelled beauty of over 19,000 tons with a service speed of 17 knots. She entered service in 1928 and became very popular. However, she was not destined for a life of any length for within three years she had been destroyed by fire while in Hamilton harbour.

But those few years had convinced the company of the viability of that service and they ordered an even larger vessel to run as her consort. This was to be the *Monarch of Bermuda* but the two ships never met, the new liner did not enter the service until four months after the *Bermuda* had burned.

During those months, whilst awaiting the new liner's debut, the company chartered an assorted collection of famous ships to keep the service operating. Among these were the *Franconia* of Cunard and the *Veendam* of Holland America Lines.

Meanwhile, a sister to the new *Monarch of Bermuda* was ordered and from 7th March 1933 she became her running mate and flagship of the line. This ship was named *Queen of Bermuda* and between them they provided a unique service to that lovely subtropical island. The most unusual aspect of these twins was the atmosphere of big ship luxury, far beyond anything else on such short distance routes anywhere in the world. The distance between New York and Hamilton was only 700 miles the round trip taking only six days, including two and a half in Bermuda.

But the seas encountered could be, and often were, heavy. The Atlantic for 700 miles to Bermuda is little different from the 3,000 miles to Europe. The ships were almost identical and at over 22,000 tons were equal to many of the famous transatlantic liners of the day. The concept of sister ships with such an advanced design made them unique. Each liner had three funnels and with curved bridge fronts and enclosed promenade decks bore a great resemblance to the mighty *Queen Mary*.

The interior decor of both was to the very highest standards of luxury. The entire accommodation being reserved for the 700 first class passengers. A small second class section, intended for only 31, was also provided. Both ships were registered in Bermuda and sailed under the British flag, the *Queen of Bermuda* sailing with an all British crew. But the *Monarch of Bermuda* had a catering and deck crew predominantly Bermudian. The service depended on speed and reliability and, although the ships were used by many as cruise ships, they were in fact liners in the truest sense of the word.

They were designed and built as passenger and cargo carriers and at times their cargo consisted of thousands of tons of fresh water which could be carried in double bottom tanks.

The 1930s was the high point of the twin ship service, each lovely liner taking turn to sail into and out of New York, there to be seen with the greatest ships of all time in the line up at luxury liner row. Their black striped, red funnels crowning the French grey hull and white superstructures, made them instantly recognisable.

When war broke out Britain recalled her far-flung fleets to the colours and the *Queen* and the *Monarch* went home too, to be converted as armed merchant cruisers and troopships. They performed their duties without mishap and when it was all over they returned to their builders to be redressed in their finery before resuming their much needed dollar-earning voyages to Bermuda.

This time it was the *Monarch*'s turn to burn and on 24th March 1947, while in drydock in Newcastle, her entire accommodation was incinerated. It was the end for her. The government bought the charred remains and had it rebuilt into an immigrant ship which was named *New Australia*. She sailed as such for 10 years and was then re-sold to the Greek Line. She was sent to Germany for rebuilding and emerged as a tourist class liner called *Arkadia*. She gave good service for a further 16 years and on 18th December 1966 was taken to Spain for breaking up.

The *Queen of Bermuda* was destined for many more years of elegant living and after her post-war refit she emerged better than ever, her gorgeous interiors beautifully restored. Her funnels slightly cut to recede gradually down into a more pleasing line she was now fully air conditioned and resumed the Bermuda shuttle alone until 1951, when a new and smaller running mate the *Ocean Monarch* was built to join her. But times were changing fast. The competition between the shipping and the airlines had become vicious.

For a time the *Queen of Bermuda* and the *Queen Mary* were to be the last three funnelled ships in the world, each of them creating a stir when seen in New York. But the company, in their wisdom, decided that the newer one funnelled *Ocean Monarch* made the *Queen* look old fashioned. So they sent her to Belfast in October 1961 to be re-boilered and modernised. She reappeared looking vastly different five months later. She now had a curved bow and one streamlined funnel and in this anonymous guise, sailed for a further four years before finally making the sad voyage to the shipbreakers in December 1966. That same month, her sister, the former *Monarch of Bermuda*, also went to the breakers. They had been, at one time, two of the most beautiful liners of their day and many thousands of people on the island of Bermuda and the city of New York will forever remember them.

Manhattan and the Washington

These two ships were the first to be built in America especially for the United States Lines. Since the creation of the company, their ships had been ex-German liners taken as war reparations including the great *Leviathan* which had been rebuilt in America to impose a yankee flavour onto her teutonic personality. But with the *Washington* and the *Manhattan*, the company had two very different liners. Their concept and atmosphere were the personification of American ideas – airy, modern and folksy – which even went so far as to have on board *Washington* a smoking room more in keeping with a cabin in the backwoods complete with a bronze bison, paintings of Indians in canoes and stuffed moose heads mounted on the walls. But apart from that monstrous room, the ships did possess a charm and a sense of modern spaciousness very much in keeping with the age, and they proved very successful in competition with the medium sized ships of the European nations.

Both ships were very attractive and well balanced, with two funnels and two masts. Originally the *Manhattan* had been built with low squat funnels to make her appear more powerful, as with the giant *Bremen* and *Europa* of Germany. These low funnels proved highly inefficient, and aesthetics had to take second place to practicality when the funnels of most of the sleek looking liners were raised in height to enable smoke and smuts to fall clear of the decks. The only ships which actually did retain their squat funnels were motor ships, like the *Britannic* and the *Georgic* of the White Star Line, whose engines did not require their funnels to be any bigger.

However, after only a few months in service, the silhouette of the *Manhattan* was changed too and new tall, thin funnels were fitted which gave her a haughty look instead of the racy one originally intended.

The *Washington* entered service with the modified shape pioneered by her sister nine months before, and both vessels looked distinctive and elegant with their countersterns and their colourful company livery.

When war came to Europe, the transatlantic service was drastically curtailed and as neutrals the American ships went to sea with huge flags painted on their hulls and on their hatch covers to proclaim their neutrality to the warring states. Their first war time voyages were made crowded with frantic tourists fleeing Europe and eager to get home. On these crossings the ships were filled to capacity, cots even being placed in the public rooms to accommodate the refugees. For a while before the United States herself entered the war, the *Manhattan* and the *Washington*, soon to be joined by the new *America*, went cruising in safe home waters before finally being called up for national service as troopships, the *Manhattan* becoming the United States ship *Wakefield* and the *Washington* being renamed the *Vernon*, both in 1941.

The only one of the twins to survive that war intact was the *Washington*. She re-entered liner service as an immigrant carrier in 1945, sailing until 1951 when she went into the inevitable American lay-up for thirteen years before finally being demolished. The *Manhattan*, as the *Wakefield*, caught fire while sailing as part of a convoy on September 3rd 1942 and although virtually gutted and abandoned by her crew, she was taken in tow and managed to reach Halifax. That was the end of her career as a liner. She was rebuilt as a permanent troopship and after lay-ups she went to the breakers at Kearny, New Jersey in March 1965.

Normandie

Never before, or since, has there been a ship such as the *Normandie*. Superlatives bathed her from her conception to the moment she was engulfed in flames, turning herself into a grotesque parody of what she once was. All the great super-liners of the 1930s were designated ships of state and were dramatic and glorious emblems of the nations which spawned them. Germany, Great Britain, Italy and France, built the biggest. Other nations entered the fray as well they could, with ships which, though beautiful, only seemed to shrink when placed next to the mammoth liners of the super powers.

At the top of the top was *Normandie*. So exquisite was she, that it seems a pity she was not placed under glass and preserved untouched forever as a monument to mankind's creativity. But that was not to be. *Normandie* was designed and built to work. To cross oceans faster than any ship had ever done before and to carry people in an atmosphere of such rare luxury that many would be intimidated by her opulence, so much so, it almost defeated the purpose of her creation.

Normandie, in the few years that she sailed, was not financially successful. Passengers preferred the cosiness of Britain's *Queen Mary*, or the legendary *Joi de Vivre* of the smaller French ships.

She was too much, almost unapproachable in her grandness. Gold and glass reflected from every pore, tapestries and embroidered furniture filled her rooms. Vast, uninterrupted spaces presenting vistas of sweeping staircases where statutory and fountains of light seemed to present an unending parade of interior splendours. Outdoor terraces and great funnels of crimson formed sensuous shapes. Steel, wrought into Gallic femininity, produced an impact stunning enough to numb the senses. A goodly part of France's national wealth was poured into her.

If she had been anything other than a ship her creation would have been hailed as a monument to a civilisation and expected to last a thousand years. But this was not to be. This monument to France afloat was available for the world to wonder at for only one thousand, five hundred and fifty days. A refugee from warfare, she was consumed by flames in the harbour of New York where she had received her greatest triumph such a short time before.

It was a waste of unimagined proportions but her legacy was the creation of a legend which seems to grow as time goes by. If any ship is to be granted the accolade of unforgettable, it is the *Normandie*, and her short life only served to enhance her fame. Whereas *Titanic* is remembered with a certain ghoulish fascination, *Normandie* brings to mind wonders untouched, fabled people gliding in and out of incredible saloons, great theatrical greetings in beautiful harbours, blue ribbons streaming in the wind denoting the claiming of a prize for being the world's fastest, finest and most fabulous.

The memories and fantasies surrounding the *Normandie* can never be tarnished for she disappeared before the ravages of time could change her. She was, and still is, the ultimate, the flagship of our imagination and for that alone she was worth the building and the extravagance. Nothing will ever dethrone her from her place as the most fabulous ship ever but she is only, in reality, a figment of our imagination. Her end came just in time to allow us to wallow in the tragic waste of her destruction which saved her from the ravages of a destructive future.

Strathmore

Between 1931 and 1938 the P&O Line built five ships with the prefix 'Strath'. They were advertised as the white sisters. The first two ships of this group carried three funnels, the middle one being the only real one. This illusion to grandeur was never worth the effort, the dummies taking up too much deck space and helping to make the ships top heavy. The buff colour of the working funnel needed repainting constantly to match the brightness of the other two unused ones. Apart from the superficiality of trying to make the ships resemble giant transatlantic liners, the *Strathnaver* and the *Strathaird* were notoriously tender ships and few were the voyages which didn't see regular bills for vast crockery replacement.

Of the other three, the *Strathmore* preceded her sister, *Stratheden*, by two years, the third ship, *Strathallan*, not being delivered until the spring of 1938. These three beauties were the forerunners of P&O's future external style which lasted until the *Canberra* was built in 1961.

On 4th April 1935 the *Strathmore* was launched by Her Royal Highness the Duchess of York whose family name the ship bore. On that day, this charming little duchess was quite unaware that through a twist of fate she was destined to become Queen of England less than eighteen months later. Eventually she would launch the biggest liner ever built and bestow on it her own regal title. The *Strathmore* and the *Queen Elizabeth* were only two of many great ships to be sponsored by her in the future, but all that was in the lap of the gods when the lovely new *Strathmore* went down the ways.

The liner lived an uneventful life and performed her duties without scandal or disaster. She developed a reputation for dependability, comfort and popularity. She spent the years of the Second World War as a troopship and when returned to her company in 1948 was, after an extensive refit, placed back into service, sailing on October 27th 1949 carrying 497 first class and 487 tourist class passengers. In 1961 she was placed into service as a one class ship while the newer members of the fleet took their turn to strut as glamour girls on the post war stage.

The *Strathmore* was sold out of the company in November 1963 and eventually went to Italian shipbreakers in September 1969 at the venerable age of thirty four.

Queen Mary

There is a museum on the coast of California which has amongst its exhibits a bronze medallion upon which is struck an image of a large three funnelled liner. Underneath this are five words written in Latin which, when translated mean "Queen Mary promised me to the seas". Those words were to herald a fabulous new era afloat and that medallion represents only one of the exhibits on view today.

The museum itself is the most incredible exhibit of all, because it is the *Queen Mary* herself, forming the centrepiece of an enormous leisure complex on the waters edge. She floats in her dock at Long Beach on the shores of the Pacific, but, unlike a building which is rooted to the land from which it grew, this museum came here by itself, after a career at sea spanning three decades.

The *Queen Mary* was always special even before she was launched. She was known to millions of people. Then only by her builders number of 534. She was to be the first liner to exceed 1,000 feet in length. She was to be the most luxurious, the biggest, the best and the most incredible thing ever created by man. But these claims had been made before in each preceding generation and always there had been a challenger waiting in the wings. However, number 534 would in this, and many other ways, be very different from any other ship.

She was the first British merchant ship to be launched by a reigning monarch and she was the first Cunarder to break with the traditional practice of having her name end with the suffix IA. It had been rumoured that she would be named the *Victoria* in keeping with Cunard tradition, but the new ships name remained a secret up to the moment of launching when it was given to her personally by her Queen. Construction began under the flag of the Cunard Steamship Company but fate took a hand in that too. The great depression of the early thirties almost finished her before she was launched and work had to stop for lack of funds. For over two grim years she sat rusting on the banks of the Clyde waiting. She became the symbol of failure to all who lived under her vast shadow. Those shipyard workers, now without jobs, were the worst affected. They were victims of that terrible period and when eventually work resumed on the hull, it was as if a cloud had been lifted, not only from Clydebank but from the entire nation.

After months of painful negotiation the government finally agreed to a loan but with certain provisos, one of which was that the Cunard and the White Star shipping companies should merge. This new company was to be known as the Cunard White Star Line and it was under their combined flags that work was restarted on 534. Sufficient funds would also be available for a sister ship to be built. The huge hull which had brooded on the stocks by the side of the Clyde now represented hope for the future. It was as if those great bones of steel had felt the fear, frustration and agony of the lean years. Caked with rust, they were at last ready to be cleaned and painted in the mantle of tomorrows optimism. She was now the workers ship and they claimed her as a symbol of a brighter tomorrow for themselves and the nation. It didn't matter that she was intended to be a gilded barge for the rich and famous she was theirs, and they put their hearts and souls into her building. The ship seemed to absorb these into her very fabric, giving her a special vitality which was never to leave her.

September 26th 1934 was a day of celebration. The great ship was about to be sent down to the seas. Heavy straight-falling rain lashed the thousands of people who had gathered to wish her well. The King and Queen were there to honour her. John Brown's great shipyard was almost silent as the moment came for the Queen to christen her and, in a tremulous voice heard for the first time on the radio by millions of her subjects, her majesty said "I am happy to name this ship the *Queen Mary*. I wish success to her and all who sail in her." With that, she cut the ribbon holding the huge bottle of Australian wine. As it crashed against the bows the great steel hull started her historic rush towards the grey waters of the Clyde.

Pandemonium reigned as the crowd roared their greetings. Horns, klaxons and hooters from ships and tugs all blasted and screamed again and again as the stateliest ship, then in being, became waterborne. The *Queen Mary*, destined to be the last of the worlds super liners to survive, was afloat at last. The secret was out. The name chosen for the world's greatest ship suited her to perfection. She was a *Queen* and the people loved it.

Millions of words have been written over the years about the *Queen Mary*, her life and her times. Suffice it to say she was almost the biggest, was almost the most luxurious, and was almost the fastest liner ever built. But in spite of not being awarded those dubious prizes, she did become the most loved, the most famous, and the most impressive liner the world would ever see. She sailed for over thirty-one years, a queen to the last, but she was not perfect. Her faults were as massive as she herself. She could roll alarmingly, especially in the early days before Fin stabilizers were invented. She vibrated massively, enough to make your teeth chatter if standing near her stern, and when, during the war, she met tragedy it was to be a devastating event which resulted in carnage.

War is not glamorous. Its destruction and death are obscenities which weigh heavily on us all. These are especially tragic if inflicted by ourselves on our own friends. That is exactly what happened on October 2nd 1942 when the great *Queen* was approaching the coast of Scotland at high speed, packed with American troops estimated at over 15,000 men, she was sailing alone on a zig zag course relying on her great speed for safety from U-boats. Naval escorts were not provided for the entire Atlantic crossing in those days. Only near the coasts were the *Queens* given naval support. On this occasion one of her escorts was HMS *Curacoa*, a light cruiser of 4,200 tons. Somehow the ships manoeuvred too closely together and, in one horrifying moment, the massive bows of the *Queen Mary* slashed through the hull of the *Curacoa* cutting her in two. She sank within five minutes taking 331 men with her to their deaths. Only 101 managed to survive. Her bows badly damaged, the stricken *Queen* could not stop to rescue survivors, the risk was too great in those submarine infested waters and reluctantly, at greatly reduced speed, she continued her voyage to the everlasting horror of those who were involved. The eventual inquiry split the blame, HMS *Curacoa* being the ship found to be most at fault.

It was not until the end of July 1947 that the *Queen Mary* re-emerged as the great ship of peace again. She was resplendent in new paint and reconditioned to perfection. She was still the fastest ship in the world even though her younger sister the *Queen Elizabeth* probably could have beaten her, but speed records were never formally acknowledged by her company. Not for her the gaudy trophies or flying pennants, she was above all that and with great dignity sailed uncrowned as the speed queen.

The post war years were the financial golden years for shipping until the 1960s when it all went badly wrong. Air travel, especially with the advent of the large jet, took over completely and the age of the passenger ship came to a shuddering stop. One by one, with unseemly haste, great liners were withdrawn from service. The *Queens* were losing prodigious amounts of money sailing with fewer and fewer passengers. They became like ghost ships, creaking and groaning eerily empty across the Atlantic. It was time for them to go.

The *Queen Mary* was sold to the city of Long Beach for use as a convention centre and museum. She was to be delivered by Cunard not, as they suggested, empty with a minimum crew but to sail there in a blaze of glory. Her new American owners wanting this final voyage to be a cruise, she sailed with over 1,000 passengers and a Cunard crew of eight hundred, still under the command of her last captain, John Treasure Jones.

Her route was to take her 14,000 miles. She was to be the largest ship with the greatest number of souls aboard ever to sail around Cape Horn. It was to be her longest peacetime voyage, through climates she was not designed to encounter. She did it magnificently at the grand old age of thirty-one, tired, rusting and old fashioned. The *Queen Mary* left her home port of Southampton for the last time on 31st October 1967. Her send off was tearful. It was the end of an epoch and, amid the exuberance of farewells, a great sadness lay over the city.

Not so in her new home of Long Beach. When she arrived six weeks later on December 9th it was to a welcome no one could have anticipated. Tumultuous, spectacular, emotional and incredible were words used to describe the scene as the great *Queen*, surrounded by literally thousands of boats, slowly came into port. She glided with aristocratic dignity to her berth. The *Queen Mary* had reached her last harbour. She had come to die as a ship and to begin her life as a fantasy.

Amra

The great British India Steam Navigation Company Limited was founded in 1856 becoming known, almost immediately, as the BI Line. It was one of the biggest steamship companies in the world. Not only did the company run fast and elegant ships from England to Africa, it also provided a comprehensive service connecting disparate ports within the orbit of Britain's far eastern empire.

The original service of the company was from Calcutta to Rangoon. It started at the beginning of the British raj in India with Burma being administered by the government of India. Most ports serviced by the company included Maliwoon, Victoria Point, Polaw and Moulmein up to the capital Rangoon.

The number of ships in the company quickly increased to enable the BI Line to eventually sail between India and Africa, India to the Persian Gulf, and from Madras to Singapore and Calcutta to Japan. An African feeder service between Mombasa, Zanzibar and the coastal ports was also inaugurated and a direct service from England to East Africa through the Mediterranean and Suez was to become a main route.

The size of ships in the company ranged between 14,000 tons and 20,000 tons. The area serviced was gradually increased as the empire grew, until the outbreak of the Second World War, when many ships of the line were lost and the empire itself started to wither and die.

In 1938, the 8,000 ton *Amra* was built by Swan Hunter and Wigham Richardson of Newcastle. She was designed for the Calcutta to Rangoon service but was not destined to remain on the route for long before the outbreak of war, at which time she was requisitioned as a hospital ship.

At the end of hostilities, with its subsequent great political upheavals and eventual breakup of the empire, *Amra* was placed on the India to Africa service. She carried 222 saloon class passengers and 737 third class. Her route now took her from Bombay to Mombasa with occasional calls at Karachi.

In 1955 she, with the rest of the fleet, had her colours changed from black hull with a white superstructure to being an all white ship, relieved only with a thin black stripe around her hull. The funnel colours remained, as always, black with a white banding. This simple colour change in itself cooled the ship by as much as 10 degrees whilst in the punishing heat.

The *Amra* sailed as one of the intermediate liners of the company, without incident or accident, until she was sold for scrapping in 1965. She was typical of the many thousands of passenger and cargo ships which were built during the days of the British Empire. She was remarkable in as much as she was unremarkable at the time, being merely another cog in the great wheel of shipping transportation.

Nieuw Amsterdam

The *Nieuw Amsterdam*, at over 36,000 gross tons, was not a giant but she was the biggest ship to be built in Holland. All that was best in Dutch design and charm went into her creation. She exhibited the same warmth and friendliness always to be found in her motherland. There was nothing of the femme fatale about her nor was she a stodgy matron.

She was known as the ship of tomorrow when first she appeared and was designed to complement the world's fair to be held in New York in 1939. In place of heavy polished woods and massive furnishings, operatic flamboyance, self conscious art deco or floating odeon, favoured by the Germans, Italians, French and British, the Holland America Line wisely decided to recruit a team of their finest young designers to create a modern interior, studiously coordinated in shades of gold, ivory, pale blue, rose and pastel greens. Her furniture was designed to create an impression of light and spacious luxury.

Her first class dining saloon was the most beautiful room aboard and, to many, it was the most beautiful afloat. All the great liners of the time were fabulous and comparisons between one and another, room for room, must only lead to argument. However, it is agreed by those who were able to compare, that everything aboard *Nieuw Amsterdam* was delightful. Her lines, her interior, her sea worthiness and her service, all were sublime. She was not remarkable in a dramatic way, she was simply a most remarkable ship. Voyage after voyage she sailed carrying the cognoscenti of ocean travellers. Her passenger lists were a virtual who's who of the famous in the worlds of the arts, industry and politics.

Whereas the giant speed queens vibrated their racy way from continent to continent in under five days, *Nieuw Amsterdam* serenely ploughed her stately furrow, providing her elegant passengers with a full week of matchless, modern luxury. The ship of peace was not destined to live her life in peace however, and only fifteen months after her maiden voyage she found herself an orphan in New York, her nation at war with Germany.

During this traumatic period in Dutch history their beautiful ship became a symbol of freedom and resistance. She was stripped of her finery and became an allied transport earning the accolade of being known as the darling of the Dutch.

She sailed in convoy many times with her former rivals of the Atlantic and was to be found in the tropic heat, of the Indian Ocean, the Pacific and then, eventually, back to the Atlantic ferrying American troops to the battlefields of Europe.

She carried over 378,000 people in miraculous safety for almost five years. Finally, it was all over and the ragged survivors of history's most destructive war could go home and prepare themselves for the work they were originally built to do. *Nieuw Amsterdam* was luckier than many of her contemporaries. The passenger fleets were decimated. Great names were lying beneath the waves or gutted by fire. Of the survivors, some would be shuffled like cards in a pack and re-emerge as completely new ships with new names and nationalities, while others would return to their homes for re-building and resume their careers better than ever.

A few days before the ninth anniversary of her launching, the Dutch welcomed *Nieuw Amsterdam* back to Holland. As she entered war ravaged Rotterdam, with her funnels specially repainted in her house colours of yellow with green and white stripes, the port greeted her with everything and anything that would float. The noise was a blood chilling cacophony of sirens and hooters, the great ship answering time and again with blasts from her mighty horns. This was a moment of triumph which heralded Holland's awareness that they were truly liberated.

Their ship of peace was home at last but it was a home exhausted by years of enemy occupation and on the point of starvation. The docks and shipbuilding facilities were in ruins but with the incredible resilience of a people who had created their own country from the sea, they started the awesome task of rebuilding their ship. It was to take fourteen months before she emerged, almost as a new liner. She was completely rewired and her beautiful decor was restored to its former glory. Her wood panelling, scarred by thousands of scratches inflicted by hundreds of thousands of troops, was planed down to a new smoothness and repolished. Furniture which had been stored in America was once more brought to Holland and placed aboard. Miles of carpet were relaid. Her magnificent dining hall, with its Morano glass lighting fixtures and padded gold ceiling, was restored to its former brilliance, beneath which satinwood chairs were placed ready for her first post war passengers.

Her second maiden voyage to New York was made in October 1947 and she immediately re-established her reputation as a very special ship, sailing, as in pre-war days, carrying three classes of passengers, her standard of comfort and service in each class being in a class of their own.

The company's advertising slogan of the time was "It's good to be on a well run ship", and to the thousands of passengers the slogan was a fact. America was hungry to travel to Europe. Students and economy conscious tourists flocked to a class named for themselves. The middle class was designated cabin class. First was all that first class should be and pampered those that demanded the best of everything. The *Nieuw Amsterdam* settled into the routine of the Atlantic shuttle. She was a happy ship creating an atmosphere of friendliness not enjoyed by many other liners.

The boom years of transatlantic travel lasted from the late 1940s for no more than a decade, during which time a new fleet of great ships were built for the mercantile nations. However, try as they might, the shipping companies were now beginning to fight a losing battle and, even though getting there was half the fun, the world was changing. Two weeks at sea, going and coming from a vacation, was not valid any more. Those two weeks were the only two weeks that most people had available. The pattern was changing. Ships which could not easily be switched to cruising were now sent to the breakers, never to be replaced.

There was much soul searching on the board of the Holland America Line. The *Nieuw Amsterdam* was no longer in the first flush of youth. The ship of tomorrow was rapidly becoming the ship of yesterday. She had periodically been brought up to date but now a complete rethink was in order.

In January 1962 she underwent another refit with a reduced first class capacity and a greatly increased tourist class. Most of her original public rooms were retained. She was still one of the most beautiful ships in the world. Her traditional ambience, and unsurpassed reputation, insured a faithful following of discerning passengers. But she was now a two class ship for the Atlantic run and could readily be opened up as a one class cruising liner when needed. This, in fact, became the norm and more and more of her years were spent in the warmer waters of the world.

She suffered a major breakdown in 1967, her thirtieth year, and the company was informed that she needed to be fitted with expensive new boilers to survive. It looked as if it was the end of her but, true to her charmed existence, she was lucky to be able to undergo a maritime heart transplant. Suitable used boilers from a defunct American cruiser were hastily purchased and installed on the stricken liner and once more she sailed. In 1971 she departed from Rotterdam on the last Holland America Line voyage to New York. She never went home again. Her registry was changed from Rotterdam to Willemstad in the Dutch West Indies and her home port became Port Everglades in Florida. She spent the rest of her life cruising to the islands of the Caribbean an island herself of old world charm and pre-war nostalgia. She was withdrawn from service at the venerable age of thirty-five and in December 1973 she sailed to Taiwan and the ship breakers.

Mauretania (1939)

The 1930s was a decade of great change for the Cunard line. It was during those few years that they and the White Star Line were to merge, and when most of their famous liners would be disposed of including the first *Mauretania*. The decade started with a devastating economic depression and ended with the beginning of World War II. The shipping world saw the entry of the great *Queen Mary* into service followed by the withdrawal of all White Star ships except *Britannic* and *Georgic*. The maiden voyage of the second *Mauretania* in 1939 was to be the prelude to the year when the gorgeous *Aquitania* would hand over her baton to the new *Queen Elizabeth* thus completing the company's modernisation plans. But all that was violently interrupted by the insanity unleashed on the world by the mad corporal then ruling Germany.

Mauretania was the first great ship to enter service following the formation of the Cunard White Star Line in 1934. She was intended to run on the London-New York route together with the remaining White Star twins *Britannic* and *Georgic*. As the great *Berengaria* had been disposed of the previous year. The new *Mauretania* was intended also to act as a stand-in for the *Queens* when either one of them would undergo their annual refit. As such, she was designed to maintain the luxury if not the speed of those two giants between Southampton and New York.

She was, therefore, unique: Not only was she to carry the world's most illustrious maritime name, her mission was also that she became a temporary *Queen* for a few weeks each year. She was destined to do both brilliantly for almost a quarter of a century.

The second *Mauretania* was very different from her famous namesake. She was larger, but slower and her accommodation was quietly elegant rather than flamboyantly spectacular. She was streamlined and modern and, with her two impressive funnels, she would resemble more the new *Queen Elizabeth* and not at all the four funnelled Edwardian beauty whose name she carried.

Mauretania was set afloat upon the historic River Mersey on 17th June 1939; she sailed on her maiden voyage to New York a hopeful symbol of the new company's determination to maintain a royal service on this old route, the surviving White Star motor ships acting as her consorts. Exchanging Liverpool for London as her home port (and thereby becoming the biggest ship to be dry docked there) it is an odd postscript to that company's saga that the only visible evidence of the historic merger was to be seen operating from that untypical port. It may seem now to have been a bad omen, for the service was to be short-lived: after only four voyages, war was declared, and the *Mauretania* was laid up in New York pending an admiralty decision as to her future.

In March 1940 she sailed for Australia where she was converted into a troopship, not to be returned to her company until 1947 during which time she steamed over half a million miles and carried an estimated 350,000 troops. Her re-emergence after the war, however, enabled her to participate in the final and greatest chapter in the long history of ocean liner transportation.

Her fleet mates now were both of the great *Queens*, and the new and opulent *Caronia*, affectionately known as the Green Goddess because of her cruising colours, the two new mini sisters *Media* and *Parthia*, the veteran *Franconia*, *Scythia*, *Samaria*, and the *Britannic* last of the White Star fleet, while the *Aquitania* was just about to go to the breakers. The *Mauretania* was lovely and deeply engrained with Cunard mystique, she sailed on unhurried voyages between Britain and America calling at France and Ireland *en route*. She was, at 35,677 tons now the third largest ship in the fleet and her intimate queen-like accommodation gave her an elegance and atmosphere second to none. She was immensely popular and loved by passengers and crew alike. Her last captain, John Treasure-Jones, reluctantly admitted to a special relationship between himself and the *Mauretania*. His gruff emotional story of her final voyage to the shipbreakers proves that ships do indeed have something akin to a soul, their lives and destruction affecting those who are closest to them as if they were living creatures. Captain Treasure-Jones always said that his favourite ship was the one he was aboard at the time, to him the *Queen Mary* was special, but the *Mauretania* was very special. She was a ship that was easy to handle, sea kindly and with a gentle personality. She was a lady at all times.

The *Mauretania* sailed into the 1960s and the decline of sea travel as beautiful as ever. As the profitability of operating a transatlantic service diminished, the *Mauretania* was placed on the Mediterranean to New York service but sadly this was not a financial success either and her cruising programmes were stepped up. She was repainted in the multi-green cruising livery made famous by the *Caronia*. She looked smart and colourful, but perhaps suited her original colours better.

Her career was coming to an end as the lifes blood drained from the haemorrhaging age of liner travel. She was not young any more, but in normal times would have had many good years ahead. However, the die was cast and she had to go. The *Mauretania* arrived at the shipbreakers in Scotland on November 23rd 1965, there to be reduced to scrap.

Captain Treasure-Jones says that when he took her to the junk yard at Inverkeithing he was filled with such a sense of melancholy when he left her there he couldn't even turn around to look or else he would have been turned into a pillar of salt. No doubt other captains have had similar thoughts at that moment of desertion when their beloved ships were thrown to the mechanical wolves waiting to rip them apart.

America

The United States of America never fully participated in the scramble for kudos on the seas. She relied on the Europeans to ship her cargoes and passengers across the Atlantic until after the First World War when, through a series of machinations instigated by the government, there came into being a company which became known as the United States Lines. This was the company which operated the vast *Leviathan* in the 1920s and early thirties. (Formerly the German liner *Vaterland*) this great ship was a financial liability due greatly to the United States prohibition laws. Not many passengers electing to voyage on a dry ship. Those laws were repealed shortly before she was withdrawn from service in 1934 at which time a pair of smaller sister ships were built for the company to replace her.

The *Manhattan* and the *Washington* were medium sized, traditional looking liners of 24,000 tons. They would prove to be successful and very popular, it was planned that they be joined in 1940 by a larger ship, more in line with the size and luxury to be found on the finest European vessels of the day.

This ship was eventually built and was called the *America*. She had a long and chequered career and is still afloat. It is not unusual for a liner to change hands after a successful career and then go on to earn the plaudits of the shipping world anew. Too often though this maritime schizophrenia proves disastrous and the vessel declines into a nautical skid-row living out her final years devoid of dignity. Sometimes fate takes a merciful hand and the ship either founders *en route* to yet another backwater or she splendidly ends her agony in sheets of flame.

This scenario could in part be applied to the *America*, a beautiful ship which in her life has had no less than five different names and towards the end was even renamed *America* once more in a disastrous attempt to cash in on her old glories. She has not gone yet. Her final act is still to be played out. She sits forlornly in a Greek harbour awaiting a doubtful future. But she will always be the personification afloat of all that is meant by being typically American.

She was, in her day, a stylish ship wearing her two distinctive funnels at a rakish angle as if they were hats brushing the brow of her face. She was sleek, modern and the pride of her nation when first she entered service in 1940 but an ill-timed debut it turned out to be. Europe went to war the day after she was launched and the *America*, named by Mrs. Eleanor Roosevelt, rather than making a maiden voyage across the Atlantic was placed safely on the cruise trade in the inter-coastal waters close to the American continent.

The United States entered the war in 1942, at which time the ship was taken over by the Navy and converted for trooping. She was re-named *West Point* and served in that role until 1946, when she was reconditioned and given her original name to take her place as the flagship of the American merchant fleet. The *America* was the largest liner yet built in that country. She was, with a length of 720 feet, only in the intermediate class of ships sailing the Atlantic. Her closest rivals were the new British *Mauretania* and the Dutch *Nieuw Amsterdam*. They could have been sisters in size and age but they were as different to each other as were the countries from which they came.

The *America* was a popular ship and even after the dramatic entry of her incredible running mate, the *United States* in 1952, continued to sail filled with discerning passengers delighted to spend a week or more enjoying the yankee atmosphere between New York and Cobh, Le Havre, Southampton and Bremerhaven.

The first time your author sailed on her was from New York to Southampton, travelling in somewhat spartan style in her tourist class. She was then divided into three classes, tourist passengers, all 160 of us, were housed forward, with little to call luxury. The deck space available was minimal, either open to the full fury of the winds forward of the bridge, or semi-enclosed in a minute promenade deck also at the bows and highly reminiscent of old time steerage. The two public rooms were more in keeping with that to be found aboard a destroyer than on a luxury liner. In spite of this the cabins were comfortable and remarkably spacious, and everything gleamed mechanically. The service was democratic and the food marvellous. I remember sneaking up to the cabin and first classes and being astounded at the difference, especially the promenade deck which was rubber under foot and had windows stretching from deck to deck. Forming a vast corridor of light and air. Her decor, very unlike that to be found aboard European ships, had touches of great luxury. She was shiny rather than cosy, comfortably efficient rather than affluent.

A few years later I sailed on her again, this time for a week at the coastal end of one of her transatlantic crossings. It was 1960 and she had then been opened up as a two class ship. In those days it was possible to sail on liners between channel ports of call for remarkably little money. I boarded the *America* early in the morning, in Cobh at the end of a voyage from New York. She arrived in company with the *Mauretania*, the two ships looked splendid as they dropped anchor in that beautiful remote Irish bay. Going aboard her was like entering a New York hotel in the middle of nowhere. The atmosphere of that frantic city seemed to wash over you the minute you stepped aboard.

This time, the improvement in the tourist class accommodation seemed unbelievable in comparison to what it had been formerly. There was space, comfort and the familiar American ambience, contributing to the makings of a memorable passage. It was during that week that the *America* showed me what a special ship she really was and I was able to understand how she had captivated the hearts of so many of her passengers.

I was sorry to learn a few years later that she had been sold. The Greeks converted her into a one class liner and renamed her *Australis* to be used specifically on the immigrant run to Australia. She quickly became known to thousands of people and was beloved by all who sailed on her. She was no longer a star among ships, all the glamour of her transatlantic years had gone but worse was to come in the days following her withdrawal from the Australian service in 1978. Since then she has declined in status, losing her forward funnel in the process, and is now a sorry shadow of her original self as she lies forlornly in a Greek harbour awaiting her eventual fate.

She will always be the SS *America* to me, a little bit of Miss Liberty afloat. The story of *Australis* is of a different ship in a different time, and is for another day.

Queen Elizabeth

The *Queen Elizabeth* remains the biggest liner yet built, even in the 1990s when cruise ships now exceed 70,000 tons and ferries of 40,000 tons are commonplace. The idea of a passenger ship 1,030 feet long and weighing 83,000 tons stretches credulity, but these were just some of the statistics which were offered to describe the immensity of the *Queen Elizabeth*. She was built as the big sister of Britain's other super ship, the *Queen Mary*, and between them they established a partnership on the Atlantic which eventually became the envy of the world.

The *Queen Elizabeth* was built to enter service in 1940 in honour of Cunard's 100th birthday but greater world events overtook her life and she became a war baby. Her sea trials in fact became her maiden voyage and under veils of grey this embattled young *Queen* sprinted across the Atlantic in secret to the safety of New York. There to briefly join her consort *Queen Mary* for the first time, their partnership was tempered in the crucible of war and they were seen on every ocean on earth as troopships before returning to their peacetime roles in 1946 as the most luxurious and greatest liners in the world.

The *Queen Mary* somehow managed to retain her well established pre-war reputation and even though her old adversary *Normandie* was gone but not forgotten she re-entered service with the confidence of her past achievements and the Blue Ribband firmly tucked into her belt.

But the now resplendent, new but well tried, *Queen Elizabeth* took her place at last as flagship of the line and supreme monarch of the sea and proceeded to try and establish herself as the ultimate ship. She almost made it but not quite. Of the two wonderful *Queens*, it was the *Elizabeth* which was the sleeker and the most classically beautiful. Her interiors were quieter and in the best of taste. Had she entered service in the year planned she would have been the natural contender for comparisons and rivalry with the *Normandie*. But fate plays tricks with all under heaven and on earth and the scenario for ships is as problematical as it is for humans.

The *Queen Elizabeth* earned and accepted the plaudits and prizes which were her due, as biggest and most fabulous ship ever created, but she never earned the popularity, love or sense of fantasy which always surrounded the *Queen Mary*. She arrived just a fraction too late on the world's stage, the best was over. She was born just in time to be indispensable in war, but she blazed like a comet for too short a time to become a true legend. Perhaps she was just too big and too splendid to be cosy or friendly, she earned respect and to many of her passengers and crew she would be their star of stars. Sadly, when the end came, it was not the dignified tear stained departure to retirement as enjoyed by the *Queen Mary*, but for the *Elizabeth* it was to years of neglect, then a painful travesty of a voyage to Hong Kong. But after only a brief glimpse of her as a gleaming possibility, she decided enough was enough and gave herself a vikings funeral in a blaze of publicity ending up as a crumpled, twisted and charred wreck in 1972 under the seas she once ruled so majestically. No book about liners would be complete without the supreme example of the shipbuilders' art being represented and that supremacy was definitely embodied in the great *Queen Elizabeth*.

Media

Cunarders always seemed to have a dynastic resemblance to each other, whether or not they were crowned with one, two, three or even four funnels, each generation was in direct line, one from another. The 'twenties to the 'forties saw the size of ships grow dramatically, the last of the giants being the *Queen Elizabeth*, intended to enter service in 1940.

The next ship to be built for the company could not have been more different. She was tiny in comparison to her big sisters and was the first transatlantic passenger liner to be built by any nation after the war and, as such, she is historically important. She and her twin, *Parthia*, were intended originally to be cargo liners for the Brocklebank line, a Cunard subsidiary. They were replanned on the stocks as passenger and cargo ships, *Media* being the first of the pair, was built at Clydebank – birthplace of the *Queens*. *Parthia*, perhaps with a certain feeling of belated loyalty, was built in Belfast, the traditional builders of the former White Star fleet.

These twins went into service in 1947 and 1948, and at 13,000 tons were the smallest passenger liners in the company. They were designed to carry only 250 passengers in one class, designated 'first' but probably nearer to cabin class in style and price. Their route was Liverpool to New York, with occasional calls at Boston and Bermuda, their leisurely crossings taking a week. They were not deluxe but were very comfortable. Their hybrid design did not enhance their stability and they earned an early reputation for being poor sea boats. Their motion was lively, so much so that the company picked the *Media* as the first in their fleet to be fitted with the newly perfected Denny Brown Fin stabilizers making her the first transatlantic liner to be so fitted. They were so successful in damping a roll that even the *Queens* were eventually equipped with them.

The *Media* looked smaller than she was, her design was beautifully compact and classic, her single mast and traditional colours made for a lovely looking little liner. The interiors were beautiful. Her dining saloon seated all passengers at one sitting which set the tone for the social life of the ship. The public rooms, all situated on the promenade deck, were typically Cunard, with exquisite wood veneers creating an atmosphere of modern, cosy luxury enhanced by fine fabrics, carpets and furniture of great quality. Even though built in the late forties, it was as if that decade had never existed stylistically.

Media, Parthia and, a little later on, the fabulous *Caronia*, were fitted with interiors similar to those in the ships of the 1930s. The *Media*, small as she was, in reality felt like a miniature *Queen* and had the edge in maritime atmosphere, possessing a club like ambience. She provided a range of accommodation consisting of smoking room, intimate cocktail bar, a long gallery, library come writing room, drawing room, and a grand saloon two decks high. Her cabins, mostly outside with private showers and toilets, were for two, some had extra Pullman berths if needed. There were no luxury suites aboard, nor were there elevators, swimming pool or cinemas. Her dining room was pleasant enough but being only one deck high, lacked true elegance. The glass enclosed promenade deck was lined with upholstered deckchairs and the open boat deck was perfect for deck sports in fine weather.

For a ship whose design was split between the needs of sophisticated passengers and no-nonsense freight, she presented a business like personality. Her fore and aft decks were a clutter of holds, king-posts and derricks, and her top deck was a magic-land created from bits and pieces guaranteed to gladden the eye of any ship lover. Open, red mouthed ventilators, a satisfying Cunard funnel, white lifeboats and davits, teak decks and one tall mast, all redolent of great passenger ships stretching back to the first decades of the twentieth century.

These sights, with clean, salt tasting breezes and a multi-mood ocean provided the ingredients for travel experiences no longer possible and very sadly missed. But the little sisters were not to be financially successful. Their rigid passenger timetables precluded full utilisation of their freight capacity which was over 10,000 tons. Too much time being spent loading and unloading to make it practical. Containers and pallets were just around the corner. Dock labour was seething with change and dissatisfaction. The *Media* and *Parthia* were neither Cunard fish nor Cunard fowl and their end came early. The company sold both in 1961 for further trading under different flags.

It is a strange foot-note to her history that after many name changes and being re-built beyond recognition *Media* was to end her life as the *Lavia* 27 years later almost on top of the remains of her former fleet mate *Queen Elizabeth*. Both were born on the waters of the Clyde and both were burnt on the waters of Hong Kong. The indignity of their final years being eradicated at last by the flames of a Viking funeral.

Orcades (1948)

The ships of the Orient Line after the Second World War were distinguished by their elegant and somewhat unconventional shapes. The company, in direct competition with the giant P&O were noted for being progressive in the design of their vessels. They were the first of the colonial shipping companies to employ a famous architect to create the interiors of a ship in its entirety beginning with the *Orion* built in 1935.

She was the first liner of the company to enter service with a corn coloured hull. This, with its green boot topping, white upper works and buff funnel was to be the livery of all Orient liners in the future.

The *Orion* was also the first traditional liner to be fitted with only one mast and this, with the single funnel and new colour scheme, placed her firmly in the forefront of modern marine architecture.

But it was her interior which put the *Orion* and her company ahead of her contemporaries. She was the first ship ever to be entirely decorated and planned by one designer. That designer was Brian O'Rorke and it was his philosophy of abandoning the hotel look for the pure ocean liner style, which made the *Orion* so unique, thus paving the way for the ships of the future. Those pre-war innovative ideas were still relevant in the post-war rebuilding programme and the ships of the Orient Line built in the 1940s still excite comment. Each one possessing some new feature which was either loved or loathed.

The first of these new liners was the *Orcades*, launched in 1947. She was a large ship, 28,000 tons, and presented a radical profile with her bridge, funnel and mast incorporated into one block placed amidships. Her hull lines were traditional, however, and with the now familiar yellow and white colour scheme, she was a powerful and elegant looking ship.

Her life was spent undramatically going about her business, sailing to Australia and, for a few months each year, on cruises from England to the Mediterranean and north Cape ports. Her only brush with international fame was her appearance among the great fleet gathered to honour the new Queen Elizabeth II at her coronation review off Spithead on June 15th-17th 1953. It was at that great event when the picture of *Orcades* was painted by Howard Jarvis.

In 1966 *Orcades* and her sisters were incorporated into the P&O fleet at the amalgamation of both companies. She was broken up in Taiwan in 1973 looking slightly less elegant in her P&O paintwork of unrelieved white.

Edinburgh Castle

The Union Castle Line emerged after the Second World War with an ageing fleet of ships sadly in need of rebuilding and replacing. The first pair of new ships to enter the mail service in 1948 were the largest ever built for the company, and at 28,705 tons were two of the most elegant liners in the world.

The first to enter the water was the *Pretoria Castle* and her South African name was endorsed by her sponsor Mrs Smuts, wife of the South African prime minister, who named the ship by radio from Pretoria. The second ship was the *Edinburgh Castle* and her sponsor was Princess Margaret, the Scottish born younger daughter of the king. These naming ceremonies underlined the importance of the ships as part of Britain's post-war programme of recovery.

The *Edinburgh Castle* was, with her sister, powered by steam, a return to a traditional source of power for the company after many years of building oil driven motor ships. This dictated their shape which was now dominated by a single, large, functioning, smoke belching funnel. This splendid red and black edifice was flanked fore and aft by two tall masts evenly spaced on a long, lean, lavender coloured hull with a white superstructure. The ships were identical and very beautiful.

Many years later the author sailed on the *Pretoria Castle* but then she was named the SA *Orange* and owned by Safmarine. She had lost her masts, her hull was rusting and her once magnificent funnel was now painted grey with black, white and yellow stripes at the top. She looked a sorry shadow of the ship of years before but her interior was still splendidly traditional Union Castle. She had hung on to a vestige of her old dignity with difficulty but ended her life in a Taiwanese shipbreakers in November 1975. The *Edinburgh Castle* sailed to her end carrying the same colours in which she was christened only six months after her sister she was beautiful and stately and very much still a Union Castle ship.

Himalaya

The post war rebuilding of the P&O fleet began with the *Himalaya* on April 29th 1946, when her keel was laid at Vickers Armstrong at Barrow in Furness. However, due to shortages of essential materials, she was not ready for launching until October 5th 1948. Her trials could not be made until late August 1949 but despite this long gestation period and the great difficulties in obtaining the stuff from which ships are made, *Himalaya* finally emerged as a liner built to the highest standards expected then from British shipbuilders. She was, true to her breeding, a typically traditional P&O ship, resembling the pre-war Straths in style and elegance.

The *Himalaya* was the largest ship yet built for the company and, at over 28,000 tons, represented a great step forward. She was also the biggest ship built anywhere in the world at that time and her maiden voyage created a flurry of excitement representing, as it did, the long awaited re-emergence of optimism to the world of glamourous travel after years of war and austerity.

She was designed as a two class ship for the England to Australia route, sailing via the Mediterranean and Bombay. Her increased size and power reduced the sailing time by five days to India and she took only 28 days to Melbourne. She became very popular and her long voyages and shorter cruises were filled to capacity for the first great years of her life.

She was the first ship to start cruising from England after 1939. Part of the incredible popularity of those cruises no doubt stemmed from the fact that British exchange controls were so severe after the war. At that time a holiday aboard a ship representing British territory was a great incentive. The maximum amount of money allowed out of the country was under £50 which made the attempt to travel abroad a mockery. Those post war cruises by P&O on their new *Himalaya*, and later on the *Chusan*, with those on new liners of the Orient Line, brought thousands of war weary people to a new awareness of the pleasures of travel aboard great ships. It was also a time for a flood of immigrants to sail to the vast island continent of Australia as well as transatlantic westwards to Canada.

The ships of P&O and Orient Lines sailed filled to capacity in their tourist class sections outbound and returned almost as full with travellers eager to see the old country. It was the start of a period of shipping richness seldom seen in the history of sea travel and, even though the staggering costs of new ship construction threatened to choke the companies, they reaped vast rewards for over a decade before the bubble burst. Competition from air travel decimated the industry. Mergers and amalgamations took place as historical and famous names disappeared forever, swallowed whole and digested into conglomerates that were no longer exclusively devoted to maritime commerce. Today, they that go down to the sea in ships, are but a small part of the mighty P&O group of companies. Nevertheless, P&O still, touchingly, harbour a deep affection and sense of pride in the ships that made them famous, maintaining a highly efficient archival department with a fine maritime art collection amassed over the years.

All this was in the distant future when *Himalaya* entered service as the first P&O liner of the new and final era in the company's shipping history. She was fitted with a Thornycroft funnel top in 1953, thus adding 12 feet to the height of the funnel, making her even more like her younger and smaller sister *Chusan*. It was not until June 1959 that she was fitted with stabilizers and, a year later, she became fully air conditioned. In the autumn of 1963 the *Himalaya* was opened up as an all tourist class ship, her line voyages being supplemented more and more by cruises from both England and Australia, culminating in 1968 when she left Tilbury for a world voyage calling at fifty-one ports and carrying nearly 15,000 passengers in all. This was to be her epic voyage. In the following year her home port would be Southampton, breaking the company's last links with Tilbury.

The *Himalaya* made her last cruise from Southampton in the spring of 1974 to the Mediterranean and at the end of that year, sailed from Sydney on her last voyage to the breakers yards at Taiwan. Her life had spanned almost three decades during which time she had heralded an optimistic era for the company after the war and lived long enough to see the end of sea transportation and her own obsolescence as a viable means of intercontinental travel.

Chusan

The *Chusan* was the last and largest liner to be built by P&O for their Far East service. Her route took her from Tilbury to Gibraltar, Port Said, Aden, Bombay, Colombo, Penang, Singapore, Hong Kong and Kobe and then back again. She was the first large liner anywhere to be fitted with Fin stabilizers and their success was such as to make them obligatory on almost every passenger ship to sail from then on.

The rather staid image of P&O belied their innovative heart and they were responsible for many new improvements in liner development over the years. *Chusan* was the second ship built as part of the company's post-war revival but due to lack of essential materials her completion too was delayed. She was expected to enter service in May 1948 but it took two more years before she was ready for her maiden voyage.

Her name was taken from a group of islands at the entrance to Hang Chow Bay south of Shanghai, a derivative of the Chinese name Chou-Shan. The ship bore a remarkable similarity to the slightly older and larger *Himalaya*, both profiles being traditional looking and unmistakably intended for the tropics. Their sleek white hulls, topped by a single yellow funnel and flanked by two tall masts, were distinctive. Tiers of open promenade decks proclaimed their promise as shady walkways in sultry far off seas.

The *Chusan* was the most luxurious ship ever built by P&O for their Far East route. She could carry 474 first class, 514 tourist class passengers and a crew complement of 572.

Her first few voyages were cruises to the Atlantic isles and the Mediterranean. Sailing fully booked on all of them. Her maiden voyage to the east was to Bombay, sailing on September 15th 1950, but it was not until November 7th of that year that she made her first trip to Hong Kong.

It was found during those first few months that her funnel did not completely dispense with all smoke and fumes, much of it returning with the down draught onto the open decks aft. It was a difficulty then common to all ships. In May 1952 she was fitted with an extension to her funnel top designed by Thornycroft. This modification seemed to work and no longer were passengers doused with smuts and fumes. However, the cure did nothing to improve the ship's appearance.

Similar contraptions were eventually fitted to other liners of the day including the *Himalaya*, and a sleeker modification of the idea was later developed into a simple dome which became familiar on later ships, including P&O's new *Arcadia*, and four Cunarders destined for the Canadian service and also the new royal yacht *Britannia*. From then on all funnels were fitted with domes, cowls or fins of some sort, it was the end of simple funnel shapes but also the end of noxious fumes sweeping the decks.

In 1953, after a period of thirteen years, the company reinstated its old service to Japanese ports, *Chusan* being the first P&O ship to enter Kobe since the beginning of the war. Her career was charmed and she was to be seen on every ocean on earth. As air travel eroded her role as a means of transportation, cruising now became more and more part of her itinerary.

In the early 1960s she was given a refit, with full air conditioning being installed. In 1963 she was transferred from the Far East to the Australian route. Her voyages now included sailings around the world, usually westward, with calls at Caribbean ports and through the Panama Canal to Los Angeles.

In 1970 she made P&O's last scheduled passenger call at Bombay, thus ending the company's passenger service to that port which had lasted for over a century. It was with a sense of loss that the shipping world heard of her withdrawal from service in 1973. *Chusan* was an immensely popular ship, she was big enough to be impressive and small enough to be cosily comfortable. Her interiors were not luxurious but were furnished with quiet good taste. Ships such as she were the backbone of the world's seaborne passenger transport system. What was at one time commonplace is now only a happy memory.

Chusan left Southampton for her final voyage east on May 12th 1973, she was to sail empty and sad to the shipbreakers of Taiwan.

United States

The quantum leap in design which separated the *Normandie* from the *Queen Mary* in the 1930s was even more evident in the 1950s when the last record breaker to be built flashed across the Atlantic on her maiden voyage.

The *United States* was everything the *Normandie* tried to be two decades earlier. This yankee flier was beautiful in a completely practical way. Gone were the movie set interiors, anything remotely combustible was taboo, the gleam of aluminium and glass replaced the wood veneers of tradition. Her accommodation was divided into three classes distinguished by their functional design. Gone too were the vast areas filled with deeply feathered luxury, instead there was a rather clinical efficient series of smaller spaces offering great comfort in an atmosphere which could only be described as modern maritime.

The *United States* was a ship through and through, no comparisons could be made with grand hotels or stately homes. She was the perfect example of Americanism and a triumph for her designer William Francis Gibbs. Her length was only 10 feet less than the mythical thousand footers of the previous decades. Her tonnage was flexible and somehow managed to fluctuate downwards without any alterations being made to the ship during the course of her life. She was, in every way, a super ship.

She was designed and built for the twin purposes of being either a grand transatlantic liner or a vast troopship capable of sailing ten thousand miles with fourteen thousand men without refuelling. Her speed was never fully disclosed. Everything about her – machinery, hull design or sub divisions – were a secret. No photographs were released of her underwater form, in fact, so secret was this, that she was even built in a United States Navy secured dry-dock and was nearly afloat at her naming ceremony. The United States government involvement, and their admitted responsibility for her incredible design and speed, was in sharp contrast to the hidden involvements of the British Admiralty before the First World War when they surreptitiously imposed their own specifications on the building of the *Lusitania* and the *Mauretania*.

The *United States* entered service on July 3rd 1952, her maiden dash across the Atlantic was made at such high speed that the paint on her water line was removed by the friction of her rush through the water. The speed record, held by the ageing *Queen Mary* for 16 years, had at last been broken and she entered the British port of Southampton wearing the Blue Ribband to a rousing reception. The return voyage to New York was also a record breaking run and the *United States* triumphantly sailed into New York as the undisputed fastest liner in the world.

The ship settled into a routine thereafter with her fleet mate *America* and competed against the Cunard *Queens* and other European liners. She became one of the most highly successful ships of all time in spite of her rather plain decor. She was in tune with the spirit of the age and, as the fastest ship ever built, attracted the new, young and affluent travellers from both sides of the Atlantic.

But the sands of time were running out for all passenger ships and, apart from the new *France* and two Italian late coming beauties, the age of the super liner was over. Jet planes ever bigger and ever faster came into service. The great ships were sent cruising and so too was the *United States*. She was still receiving government subsidies and she sailed the world until she was unceremoniously withdrawn from the arena and sent to be laid up at her birthplace of Newport on November 8th 1969. She lay there for five years before being moved to Norfolk, Virginia, where she is still to be seen decaying and forlorn without any decision having been made as to her eventual fate.

It seems to be an undignified situation for one of the world's greatest maritime achievements. She was, and is, a great ship carrying the name of a great nation, she deserves better than the sleazy fate she seems to be consigned to.

Orsova

Orsova was built in 1954 and completed Orient Line's post-war building programme. The design feature which distinguished her from the rest of her fleet mates was her lack of any kind of conventional mast. She was in fact the first large mastless liner, her funnel with its 'Welsh hat' top serving the double role of mast and smoke dispenser. The *Orsova* was the link between the *Orion* of pre-war days and the futuristic *Oriana* which would follow as the greatest and last liner to be built for the company.

Her lack of mast gave her a silhouette which was instantly recognisable but when flying her signals, rigged between the bridge top and her funnel top she looked untidy, the lack of height making the bunting appear more like washing on a line than flags proudly flown from a masthead. Nevertheless the ship was sleekly modern, the use of her all-welded construction resulted in a smoothness never before seen on the hull of such a large liner and gave her a crisply tailored look, even when seen in close-up. Her career followed that of most post-war liners, gradually relinquishing the role of transport to the jet plane. *Orsova*'s voyages around the world were interrupted in the summer when she would cruise from Southampton on shorter voyages to the Mediterranean and Scandinavia. This pattern continued until 1974 when she was sold to the breakers, arriving in Taiwan on February 14th.

Uganda

On May 20th 1986 a pathetic looking ghost of a liner sailed out of the River Fal and headed out to sea. As she passed the historic town of Falmouth she was greeted by a small flotilla of tugs spraying fountains of water and sounding their sirens in tribute to her passing. The name *Triton* was crudely painted on her bows but it had no ring of familiarity about it. Once pristine white, the ship was now heavily rusted. She was dressed overall in a brave attempt to appear festive while black oily smoke poured from her funnel with the exertion required of her tired engines. For this maritime vagrant was, in fact, the once beautiful *Uganda*, the former flagship of the British India Steam Navigation Company Limited.

This was the beginning of her final voyage, to be ended by the wild winds of a typhoon which capsized her as she lay in the hands of the ship breakers off the coast of Taiwan. It had been 34 years and 4 months since the happy day of her launch to the day of that final departure from the shores of England.

The *Uganda* was the 450th ship built for the famous British India Company. She was one of a pair, her earlier sister, the *Kenya*, being almost her pea pod twin: the only way of telling each from the other was that *Uganda* had been fitted with a taller funnel.

They were traditional ships of 15,000 tons, built with the classic lines favoured by their company. Designed for the United Kingdom, East Africa route they were the largest in the fleet and their two class accommodation was typical of the high quality found aboard British Colonial liners of the 1930s to 1950s.

Uganda was especially charming, with her wealth of African inspired art works and her panellings of rare wood veneers. The ships entered service in the original livery worn by the fleet of the time – black hull, white upper works, black and white striped funnel and red water line. A thin white line encircled the hull to give an elegance never quite equalled. *Kenya* and *Uganda* sailed regularly for 15 years on their original routes but economics, politics and progress conspired to finish their reason for being, and in January 1967 the *Uganda* was withdrawn from service to be rebuilt for a new life.

The BI Line had inaugurated a schools educational cruises service in the 1920s. These cruises were originally operated aboard troopships no longer needed and operated by the company. *Uganda* was to be the latest in this line of specialised ships. Her original first class and cabin class accommodation was to remain virtually intact to accommodate some 300 fare paying passengers. New accommodation was built into her former cargo space to enable the carriage of 900 students in dormitory accommodation. That and the lecture rooms were completely separated from the accommodation provided for the cruise passengers.

When she entered this new service, her familiar, lovely, classic lines had almost disappeared. A superstructure had been built upon her stern, her promenade deck was extended forward, her twin masts had gone and her bridge structure was altered. *Uganda* was recognisable now only by her hull lines and her original funnel but she was still an attractive looking ship.

The most delightfully surprising result of her refit was that, despite all the newness, her original passenger accommodation was left almost intact. The *Uganda* sailed into the age of the new cruising market of the 1970s as an anachronism among the glossier ships of the day. Her fares were pitched lower than on the new built holiday ships she was to compete against. She was no longer classified in the language of modern travel as luxurious. She was old fashioned, traditional and classic. Her style of service aboard was still colonial. She was quietly charming and offered her discerning and knowledgeable cabin passengers nostalgia and elegance at a price which would have been cheap, even if doubled. These assets were the secret of her success and successful she undoubtedly was.

At the end of her commercial life she was mourned by her many admirers in a way that falls to few ships. A preservation society was formed in a vain attempt to preserve the liner. Originally called the Uganda Society, it has now evolved into the Passenger Ship Enthusiasts Association, an organisation dedicated to the life and times of passenger liners past, present and future.

Uganda's commercial life ended in 1982 when she was quickly taken out of service in the midst of a Mediterranean cruise and sent to Gibraltar for conversion into a hospital ship. The war for the Falkland Islands had broken out between Britain and Argentina, and in an emotional upsurge not seen since the 1940s, an armada of British ships was assembled to sail half way across the world to fight for the liberation of those invaded islands. The great liners *QE2* and *Canberra* had both been requisitioned as troopships and with a fleet comprised of aircraft carriers, frigates, ferries and submarines, sailed for the South Atlantic.

Uganda sailed independently, meeting up with the fleet near the Falklands. She was now painted white overall with the red crosses of a hospital ship on her funnel and hull. Many men were killed and maimed on both sides during that brief conflict – war in the 1980s being no different to wars of the past. In the hospital wards aboard *Uganda* the wounded were relieved of their tragic suffering by the skill of her doctors and nursing staff.

The ship never really recovered from the trauma of that war and she was virtually to end her life in the South Atlantic after Britain's victory. She gradually ground herself down into exhaustion, running a shuttle service as replenishment ship and troopship, constantly sailing between Ascension Island and the Falklands, until her services were no longer required and she was almost ignominiously deserted in a lay-up berth of the River Fal in Cornwall until that sad May day when she finally sailed for an ending in the Oriental ship breaking yards.

Southern Cross

Few British ships have been sponsored by reigning monarchs, many have been launched by consorts, princes and princesses. In Germany the kaiser and his family stood many times at the bows of their finest liners to send them down the ways. In Holland, the beloved Queen Wilhelmina launched their gorgeous *Nieuw Amsterdam* in 1938 and in Britain the supreme accolade of naming a ship after themselves and then launching it went to the reigning consorts of two British kings but it was not until August 17th 1954 that a liner was launched, for the first time, by a reigning British sovereign.

Queen Elizabeth II launched the *Southern Cross*, not because it was a ship of record breaking proportions but more as a mark of her favour to the shipping company for their service to her in the year of her coronation. The Shaw Savill and Albion Line had carried the queen around the world on their liner *Gothic*, then designated a royal yacht for the voyage, and now her majesty had come to Harland and Wolff's shipyard in Belfast to wish god's speed to the company's newest ship. The *Southern Cross*, even though not a world beater in size and speed was, however, a ship of great importance. Her design was revolutionary as was her concept and she was truly a forerunner of today's cruise ships, though at the time of her entry into service, the idea of building a ship for anything other than transportation services was rare. The *Southern Cross* was the first liner to have no provision for the carrying of cargo. This was especially significant, for her intended route was to sail from Britain to Australia and New Zealand and then home around the world. This traditional, colonial route had formerly been one based on carrying goods to the colonies from the mother country and returning with their produce. The carriage of passengers to and fro was of equal importance and both previously had usually sailed together aboard the same ships. But now all that was changing.

The *Southern Cross* was designed to carry 1,100 passengers, all in tourist class. Her accommodation ranged from single cabins to dormitories and her passengers from immigrants to those voyaging purely for pleasure. Her design was novel too. She was the first liner of over 20,000 tons to have her engines placed near the stern. Consequently her funnel was placed aft too. This left the rest of the ship's space entirely free for the accommodation, resulting in an uncluttered series of public rooms and spacious open decks.

The concept found favour in some of the great liners which followed her but she was not the ship that shaped the future as had been suggested at the time. The future was, even then, being shaped by the airlines. Nevertheless, in the few years left to the age of the ocean liner some exceptional ships would be built using the *Southern Cross* as the role model. A consort to herself was eventually launched and called the *Northern Star*. She too was an aft funnel ship. The Dutch adopted the idea for their beautiful new liner the *Rotterdam*, launched in 1958. She was the first and only transatlantic liner to have engines aft and fitted with twin uptakes instead of funnels. She is still sailing with her original name as a cruise ship and when P&O built their newest and biggest liner *Canberra* in 1961 she too was built with engines aft and carried twin funnels at her stern. She also sailed into the 1990s much as she did originally, and still sails under her original flag and name.

The *Southern Cross* was very successful and popular and with the ending of passenger ship trading was sold out of her company and into the cruising trade. First to the Greek Ulysses line and renamed *Calypso* and now sailing under the flag of Panama she is named *Azure Seas*, her time being spent on the Pacific between Los Angeles and Mexico. These are seas that she knew well in her heyday. She was, and still is, a lovely looking ship instantly recognisable by her distinctive profile. Her running mate, the younger but larger *Northern Star*, never caught the imagination of the public and sailed for only thirteen years before going to the breakers. The *Southern Cross* is now thirty six years old and is a floating tribute to the skill of her Belfast builders.

Windsor Castle

The *Windsor Castle* was the biggest liner to be built for the Union Castle Line and the third to bear the name. She was launched by HM Queen Elizabeth the Queen Mother on the 23rd June 1959 and was the largest ship launched in Britain since her majesty had launched the Cunarder *Queen Elizabeth* in 1938.

The *Windsor Castle* was a graceful, streamlined vessel and looked every inch a conventional Cape ship. She had a balanced profile with a tall superstructure topped by a single funnel, a curved bow on an elegant hull, ending in a cruiser stern, presenting lines worthy of a steam yacht.

Those beautiful shapes were enhanced by the typical but quirky colour schemes of the company; lavender hull, white superstructure and a red, black topped, funnel.

This gorgeous looking liner was intended as the penultimate new build for the company of that period. A running mate was being built at Barrow-in-Furness and was to be called *Transvaal Castle*. She was to be the first hotel class ship in the fleet but she, at an early age, was taken over by the newly formed Safmarine of South Africa and re-named the SA *Vaal* which then left the *Windsor Castle* as the last great ship to be built by the company.

Her intended service was the fast mail run from Southampton to Cape Town. Her speed enabled her to improve the time for the voyage from 13½ to only 11½ days.

Her accommodation was designed to take account of the cruise nature of the route, her tourist class passengers outnumbering those in first class, the quality of accommodation and space per passenger being almost equal.

The *Windsor Castle* entered service on August 18th 1960 in what was to be the last of the shipping world's major year-round liner runs. She, and her surviving sisters, sailed on the route until 1977 when passenger service was abruptly terminated to be replaced by huge container ships for a freight only service. The *Windsor Castle* left the company of which she was the glorious flag-ship, to become a hotel for Middle East oil riggers under the Greek flag. Her near sister, the *Transvaal Castle* still cruises from Miami as the *Festival* of the Jubilee Cruise Line.

With the withdrawal of these ships from the Cape service, ended the fabulous history of Britain's mail ships south of the equator. The seven seas are sadder without them.

Canberra

The remaining ships still sailing in this last decade of the 20th century which were built in the days of liner service are few and far between. Most of them are now almost unrecognisable from the days of their youth. They now sail with new names and under different flags, having been rebuilt into cruise ships. A very small number still retain the distinctive shapes which gave them their character. Of these the great liner *France* of 1962 is probably the most famous. She now sails as the cruise ship *Norway* and very seldom crosses the Atlantic. The former Canadian Pacific liners, *Empress of*

Britain and *Empress of Canada*, and the Union Castle liner, *Transvaal Castle*, still sail as lovely cruise ships with the air of old time ocean aristocrats surrounding them but now with different names.

P&O's liner *Canberra* is the only one left much as she was when built. She carries the same colours and still sails with her original company flag under which she started her career in 1961. She is the last British passenger liner in service which was designed and built as part of the global transportation system. Her intended route being to Australia and around the world. The later and larger Cunarder *QE2* was built for a different life being designed as a cruise and part time transatlantic liner and was never part of the old liner traditions.

Canberra and her running mate *Oriana*, of the now defunct Orient Line, were the largest ships built at the time for any route other than the transatlantic. They were futuristic and radical in design and although *Oriana* was built in the modernistic traditions of her company, it was to *Canberra* that the prize went for a completely new departure in liner design. Even today, after almost thirty years at sea, she appears as modern as ever, her distinctive shape instantly recognisable wherever she is seen.

The *Canberra* is a large ship, being over 45,000 tons, and is still enjoying great popularity with her predominantly British passengers. Her ambience is down-to-earth, comfortable without glamour, and for such a large ship is friendly and cosy in a very traditional British way. Her days as a troopship in the dangerous waters around the Falklands crowned her reputation and she is now considered one of the nations treasures, commanding respect as well as affection from those who sail in her.

But those feelings, lofty as they might be, will not keep her sailing forever and her days must be numbered. Some doubt that she will sail into the new century but her image and reputation will live in the hearts of ship lovers for many years to come. She is a ship of character and one of the greats of all time.

Canberra was built in Belfast and was designed to carry 548 passengers in first, and 1,650 in tourist class. Her crew numbered 900. The ambitious maiden voyage around the world took her from Southampton to Sydney and Auckland, then across the Pacific to the west coast of the United States, through the Panama Canal and back to Southampton. She plied this route until her company decided to place her on the year-round cruising circuit in 1973. Since then she has operated as a one class ship, sailing regularly from the port of Southampton, the last British ship to do so on a regular basis.

Over the past thirty years, *Canberra* has reassuringly appeared in various ports around the world and the sight always brings an instant feeling of familiarity as if a friend had been spotted in a strange city.

Queen Elizabeth 2

The naming of a ship has great significance especially if she is important enough to represent the nation which built her. This was especially true in the days when liners were pre-eminent in the transportation system of the world. Then, a ship of state was a floating embassy and a source of national pride with her name underlining this. Today, all is quite different and a cruise ship is named as if it were a product to be sold in the mass market place, carrying new and trendy names more in keeping with hotels or funfairs. Every name under the sun but dignified names are placed on the bows of huge new ships, not to impress but to amuse the passengers they must attract.

Occasionally, a ship will appear which has been created to reflect the continuity of an age old shipping company with her name proudly carried, denoting quality and a sense of tradition. Somehow those ships seem to carry themselves a little more elegantly and their presence lends dignity to their surroundings.

One such vessel sailing today stands out among her peers as a ship apart, she is the mighty *Queen Elizabeth 2*. She is the last great liner to have been built upon the traditions of a noble line and even though intended to spend most of her time cruising she still fulfils her role as a transatlantic liner, operating a regular schedule of voyages between Southampton and New York. She is the last of the great liners to have been designed and built in the days when there were others to compete against.

She was intended to be a replacement for two of the finest ships ever seen. Historic and nationally loved floating palaces built in the 1930s and named after the consorts of Britain's reigning monarchs of the time.

The *Queen Mary*, the first great supership to exceed 1,000 feet, was given her name by the wife of King George V in 1934 and the *Queen Elizabeth*, the largest liner the world has yet seen, was launched by the consort of King George VI in 1938. Those two unique and magnificent *Queen* liners carved a niche for themselves in maritime history and created their own legends inseparable from that age of sea travel. They were the high point in the ambitions of the Cunard Steamship Company and became synonymous with all that was finest afloat. It was only natural that when they were to be replaced, those ships should be honoured by designating the last great ship of the era – a *Queen* too.

The *QE2*, as she became known, was named by the monarch herself in 1967. Her majesty did not in fact give the new liner her own name but instead named the ship after the one named for her mother. This was believed to be an act of diplomacy mixed with sensitivity, for even though the Queen is Elizabeth II, historically she is not the second Elizabeth to rule Scotland, and as the new ship was being built on the Clyde, it was thought polite not to raise any Scottish objections to the name.

The new liner was, when built, not a resounding success. Her entry into service was plagued by troubles. Her builders were in financial trouble and the ship was not accepted by Cunard on her due delivery date. Her trials developed into a series of minor disasters. There was trouble with her turbines, bits and pieces of the ship herself were found to be missing, taken by the ton as souvenirs by the men working on board. Eventually she sailed as the ship of tomorrow, not as a direct descendant of the old *Queens* but with a new philosophy that broke with old traditions, even the company livery was changed, and, for the first time in its history, the flagship of the Cunard Line did not sail carrying the famous red and black funnel. Instead, the ship was painted deep grey with white upper works and her stove pipe funnel was painted white with a black top. The only concession to tradition were a few touches of Cunard red which appeared on the base of the funnel and the Cunard logo painted on her superstructure. She also flew the famous lion rampant flag.

Nevertheless, she was very beautiful and entered service as a *Queen*. She had her critics who mourned the greatness and elegance of the past, but as she entered New York on her maiden voyage to an enthusiastic greeting, she presented a vision of majesty and graceful power. She was a liner with an uncertain future, trying desperately to find a reason for being. Her immediate competition was the *France*, the last pure transatlantic liner built earlier in the sixties.

At the same time the warm water route from New York to the Mediterranean was impressively sailed by new Italian twins, the *Michaelangelo* and the *Raphaelo*, which, as in the case of the *France*, were heavily subsidised by their respective governments. Soon, they became bogged down with heavy losses and, in the early 1970s, they were withdrawn from service leaving the new *QE2* as the sole surviving liner crossing the ocean on a semi-regular basis.

Over the years the *QE2* has endured much. Her original company changed hands and direction, her builders disappeared, her character was changed but not for the better, in an attempt to generate income. She even went to war in the Falklands as a troopship and then continued to sail the oceans of the world increasingly alone as her contemporaries disappeared.

New, flashier cruise ships jostled her for the position of *Queen* of the seas and it was only within the last few years that a change has taken place which has profoundly altered the direction of her destiny. The Cunard Line, at last realising that elegance, tradition, quality and nostalgia have a place in modern commercial thinking, have rebuilt the *QE2* into the *Queen* she should always have been. She is now the true successor of the *Queen Mary* and the *Queen Elizabeth*, with glimpses of the old *Mauretania* and *Aquitania* peeping through.

The ship, now in her twenty-third year, has matured into a vessel of regal magnificence. She has been re-engined to reduce fuel consumption. Her tired interiors, motel like and ordinary, are filled once more with the opulence and luxury traditionally expected aboard an ocean liner. Her crew provide a service equal to the legendary ship board pamperings of yesteryear and not least of all her reincarnations is the crown she at last rightly wears. It is a funnel of noble proportions towering above a gleaming white superstructure. A Cunard funnel, resplendent at last in the traditional manner of crimson red with two black bands and a black top.

Thus crowned and enthroned as *Queen* of the seas once more, and flagship of her line, the *QE2*, during July of 1990, progressed around the traditional Cunard ports of Britain joining the old world with the new as part of the 150th anniversary of the founding of her company.

It was in July 1840 when the first Cunard steamer, the little paddleship *Britannia*, wearing the same livery, sailed on the inaugural voyage between Liverpool and Boston. Today, the Cunard line looks towards a bright future as with a fabulous *Queen* leading the fleet, they celebrate one and a half centuries of being the first and the last of the steamship companies to sail across the Atlantic.

HMS Ophir

In 1901 Edward VII had succeeded his mother, Queen Victoria, to become ruler of a vast disparate collection of peoples around the world. His empire comprising lands as far apart as Canada and Australia were joined together by a communication and transportation system which was to become the envy of the world.

Telegraph cables, laid under the oceans, were now connecting every land in the empire. Mails were swiftly carried by fleets of ships which themselves carried settlers to populate those lands. Administrators were trained and despatched to those far flung corners of civilisation in their thousands and when the new king had been crowned, his government suggested that it was time for the monarch to be seen by his scattered subjects.

An epic voyage was planned to visit almost every corner of the realm. However, it was not to be undertaken by the king himself. His son and heir, the Prince of Wales, was to undertake this vast journey on behalf of his sovereign. Known then as the Duke of York, he and his Duchess sailed from Portsmouth on 16th March 1901, aboard the Orient liner *Ophir*.

This beautiful little ship of only 6,800 tons had been chartered from the Orient Line and reconditioned to be worthy of her illustrious passengers. The voyage was to take eight months. Their Royal Highnesses were to show themselves to the peoples of Gibraltar, Malta, Aden, Ceylon, Singapore, Australia, New Zealand, Mauritius, South Africa and Canada, before returning to Portsmouth in November of the same year. As a royal yacht the ship sailed with a crew greatly different from her usual complement.

She became known as HMS *Ophir* sailing under the direction of the Royal Navy. Her ships company included 125 sailors, 100 marines, 37 bandsmen, 20 boys, seven engineer officers, 88 stokers, 2 pursers, 50 stewards, 9 cooks, 3 bakers, 2 butchers, 1 laundryman and his wife, 1 printer, 2 barbers, 1 cowman and 3 cows. *Ophir* sailed under the command of a commodore, with 21 other naval officers in attendance. The members of the royal suite numbered 54. The ship then represented a perfect example in miniature of the social strata of the nation at that time with the monarchy at its head. In letters sent to his father during the tour, His Royal Highness lends a note of humanity to the pomp surrounding this regal journey. He noted that he and his wife, Mary, were separated from home and children for 231 days.

In his first letter sent from Gibraltar, he wrote: "May and I came down to our cabins and had a good cry and tried to comfort each other." In another letter to his mother, Queen Alexandra, written half way through the tour, he said: "It is all very well for you and papa to say we musn't do too much but it is impossible not to do so. Our stay in each place is so short that everything has to be crammed into it otherwise people would be offended and our great object is to please as many people as possible."

The 'too much' mentioned in this letter was in fact chronicled later and added up to quite a formidable list of duties. The Duke and Duchess in those 231 days laid 21 foundation stones, received 594 loyal addresses, presented 4,329 medals, reviewed 62,000 troops and shook hands with 24,855 people at official receptions alone.

That gruelling tour set the pattern for all future royal tours of the empire and commonwealth. The days at sea between ports were a thankful respite in that timetable. On their return to England they were met by the King and Queen who came out to meet them aboard the Royal Yacht *Victoria and Albert* which then led *Ophir* in triumph into Portsmouth.

HMS Balmoral Castle

In the first decades of the 20th century, Britain's Empire, which in reality was a collection of colonies and self governing states, was brought under centralised control. This took the form of combining those territories into larger, more manageable, units. The names for these blocks of combined states varied. Some were called unions, others were dominions, colonies or commonwealths. All were collected under an umbrella known as the Empire.

Whatever else were the motives for all these lands being annexed under the British crown, the professed motive was that Britain considered herself the civilising influence to an uncivilised world. A paternal force supplying goodness, culture, godliness and unity. If, in the meantime, the mother country received in return free trade and riches, as a little thought of by-product, then so be it. But peace did reign and the sun never did set on the British Empire.

Among the many new nations being created under the kindly gaze of the monarch, was a combination of territories in southern Africa. These were united under one government which was to become the Union of South Africa, a self governing nation administered indirectly by Britain with a parliamentary system exported from London. To open this new parliament, King Edward decided that his son would again be his representative and it was planned that he and his Duchess would sail to Capetown on October 11th 1910. But fate took a hand and in May of that year King Edward died. At that moment the Duke and Duchess of York became King George V and Queen Mary, Emperor and Empress of India and sovereigns of all British lands and territories across the seas.

The tour of South Africa could not now be undertaken by them but the new king's uncle, the Duke of Connaught was sent as his envoy. As originally planned, they sailed from Portsmouth aboard the Union Castle liner *Balmoral Castle*. For this voyage, the duration of which was measured in weeks rather than months, she was completely refurbished to become a royal yacht. Her funnels and masts were painted yellow and her hull white. She flew the white ensign from her stern and became HMS *Balmoral Castle* for the duration of the voyage.

The ship was almost brand new when chosen to be elevated to royal status. Of 13,661 tons she was a handsome vessel and the largest ship in the fleet. She was also the first of her line to be fitted with wireless telegraphy. Her name, with its associations with the royal house, could not have been bettered. She sailed throughout, amid pomp and naval ceremony, and fulfilled her role admirably without drama or special cause to be remembered. Her period as a royal yacht has been forgotten, due in part to the almost anonymous position of the Duke who sailed in her.

That South African tour was eventually over-shadowed by the next royal voyage which was the prelude to an imperial extravaganza, the likes of which were never before seen nor never again repeated.

HMS Medina

Medina was destined to be the most regal of all the liners requisitioned for royal service, she was the only one ever to carry the King Emperor himself on a royal tour. She was built for the P&O line and launched on May 14th 1911. Her maiden voyage was undertaken as a royal yacht, a third mast being fitted for the occasion from which to fly the royal standard. This mast was borrowed from the new liner *Nanking* which was being built at the same yard, for amid great state splendour runs a streak of parsimony. It was not unknown for vast amounts of money to be expended on ceremonials but at the same time deals would be struck to cut down costs. Things were borrowed, leased or altered, and governments, with an eye for a bargain, were known to ask for gifts from their host country from which to defray their own costs.

Such was the case when King George V and Queen Mary sailed to India for the great durbar in Delhi in 1911. British law forbids the crown jewels leaving the country and as the Emperor and Empress of India were to appear among their peoples robed and crowned, a new imperial crown had to be created. India itself donated the gems to encrust those wonderful symbols of majesty but the crowns were never destined to remain in India – they can still be seen amongst the crown jewels in the Tower of London.

When the Indian subcontinent was finally absorbed into the sphere of influence controlled by Britain, the great Queen Victoria was eventually proclaimed Empress and her son, on his succession to the throne as King Edward VII, inherited this title. Neither of them ever saw this great jewel in their crown but King George V and Queen Mary declared that they would not only visit this great and exotic land of theirs but would show themselves to their Indian subjects in a manner befitting their supreme status.

India was vast, combining many sovereign states each with its own ruler. These princes and maharajahs with access to the world's greatest jewel mines, were resplendent in their own state dress, splendour being the watchword. Palaces throughout the land vied with each other in magnificence, all was intended to convey power and influence and therefore command respect.

For the first appearance of their supreme ruler in their midst, it was deemed necessary that the Emperor and his Empress should show themselves more splendidly than even India had ever seen before. Part of that progress was obviously the voyage there and back especially with its historic moments of arrival and departure. A ship of stature and presence was required and one with an Indian connection if possible. What better choice could be made than the new flagship of the company which epitomised the British raj to perfection, almost a navy in itself – the great P&O line.

As the arrangements for the royal journey were being made, the *Medina* was being fitted out by Caird and Company of Greenock. She was a handsome ship of 12,358 tons and her internal fittings were of a particularly high standard. A week before her intended departure for India, Queen Mary spent an afternoon aboard in Portsmouth, seeing to the final arrangements of the royal apartments. The colours chosen for these were predominantly blues and greys and much of the furniture and fittings were transferred from the royal yacht *Victoria and Albert*. Like ships on previous royal tours, *Medina* was commissioned into the Royal Navy and her crew was mainly naval personnel.

She was beautiful, painted in her white livery with a double band of royal blue and gold around her hull. The boot topping was red and her twin funnels were painted buff. The third mast, mounted in front of the fore funnel, gave her an added air of dignity much in keeping with her new status. All her engineer officers were P&O men but the firemen and greasers were navy stokers.

Like other ships of her class *Medina* was a twin screw vessel powered by two sets of reciprocating engines developing 15,000 horse power which gave her a service speed of sixteen and a half knots. She sailed at 3pm on November 11th 1911 with the King and Queen aboard. It was a dull autumn day but, undeterred by the pouring rain, thousands of people turned out to see her off.

The voyage to Bombay took three weeks. After the first few days of storm and sea sickness, the waters grew calm and the sun shone. The King enjoyed listening to the band of the Royal Marines, while Queen Mary spent most of her time reading – amongst the books were those of her favourite author Rudyard Kipling. The voyage was uneventful with calls at British colonies or protectorates along the route. Gibraltar, Malta, Suez, Aden and finally Bombay where George V was to receive the homage of his Indian subjects on their native soil.

The durbar itself, at Delhi, was splendid, it was, in effect, an Indian coronation, even more spectacular than that which had taken place in London the year before. The description of the great occasion by the Times stated that: "the great coronation durbar which has occupied the thoughts of India for more than a year, has involved the most elaborate preparation and has brought a quarter of a million people together from every part of the Indian empire, was held today on the vast plains beyond Delhi. Enthroned on high beneath a golden dome looking outwards to the far north whence they came, their majesties the King Emperor and Queen Empress were acclaimed by over a hundred thousand of their subjects. The ceremony, at its culminating point, exactly typified the oriental conception of the ultimate repositories of imperial power. The monarchs sat alone, remote but beneficent, raised far above the multitude but visible to all, clad in rich vestments, flanked by radiant emblems of authority, guarded by a glittering array of troops, the sinecure of the proudest princes of India, the central figures in what was surely the most majestic assemblage ever seen in the east. It was a sight which will remain indelibly engraved on the memory, not a soul who witnessed it, not even the poorest cooly who stood fascinated and awed upon the outskirts of the throng, can have been unresponsive to its profound significance. There can be only one verdict upon it, the durbar has been far more than a mere success it has been a triumphant vindication of the wise prescience which conceived and planned it. The King Emperor's mission to his Indian peoples has been fulfilled with a completeness which places it beyond the reach of criticism." The king himself in his diary said: 'It was the most beautiful and wonderful sight I ever saw.' At the end of the ceremonies, he says: 'We reached our camp at 3 o'clock, rather tired after wearing the crown for three and a half hours – it hurt my head as it is very heavy. Afterwards we held a reception at a large tent, about 5,000 people came. The heat was simply awful. I was in bed at 11 and quite tired.'

With all the pomp and ceremony over, the King and Queen once more boarded *Medina* in Bombay and set sail for Portsmouth. At Port Said a luncheon was held on board for the khedive of Egypt and there was an enthusiastic welcome in Gibraltar.

The royal tour ended at Portsmouth on February 5th 1912 and so did *Medina*'s highly publicised service with the Royal Navy. She then returned to Caird's at Greenock to be refitted for her usual P&O service. Her borrowed third mast was removed and fitted to the *Nanking* from whence it came. Her hull and funnels were painted black and she sailed from Tilbury on her maiden voyage for P&O bound for Australia on June 28th 1912.

Medina did not live into old age. She was attacked and sunk by a U-boat on 28th April 1917. Her ignominious end being in sharp contrast to the splendour and glory of her beginning.

RMS Gothic

The coronation tour of the commonwealth in 1953, by Her Majesty Queen Elizabeth II, was the most extensive ever undertaken by a British monarch, she being the first ever to circumnavigate the globe.

The ship chosen was a vessel converted for duty as a royal yacht once before but never used. She was the *Gothic*, a passenger cargo vessel owned by the Shaw Savill Line. She had been fitted out to a royal standard for a tour originally planned for 1951 by King George VI to the commonwealth, but ill health forced a postponement. His daughter, Princess Elizabeth, with her husband, the Duke of Edinburgh, eventually were to go instead, intending to board the ship in Mombassa after a tour of Kenya. But fate decreed otherwise. The King's sudden death in February 1952 compelled them to immediately return to England with the subsequent cancellation of the remainder of the tour, the Princess went home as Queen and the ship continued its voyage to Australia and New Zealand without ever raising the royal standard.

However, 21 months later *Gothic* was prepared yet again for a royal tour, this time to carry the young Queen and her husband on their delayed epic voyage. Previous royal tours had always been made sailing under the white ensign in ships transferred to the navy. But this was different. Times had changed. No longer was the sovereign merely an icon, an unknown and remote figure weighed down within an atmosphere of mysticism. Under the crown was a face now known to millions through the magic of television. A young woman with a family, loved by those over whom she reigned.

The choice of ship to be used for her first tour as monarch reflected this new thinking and established the tenor of her reign. Whereas her grandfather and her great grandfather sailed to their empire in great pomp, her own father and mother had meanwhile, in their reign, softened the face of kingship, thus preparing the way for a new style of monarchy more in tune with the changing social and political life of the nation.

Her Majesty Queen Elizabeth II, aboard this cargo passenger liner, somehow presented an image of approachable dignity without reducing the effect of her station. This was not to say that the ship was ill-equipped for her duty but, unlike the other liners previously employed as royal yachts, in their day, the newest and largest in the fleets and possessing considerable status, *Gothic* was, by comparison, merely one of a class and never built to be a flagship with any pretensions to grandeur.

She was, however, a steady ship at sea. Her accommodation originally built to cater for only 85 passengers in first class, was comfortable rather than luxurious. This was modified to bring it more into line with the requirements of the Queen and her suite. The result was a home of incomparable taste and solid comfort, not at all like a floating palace to be used solely for ceremonials. This was a reflection of the person rather than the position of the Queen and for the first time in British history this cosy side of the sovereign's life was allowed to be glimpsed by her people.

However, this new lowering of the veils of pageantry did not reduce the impact of the voyage or the majesty of the occasion. This time, *Gothic*, in every respect a royal yacht, was to sail under the British merchant ensign, with her usual merchant crew, and carry outward and homeward cargoes as on a normal voyage. This was at the special request of the Queen herself, she believing that in post war austerity Britain, it would not be right for her to preclude the ship from carrying on its usual business even though she was aboard.

Before embarking on her royal appointment, the *Gothic* loaded some 6,300 tons of general cargo at Liverpool and London, and commenced her voyage from the latter port in November 1953, bound for Kingston, Jamaica. She sailed looking very much as she did prior to her elevation in status. Her funnel had been raised a few feet to help eliminate smoke and smuts from her decks. She had been re-painted white with a green boot topping at the waterline. But her funnel still carried the buff, black topped colours of her company. No third mast for flag etiquette, like that fitted to *Medina* in 1911, was fitted to *Gothic*. She remained as she was. Only whenever the Queen was aboard did the ship fly the royal standard, (the sovereign's personal flag) and the flags of the flag officer royal yachts. The British merchant ensign and the Shaw Savill house flag completed her bunting.

Internally most of the furniture for the royal apartments was transferred from the *Victoria and Albert*. Sections of the original accommodation were altered to provide day rooms, sleeping rooms, dining cabins and anti-rooms. In addition to the *Gothic*'s regular crew, apart from the royal couple, extra accommodation was provided for other members of the household, Royal Navy officers and ratings, press correspondents etc.

Apparently, during the conversion work, the doors to the royal apartments were fitted with door knobs having milled edges, whilst all those on other apartments had smooth ones. This would indicate to an unknowing crew member that he was opening the wrong door.

The *Gothic* presented a striking appearance in her livery and presented a beautiful sight wherever she appeared. All the royal apartments were comfortably air conditioned – an innovation for the time. Additional boats carried, especially for the tour, were an admirals 35 foot barge and the 45 foot royal barge taken from the *Victoria and Albert*. These were handled by the ships derricks. In all, the total complement for the voyage had grown from the normal 124 to 283. This was made up by an augmented crew of 168, 51 passengers, 29 royal naval ratings, 32 royal marines and 3 telephonists. The ship was commanded by the master of the *Dominion Monarch*, commodore of Shaw Savill line, David Aitcheson. This was in sharp contrast to previous royal tours and was the beginning of a new, more relaxed atmosphere surrounding the sovereign and her presentation to her peoples.

After a 12 day Atlantic crossing the *Gothic* arrived in the West Indies where the Queen and her husband joined the ship having flown out from the United Kingdom. The tour was to last six months during which time *Gothic* would transit the Panama Canal and then visit Fiji, Tonga, New Zealand, Australia, Ascension Island, Colombo and Aden. Throughout the voyage, *Gothic* was escorted by ships of the Royal Navy and the navies of the commonwealth nations, each taking up duty in their own sphere to protect their sovereign.

In each port visited, vast crowds thronged the waterside to greet their Queen. Her Majesty and the Duke finally disembarked in Aden and flew to Tobruk where they boarded the new Royal Yacht *Britannia* which had sailed from England to meet them. Their return to England aboard this beautiful ship ended with a spectacular and triumphant procession up the Thames into the pool of London.

A postscript to that epic coronation voyage was that on May 4th, after having been given priority for a rapid transit through the Suez Canal, *Gothic* arrived at Malta to be there at the same time as *Britannia*. Here, all the furniture from the old royal yacht *Victoria and Albert*, which had been placed aboard *Gothic* for the duration of the voyage, was finally transferred to the new royal yacht, thereby completing her furnishings for the voyage back to England.

Later that month, *Gothic* berthed at Tilbury. She had certainly distinguished herself and her crew and had been a credit to her company. Now, all that remained was to send her to Birkenhead to be put back to her original cargo status. She then rejoined the fleet, her days of glamour gone but never forgotten. In August of 1969, she made her last voyage; to the breakers yard, so ending the last of a line of special British merchant ships which had been, for a short time in their lives, very special ships indeed.

The Royal Yacht Britannia

As the 20th century enters its last decade, one beautiful ship still sails upon the oceans of the world much as she did when first built almost forty years ago. At that time she was considered rather unexciting in appearance, too traditional and not modern enough to satisfy the expectations of her critics.

However, the years have proved how right her designers were and today those who are lucky enough to see her as she performs her duties, are treated to the sight of a ship which looks as a ship should look, a living piece of maritime history in more ways than one. For this lovely vessel is the Royal Yacht *Britannia*, presented to Queen Elizabeth II as a coronation present from the Royal Navy in 1954. Since then, the yacht has travelled thousands of miles carrying Her Majesty and members of her family on countless voyages to every corner of the globe.

The ship is a perfect example of the thinking behind the shapes of most passenger liners built early in this century, very few of which still remain afloat. Her contemporaries were mostly victims of the age of air travel and if not that, the ravages of commercial life and age would have ensured their departure from the scene by now. However, *Britannia* was built for a life of tender loving care, to be impeccably maintained, polished and pampered by the Royal Navy as if she were a jewel to be treasured. She will no doubt sail for many decades yet and as time goes on, become even more appreciated as a monument to the traditional values once familiar at sea.

The Royal Yacht *Britannia* first entered service towards the end of the Queen's coronation tour of the commonwealth which was undertaken aboard the temporary royal yacht *Gothic*. Her Majesty had disembarked from *Gothic* at Aden, flying with the Duke of Edinburgh to Tobruk in Libya for a state visit before boarding the new royal yacht which had sailed from Britain to meet her. In fact, the first members of the royal family to sail aboard this ship was not the Queen herself, but her children Prince Charles and Princess Anne. They sailed with *Britannia* to greet their parents and were aboard when the Queen made her triumphant entry up the Thames to London on the completion of Her Majesty's epic voyage.

Britannia since then has been an integral part of royal pageantry. Her sleek shape is familiar wherever it is seen – and what a lovely shape. She has a slender hull with clipper bow and counter stern. Her muted colours are the perfect foil to her silhouette, royal blue hull over a red waterline. A thin gold band around her waist, a white superstructure and three yellow masts, her elegant yellow funnel is topped by a black dome. The royal coat of arms, vividly painted, forms her figurehead, but nowhere does her name appear upon her structure. So special is this ship that her name is quite unnecessary, she being immediately recognised for what she is anywhere in the world.

Since being commissioned no other merchant ship has taken on the role of royal yacht, the *Gothic* being the last. Those which formerly performed that special duty have now been consigned to maritime history their one time exclusive role now almost forgotten.

Jervis Bay

Of all the ships converted from peace to war, none tells the story more poignantly than that of the *Jervis Bay*. Whereas some of the liners used as transports or armed as merchant cruisers were well known and glamorous, the *Jervis Bay* was at the other extreme and typified the mass of anonymous, small British liners which sailed the seas before both great wars. They were the ships, manned by the crews which gave substance to Britain's worldwide empire. Sailing virtually unknown and functioning as small cogs in an enormous wheel. Therefore, the saga of this special ship should be more fully told here and through her the story of other liners in wartime, most of which came through unscathed but not untouched by the horrors which were common to all at that time.

The *Jervis Bay* was no sleek greyhound of the sea, she was a workhorse of a liner of 13,839 tons, accustomed in her peacetime role to carrying some 600 passengers between Britain and Australia. On her outward bound passages her holds were filled with British goods from machine parts to gramophone records. Homeward bound from Sydney she carried Australia's meat and wool. Although, unlike a warship, she had no armour plating, she had been built to a heavy standard by designers who had noted the service of armed merchantmen in World War One and thought it expedient to make her easily convertible to similar work in the uncertain future.

By 1939 one of the few factors about her which could reasonably be called modern, was that she was oil fired with six huge boilers providing the power for her two turbine engines, each of which drove one of her twin screws. She was a steady ship, even in bad weather. But the conversion the admiralty wished upon her when she was called up for war service was not calculated to inspire confidence. Shipyard workers fitted her with seven six inch guns, hastily gathered from a variety of holes and corners. Four of the guns were placed forward and three abaft the bridge, one on either side of the ship with the third mounted on the poop. But it was the dates engraved on the guns that caused some anxious thoughts – two dated back to the 1890s and others were inscribed 1901.

On her boat deck the ship carried two anti-aircraft guns salvaged from a cruiser, wrecked in 1921. The *Jervis Bay*, and all other converted merchant ships were being pressed into service as frail substitutes for the convoy-guarding cruisers which Britain had failed to provide for herself. However courageous their crews, these ships were incapable of being properly equipped for modern warfare.

The situation for *Jervis Bay* was typical. It was impossible to fit her with the gun turrets and technology that was vital to a fighting ships fire power, much of the ammunition had to be man-handled and the limited number of watertight compartments meant that any heavy water-line damage to the ship would be fatal. All individual cabins for ocean-going passengers had been dismantled to make way for mess decks, where the wartime seamen were to eat, rest and sling their hammocks.

A cage with wooden slats to house prisoners captured from enemy merchant ships was built on mess deck one. *Jervis Bay* acquired a complement of 255 officers and men, 66 more than in peacetime. Some were members of her previous ships company who were simply transferred overnight to Royal Navy ranks. Many others were also ex-merchant navy men and one or two moved over from ships of the Shaw Savill Line, the parent company of *Jervis Bay*'s owners. There was no doubt that the ship was in capable hands and no doubt either that she was badly needed for the crucial task of escorting convoys carrying food and raw materials to Britain. But many who observed her tall, liner-style superstructure, with its bridge two thirds of the height of her funnel, thought how easily visible and vulnerable she would be to enemy surface ships and boats.

Her conversion completed, she was first ordered south to escort homeward bound convoys from West Africa. Then, in the spring of 1940, she steamed to Halifax, Nova Scotia to take up North Atlantic duties under a new commander, Captain Edward Stephen Fogarty Fagan, Royal Navy.

Captain Fagan was 47, a tall, toughly built man with the handsome rugged features of a western movie hero. On April 2nd 1940, the day after he first set foot on the ship's deck, he called his officers and men together and told them: 'So far we haven't seen any real action, but I promise you this much, if the gods are good to us, and we meet the enemy, I shall take you in as close as I possibly can.' Six months later, at six in the evening of Monday October 28th 1940, thirty-eight merchant ships – British, Norwegian, Polish and Greek – took station together off Halifax and began the long plod eastwards to Britain, under the collective title of convoy HX84. They were in the charge of three ocean escorts, two Canadian destroyers and HMS *Jervis Bay*.

After three days out, the Canadian warships were to put about and the *Jervis Bay* continued as HX84's only guardian. According to the procedure plan the convoy would be met on the other side of the Atlantic on November 8th by Royal Navy anti-submarine escort vessels which would stay with it on the final leg to Liverpool.

All convoys to Britain were of the utmost value, but HX84 was particularly important. Eleven of the 38 ships were tankers filled with a total of 126,469 tons of crude oil, fuel oil and petroleum. The other ships carried a mixture of supplies, equally sorely needed by beleaguered Britain. The cargoes themselves told their own story: 3,700 tons of chilled meats, 3,900 tons of canned meat, 31,000 tons of grain. There was copper and pit props, 43,000 tons of steel and chemicals, aluminium and asbestos. There was 768 tons of tobacco. To help keep people informed of the war's progress 5,300 tons of newsprint. One ship carried 12 fighter aircraft, others had tractors and trucks. The cash value of the total cargo of 127,600 tons, in addition to the oil carried by the tankers, ran into many millions of pounds. But the symbolic value was incalculable, every item being earmarked for a vital place in Britain's war economy.

Most of the vessels in the convoy kept scrupulously to their stations, steaming in nine columns with a distance of 600 yards between each. *Jervis Bay*'s station was between the fourth and sixth columns and there, and there only, the columns were 1,200 yards apart in order to give the escort comfortable room for sudden manoeuvre. Day and night the convoy steamed onwards through deserted seas, with all radios silent in an effort to protect the secrecy of its presence. During darkness the ships played the hazardous game of convoy tag – each helmsman keeping his eye glued on the faint blue light burning on the ship ahead – the only sign of nightlife any vessel was allowed to display.

The monotony and natural anxiety of the voyage went undisturbed until, on the morning of November 5th, smoke was seen on the horizon away to the southwest. The eyes of the lookouts concentrated on the distant smudge. Admiral Maltby, the convoy commodore, and Captain Fagan waited until they could decide whether the stranger was friend or foe. A few minutes later the smoke was followed by the outline of a single funnel and a superstructure. The newcomer was then identified as the SS *Mopan*, a banana boat. The *Mopan* was alone and Captain Fagan signalled asking if she would like to join the convoy, but her master, worried about the effects of delay on his perishable fruit cargo, refused the

offer. Silently the men in the ships of HX84 watched as the *Mopan* forged ahead of them, and finally disappeared over the next horizon, going, had she but known it, to her doom.

Less than 100 miles away other eyes were anxiously scanning the ocean, they were German eyes, the eyes of the lookouts in the 10,000 ton pocket battleship *Admiral Scheer*, one of Hitler's most formidable seagoing strike force. Her commander, Captain Theodore Krancke, was among the German Navy's most brilliant and courageous officers who invariably appeared on his bridge, chomping on a black cigar. On that particular morning he was looking for something the sea would deliver to him. Convoy HX84 was not the secret its planners had hoped it would be. German intelligence knew of it and had been able to give the *Admiral Scheer* an approximation of the position.

The *Scheer* expressed power and speed in her long sleek lines. She carried tremendous fire power with six eleven inch guns, three set in a turret mounted forward and three in a turret aft, to add to that punch she also had eight 5.9 inch guns, anti-aircraft guns and a catapult reconnaissance sea plane. At a maximum speed of 28 knots she could outpace most battleships afloat and could operate over a range of 19,000 sea miles before needing to take on more fuel for her thrusting diesel engines.

Just before noon, Captain Krancke ordered the *Admiral Scheer*'s sea plane to take off and patrol immediately to the south of the battleship. If the information from Berlin was correct, then convoy HX84 must have been somewhere in that area. The sea plane had been told to return to the ship at 1300 hours but, to Krancke's surprise, she appeared over the deck 20 minutes early. As she flew by her signal lamp flashed: 'Convoy, 88 sea miles'. The freshening wind had developed into a gale and a moderately heavy sea had begun to run. Krancke, consulting with his navigation officer, decided that he would have to make his greatest possible speed if HX84 was not to gain advantage from the gathering darkness. But his timetable was soon to be upset. Just before 1430 one of the lookouts spied smoke on the southern horizon, followed quickly by the silhouette of a vessel of around 5,000 tons coming up at a good turn of speed with her stern to the gale. She was the hapless *Mopan*, who was about to swim into the *Scheer*'s net.

Krancke put three shots ahead of her and ordered her master to send no radio message. He was to abandon his ship and bring himself and his crew over to the *Admiral Scheer*. His crew received all 68 men from the *Mopan* and gave them cigarettes and warming drinks. Then, at 1600 hours, they turned their guns on the banana boat and sank her. As *Mopan* slipped beneath the surface, he ordered *Scheer*'s engine room to pile on the speed and resumed his search for the known approaching convoy. He found it, only a few minutes later, the columns of ships clearly visible some 12 miles away.

Aboard the *Jervis Bay*, Captain Fagan snapped the order: 'Sound action stations'. But there was still some doubt in the convoy about the approaching warship's nationality – many thought she could have been British. Fagan ordered his ship to leave her station and move ahead of the convoy. As she did so, he called for the recognition signal to be flashed out - the letters M A G. There was a few seconds interval, then the warship replied with the same quick letters. Captain Krancke could not sustain his bluff. A moment or so later his radio operators picked up a coded message coming from the convoy. It was from *Jervis Bay* and, decoded in London, read: 'From *Jervis Bay* to Whitehall WT. One enemy battleship bearing 328 distance, 12 miles, course 208, position 52 degrees 45 minutes north, 32 degrees 13 minutes west.' Fagan now had only one overriding duty, to do everything in his power to protect the convoy.

The first essential move was to enable the speedier ships to put it to the use of themselves and their precious cargo. From *Jervis Bay* fluttered the flag signal 'prepare to scatter'. The ships turned away and the convoy columns broke up. Captain Fagan issued another immediate order to his own officers: 'Make smoke'. At once, from a dozen smoke floats on the forecastle rose a dense and oily murk, shrouding the ships around the *Jervis Bay*. His next command was that the *Jervis Bay* would stay on her course, towards the *Admiral Scheer*.

From that moment there could be no doubt about the outcome. One shell from the *Scheer* landed short of *Jervis Bay*, a second passed over her, a third struck her amidships, blowing away part of the bridge and cutting the link between the helmsman's wheel and the rudder. To *Scheer*'s gunners their opponent was a suicide ship, their shooting was deadly accurate and high explosive shells were raining down on the merchant cruiser.

Soon, the *Jervis Bay* took on the appearance of a derelict, her tall superstructure, which made her such an easy target, was shattered, iron work was twisted like scrambled twine, fire sprouted throughout her entire length. Men began to die quickly and agonizingly. Direct hits took a murderous toll in the forepart of the ship and above and below decks the only scene was one of carnage. For 22 minutes and 22 seconds, the *Admiral Scheer* poured her fire into the *Jervis Bay*. Captain Fagan, having escaped the first crushing blow, did not long survive. He was seen making his way forward from an inspection of the ship's after control when a shell burst on the decks nearby. Fagan, and his chief yeoman of signals, died together. Other officers and men also died together at their stations.

Soon after the captain was killed, the navigating officer, Lieutenant Commander G.L. Roe, who had served in *Jervis Bay* before the war, was the only surviving officer in the ship. The engine room took much of the fury of the bombardment and, long before the brief and bloody action was over, the engines had ceased to turn. Riddled, the sea pouring into her hull that now resembled a colander, *Jervis Bay* lay helpless in her death agony.

At the end of the ordeal, Lieutenant Commander Roe gave the order 'abandon ship'. Ignoring the ship's boats which had splintered to matchwood, the survivors began manhandling life rafts over the side. Many men who escaped the shambles in the ship died in the turbulent and icy seas. Some swallowed fuel oil and then perished. Night came on and, in the darkness, the Swedish ship *Stureholm*, rescued a handful of men and picked up more at first light the following morning. Altogether, out of the ship's company of 254 only 65 were saved and, of those, one man, an engineer, died back in England a few weeks later.

After the *Jervis Bay* had been overwhelmed, the *Admiral Scheer* turned her attention to the scattered ships of the convoy, but she sank only five of the 37 ships, a total of 47,500 tons of shipping. The convoy's escape was due to Captain Fagan and the officers and men of the *Jervis Bay*. By steaming towards the *Admiral Scheer*, with no hope of saving their ship or themselves, they had bought lifesaving

time for the 32 ships, their crews, and their cargoes, that had escaped.

Captain Fagan was posthumously awarded the Victoria Cross and the master of the Polish steamer *Puck*, the smallest ship of the convoy, summed up the feelings of other masters of HX84 when he wrote, in a letter to the London Times: 'The fine example set to us by the British crew of the *Jervis Bay* who, through their valuable sacrifice, saved a lot of valuable tonnage and very valuable cargo, fills us with deep admiration and makes us their spiritual debtors.'

Rawalpindi

The age of great empires seem lost in the mists of time, yet it is but a few decades ago that Britain ruled over the biggest empire the world had ever seen. The great prize was India and to serve the needs of that empire one great shipping company fitted the bill to perfection. This was the mighty P&O. P&O ships were designed and built to serve the company with distinction and were often called upon to do so for their country in time of war.

From England to Suez, China and Australia, the ships of the P&O sailed as regularly as trains upon a track. But it was from India itself that the company was to receive its exotic personality. The names of many ships reflected this to a remarkable degree. Not least was the beautiful *Rawalpindi*, whose name was taken from a town in the province of the Punjab – then part of British India – but the name was to be remembered for a reason other than its exotic charm. The ship which bore it was to enter maritime history as a symbol of Britain's David pitted against the Goliath of Hitler's Germany.

The *Rawalpindi* was built in Belfast in 1925. A handsome ship of 16,619 tons and fitted with twin black funnels. She was painted in the then traditional P&O colours of black hull with tan upper works. She and her sister ships ran on the London-Bombay-Far Eastern service carrying 301 first class passengers and 290 second class. Her crew numbered 380. She plied this trade carrying sahibs and memsahibs on voyages reminiscent of Somerset Maughan for almost 15 years, until August 1939 when she was requisitioned by the Royal Navy just prior to the outbreak of war. She was quickly converted into an armed merchant cruiser. One funnel was removed and she was painted warship grey. She was fitted with eight 6 inch and two 3 inch guns – left-overs from the First World War. Her crew was supplemented by naval personnel and she sailed flying the white ensign as a fighting ship of the Royal Navy.

HMS *Rawalpindi* was one of the armed liners sent to impose a blockade on trade with Germany and three months after the outbreak of war she, under the command of Captain Kennedy, was to be found on station between Iceland and the Faro Islands. It was on November 23rd that she was to meet her fate. Dusk was falling, visibility was poor. The mists were rolling in when a large dim shape was seen approaching. It was soon realised with horror that this was the German battle cruiser *Scharnhorst*. A powerful new predator who, with her sister *Gneisenau*, was one of the prides of the new German Navy. These great ships had a speed of 32 knots and a range of 10,000 miles and their armaments were capable of reeking havoc on any ships they encountered, comprising nine 11 inch and twelve 5.9 inch guns.

As soon as Captain Kennedy recognised what was coming out of the mists towards him he turned the *Rawalpindi* away while radioing the sighting to the Home Fleet at Scapa Flow. As the story went, he was hoping to reach the shelter of a fog bank but was dismayed to find his way blocked by the appearance of another warship. The *Scharnhorst* flashed signals to him ordering him to stop but he decided not to surrender but turn and fight. The odds against him were overwhelming. The second ship was, in fact, *Gneisenau* and with his puny guns blazing he engaged the enemy. *Rawalpindi* scored at least one hit on the *Scharnhorst* but both warships repeatedly pumped shells into her. After only fourteen minutes she was finished. Her captain was dead as were 54 of her P&O crew. Only eleven of the entire ships company survived the massacre.

Neville Chamberlain, the British Prime Minister, told the House of Commons a few days later: "they didn't think of surrender, they fought till they could fight no more. Their example will be an inspiration to those who come after them." It was not long after this action that the British government decided that passenger liners were no match for the superior fire power of Nazi Germany's Navy. The *Rawalpindi*'s sacrifice was not completely in vain, her prompt radio report of the sightings to Britain's naval intelligence served to compel the German ships to abandon their breakout into the Atlantic. They returned to the fatherland not to make the attempt again for many months. The strategy of using surface raiders was later abandoned in favour of the U-boat which led to the sinking of many millions of tons of allied shipping and almost brought Britain to her knees.

Rangitata

The two funnelled motor ship *Rangitata* with her sister ships *Rangitiki* and *Rangitane* were the last word in luxury when they entered service between Britain and New Zealand in the early 1930s. They were combination ships built to carry cargo, mails and passengers, and with their black and white hulls, buff funnels and exotic Maori names, were an attractive and intriguing sight when seen in port.

The *Rangitata*, at just under 17,000 tons, had accommodation for 123 passengers in first class and 284 in tourist class. The route on which she sailed was perfect for sun starved Britains to make use of while trying to escape the British winters.

The New Zealand shipping company were among the originators of long distance pleasure cruising but, in those days, it was not known as such and passengers lucky enough to do the entire round trip would be aboard merely for a long sea voyage.

The time taken for such voyages from London to Auckland and back would be approximately 100 days with calls at Curacao, through the Panama Canal to Fiji and then on to Wellington and Auckland, where the ship would stay for about a month.

The round trip passengers could use the ship as a hotel while she was being loaded with her 8,000 tons of cargo, mostly consisting of lamb and butter. The ship would then return to Britain calling at

the same ports to that on the outward journey but this time including Kingston in Jamaica, Port Everglades and Bermuda, then to Southampton where passengers would disembark before the ship proceeded to London docks for the unloading of its cargo.

The charm of those voyages were their relative simplicity and business-like atmosphere. These were not cruises in the true sense of the word and although some shipping companies in the 1930s were diverting some of their liners to cruising in the off season, there were many people who preferred to be aboard a ship going about its usual business and not catering especially for the whims of its passengers.

These traditional, languid patterns of global sailing schedules were interrupted during the war and were resumed in the post war period but it was only to last another couple of decades before becoming uneconomical. The fleets of ships dwindled and in the mid 1960s passenger sailings were terminated. From that time on, only vast container ships would be seen sailing their lonely voyages across the suddenly empty seas, packed with their sealed boxes and looking like badly wrapped parcels when compared with the sleek lines of the ships they had replaced.

Dunottar Castle

Two pioneering shipping companies opened the trade between South Africa and Britain in the late 19th century. The Union Line and the Castle Mail Packet Company Limited, in their early days produced ships which vied with each other for supremacy on the route. In 1890 the Castle Line produced its greatest challenge by placing into service the *Dunottar Castle*.

She was the first two funnelled ship built for the company and was designed to carry 360 passengers, in three classes. She was directly descended from the days of sail, carrying yards on her foremast and being barquentine rigged. She measured 5,625 tons and had a speed of 17 knots.

Her maiden voyage was from Dartmouth, where the company had taken on mails for the previous twenty years. However, in 1891, they changed this making Southampton the first port after London for picking up mails. The new flag-ship, the *Dunottar Castle*, being the vessel to inaugurate that service on 20th June 1891. It was the beginning of an era of co-operation between that port and the company which was to last until the end of the mail-ship service.

To counteract this challenge by the *Dunottar Castle*, the Union Line built the most beautiful ship yet seen on the South Atlantic. She was the yacht-like *Scot* and she broke the speed record for the run on her maiden voyage in June 1891 by sailing from Southampton to Table Bay in 15 days 9 hours and 52 minutes, thus beating her rival by over a day. She was the most elegant and popular ship of her age to sail on that route but she was also the most expensive to operate, never being profitable for her owners.

The two companies merged in 1900 to become the famous Union Castle Line and the destinies of South Africa and the company were to be intertwined from thence forward. The history of that company in the 20th century is one of the shipping worlds greatest successes. The ships themselves grew in size and luxury, and at the very peak of their achievements, still sailing their traditional route and with no decrease in the quality of passenger service, the lines suddenly stopped operating.

The greatest Union Castle liner of them all, the *Windsor Castle*, sailed out of the Solent for Cape Town on Friday 12th August 1977, for the last time. Only 17 years, almost to the day, after her maiden voyage, and 77 years after the *Dunottar Castle* had sailed from the port for the first time.

Titanic

There are very few words which alone can describe some momentous events, no matter which language is spoken, those words need no explanation. They immediately produce a shudder to all those who hear them. Hiroshima and Belsen are words which can turn man's blood to ice, and the word *Titanic* needs no explanation to conjure up scenes of horror.

The *Titanic* was a ship which will live throughout history for all the wrong reasons. She was one of a trio of liners intended to be the biggest and best on the oceans of the world, now only remembered as the loved, the damned, and the forgotten.

The company which conceived and built them started life in the days of sail. It was a company which grew to become one of the greatest steamship companies in the world. The White Star Line established a relationship with the Belfast shipbuilders of Harland and Wolff which was unique, no other builder ever created a White Star liner throughout its history apart from the German ships which entered the company as war reparations.

Their business arrangement was virtually a partnership, each ship of the fleet being built to quality and not to price. Their costs would be established and a percentage of profit added. That was what the White Star Line paid. It was a simple formula which worked well for all concerned and resulted in ships of exceptional luxury.

The philosophy of the company for the second decade of the 20th century, was to give passengers a transatlantic crossing in the most comfortable and biggest liners then in existence. This luxury was not to be sacrificed for record breaking potentials. All that was left to others, including the Cunard Line which had recently taken the Blue Ribband of the Atlantic with their new *Mauretania* and *Lusitania*.

In October 1910 the first of the great trio for the White Star Line was launched. She was also the first ship in the world to exceed 40,000 tons and she was named *Olympic*. When she entered the water she left behind the unfinished hull of her twin on the building berth next to her. This was to be the *Titanic*, she would not be ready for launching for another seven months, at which time she would then be the biggest afloat. She in turn left the third sister to be named *Britannic*, building on the berth vacated by the *Olympic* months before. These then were to be the three shipping wonders of the world, all being created for a service that would dominate the Atlantic.

The *Olympic* quickly established herself as the great liner she was intended to be and the world wondered how she could ever be improved upon. The promise was that the *Titanic* would be even better. She was launched without ceremony on May 31st 1911 and was completed and delivered to the White Star Line on April 2nd 1912. The *Titanic* sailed quietly without fuss from Southampton at the start of her maiden voyage on April 10th. She called first at Cherbourg for continental passengers and then Queenstown in Southern Ireland to pick up the remainder.

She sailed out of that Irish bay shortly after noon on Thursday April 12th, and was never seen again.

The sinking of the *Titanic* was a salutary lesson indeed and it resulted in far reaching changes being made to the laws of safety at sea. From that time on, no vessel could leave any port without sufficient life-saving equipment for all passengers and crew. The requirement for life-saving drill to be held aboard all ships every week was then made maritime law. An international ice-patrol was set up in the North Atlantic to warn of impending danger from icebergs and a winter and summer sailing track was devised to cut down on possible ice encounters.

Radio demonstrated its usefulness in emergency when the *Titanic*, for the first time, summoned help by using the emergency call sign SOS. It was also decreed by international law that no longer would passengers be imprisoned behind locked barriers. It was the first faltering steps to democracy afloat.

The Great War which followed shortly after the disaster, crumbled, even more, the social barriers then prevalent. Changes were set in motion which even today are being acted upon. The disaster which befell the *Titanic* on that April night in 1912, seemed to symbolise a need for universal change in human behaviour. Perhaps that is the secret of its incredible hold over the imagination and conscience of us all. The tragedy of *Titanic* stopped the world and made it think for just a moment.

Leviathan

There is little that can be written about this incredible ship that has not already been written by Frank Braynard. Every rivet, nuance, quirk and moment of her existence has been scrutinised and set down by him, in an encyclopedic work which fills six large volumes. That feat of maritime historical scholarship is as awe inspiring in its magnitude as was the ship herself.

The *Leviathan* started her life as the second of the Hamburg America Line's three great symphonies of steel and known at the time as the Ballin Three. Launched by Prince Rupert of Bavaria in April 1913, and named the *Vaterland*, she was the largest ship in the world at that time and some say she was the most magnificent. There is no doubt about her impressiveness and at 54,282 tons she was massive. She didn't quite reach the magical 1,000 foot mark, falling short by only 50 feet, but her length was enough to span the largest Atlantic waves which, theoretically, were the barriers to high speed regularity for the crossing of that ocean.

Possessing an appearance perfectly matched to her teutonic personality, the *Vaterland* entered service only a few months before the outbreak of the First World War. Fate was to allow her and her older sister, the *Imperator*, to sail under the Kaiser's flag for only a short time. Their unborn triplet never did sail as a German liner and although launched and named *Bismarck*, she was to sit unfinished at her builders yard until the end of hostilities, at which time she would be renamed *Majestic* and sail under the British flag in the White Star fleet.

The older ship would eventually be renamed *Berengaria* and become the flag ship of the Cunard Line while the *Vaterland* would sail under the American flag during the war but under the name *Leviathan*.

The United States Navy had seized her while she lay in New York harbour in 1914 and there she remained, but it was a struggle to prepare her for sea after her long lay-up. She did good service in her role as troop transport and when it was over she was virtually rebuilt as America's first superliner and sailed under the flag of the newly formed United States Lines. When the *Leviathan* sailed at last as part of the American fleet, she had to face very severe competition, not least from her sisters sailing for the British companies.

America's crazy prohibition laws did not help and the drying up of the mass immigrant passenger trade only aggravated the situation. She was a loner, with no comparable partner in her company to balance her sailing schedules. But in spite of these shortcomings she was one of the wonder ships of the world and her passenger lists were a who's who of American and European high society.

Her new tourist class, created from the caverns formerly filled with the huddled masses, was now gloriously crowded with yankee youth, heading for the delights of European sophistication and *joie de vivre*, and in many ways she was a success. But financially she was no asset and without her government subsidies she would have been awash in a sea of red ink.

The break-up of Germany's mercantile fleet and especially the Hamburg America's big three, was such a blow for Albert Ballin that he ended his own life. He was the mastermind behind their conception and it was his genius which was the moving force which gave those great ships life, but it all came to nought in his eyes, even though his creations lived on and did the work intended for many more years.

The ships, even though awe inspiring, were not beautiful. Of the three the one most suited to her new livery was the *Leviathan*. Her three tall, massive funnels looked less overpowering in their red, white and blue than did those on either the *Berengaria* or the *Majestic*.

The *Leviathan* eventually became a victim of the great depression and in the early 1930s was withdrawn from service. But in 1934, in answer to public demand, she undertook a few voyages carrying first and tourist class passengers only. But the end was in sight as she proved too costly to continue as normal, so once more she was laid up in Hoboken and became ever more decrepit. She was to sit awaiting her final fate for almost four years. America, that great consumer and inventor of the throw away society, always seems to be reluctant to throw away her old ships and they are condemned to lie in ever depressing states of decay before finally being given a dignified end.

The *Leviathan*'s day of reckoning came on January 25th 1938. She had been sold to the Scottish shipbreakers Thomas Ward and Company at Inverkeithing and to enable her to pass under the Forth Bridge her masts and her funnels had been cut down. She was a sorry sight as she sluggishly limped out of New York harbour belching clouds of black smoke. Her captain for this last, sad transatlantic voyage was Captain Binks who was one time captain of the great White Star liner *Olympic*.

The *Leviathan* left America flying the red ensign of Great Britain. She was a lonely shadow of what she once was as she headed for her appointment with her demolishers. Today, history repeats itself with the even more sorrowful plight of the greatest American ship ever built. The incomparable SS *United States*, or what remains of her, lies waiting for her agony to end, as did *Leviathan* so many years before. But the years of neglect for this, the last of the Blue Ribband holders, can now be counted in decades and no end is in sight for her. If ships have a soul, and many people think they do, then is it not time to put the *United States* finally into the history books, and close the chapter in a dignified manner and give her peace at last?

Paris

The *Paris* was the ship of the hour for France during the early 'twenties. Never intended to compete with the German or British giants on their terms, she created a style and ambience of her own which eventually changed the stylistic direction of liners for the future. The ship is an example of how the fates rule everything under creation.

Her life was a story of almosts, nearlys and never quites. She was *almost* built before the First World War but had to lie as an empty hull for six years before completion. She only entered service as late as 1921. She was *nearly* a pure, pre-war art nouveau palace but those empty years had seen a shift in styles and a new art deco was all the vogue as she was preparing for her debut in the Atlantic.

That style too was then incorporated in her decor before completion. She was *never quite* free to live an untroubled life. In 1929 her interior was gutted by a fire and five months had to pass before she could sail again. But this was only a rehearsal for the real thing which overwhelmed her ten years later. In April 1939, as if she wanted to avoid another war, the *Paris* caught fire with a vengeance and filled with the charred remains of exquisite things, rolled over and sank, lying where she died, unmoved and unloved, until broken up in 1947.

Largely forgotten in the annals of great transatlantic liners, the *Paris* was a bridge between the old and the modern. She lived long enough to sail beside the *Ille de France* and the *Normandie*, both ships owing their fabulous reputation to the pioneering spirit of the designers of the *Paris*. All that we know today as modern and associate with the ocean liner style, was born with that beautiful, sleek, Parisian femme fatale.

Technical Details

America
United States Lines

Builders: Newport News Shipbuilding & Dry Dock Co
26,454 GRT | 723 x 93 feet
Passengers: 543 cabin; 418 tourist; 241 third; crew 643

1939	August 31, launched
1940	First voyage, cruising American waters
1941	Converted to troopship
1942	Renamed *West Point* for duration of war
1946	November 14, maiden voyage New York–Le Havre as *America*
1960	Remeasured at 33,961 GRT, passengers: 516 first; 530 tourist
1964	Sold to D&A Chandris of Piraeus, renamed *Australis*
1978	Sold to America Cruise Line. Renamed *America* but later returned to Chandris and renamed *Italis*. Laid up Piraeus
1980	Sold, renamed *Noga*
1984	Renamed *Alferdoss*
1988	October 29, developed leak and beached Piraeus.

Amra
British India Steam Navigation Co Ltd.

Builders: Swan Hunter & Wigham Richardson, Newcastle
8,314 GRT | 461 x 61 feet
Passengers: 222 saloon; 737 third

1938	Launched. Calcutta–Rangoon service
1940	War service, converted to hospital ship
1946	Route India–Africa
	Bombay, Mombasa, Dar-es-Salaam and return
1965	Sold for breaking up.

Aquitania
Cunard Steamship Co.

Builders: John Brown, Clydebank
45,647 GRT | 901 x 97 feet
Passengers: 618 first; 614 second; 1,998 third; crew 972

1913	April 21, launched
1914	maiden voyage Liverpool–New York, war service
1919	First post-war voyage
	June 14, Southampton–New York
1919	November, converted to oil fuel
1926	Passenger capacity changed: 610 first; 950 second; 640 tourist
1939	November, converted to troopship
1948	May, first voyage as emigrant ship Southampton–Halifax
1950	February 21, arrived at Faslane for breaking up.

Arcadia
P&O S.N. Co.

Builders: John Brown, Clydebank
29,734 GRT | 721 x 90 feet
Passengers: 675 first; 735 tourist; crew 710

1953	May 14, launched
1954	February 22, maiden voyage London–Sydney
1959	October 19, first round the world voyage
1970	Converted to one class for cruising
1979	Sold for breaking-up.

Atlantis
Royal Mail Lines

Builders: Harland & Wolff, Belfast
15,620 GRT | 589 x 67 feet

1913	May 8, launched as *Andes*
	September 26, maiden voyage Liverpool–Chile for Pacific Steam Navigation Co, then Southampton–La Plata service for Royal Mail S.P. Co.
1915	Taken over by Admiralty as auxiliary cruiser
1919	Resumed passenger service
1930	Refitted as cruise ship and renamed *Atlantis*, passengers 450 first class, oil fired and painted white
1939	Converted to hospital ship
1941	Sold to government
1948	Reconstructed as emigrant ship to carry 900 passengers, used on Australasian service
1952	Sold to be broken up at Faslane.

Balmoral Castle
Union Castle Line

Builders: Fairfield, Glasgow
13,361 GRT | 590 x 64 feet
Passengers: 320 first; 220 second; 270 third

1909	November 13, launched
1910	February, maiden voyage Southampton–Capetown
	November, converted to temporary royal yacht
1911	Resumed company service
1917	Converted to troopship
1919	First post-war voyage Southampton–Capetown, passengers: 120 first; 68 second; 200 third
1939	Broken up.

Berengaria
Cunard Steamship Co.

Builders: Vulcan, Hamburg
52,117 GRT | 909 x 98 feet

1912	May 23, launched
1913	June 10, maiden voyage as *Imperator* of Hamburg-America Line Cuxhaven–New York
1914	Laid up at Hamburg for duration of war
1920	February, handed to Britain as war reparations
1921	February, sold to Cunard, renamed *Berengaria*, refitted to carry 972 first; 630 second; 606 third; 515 tourist class passengers, oil fired
1934	Cunard & White Star Lines amalgamate
1938	Damaged by fire in New York, returned to Southampton without passengers and sold for scrap
1939	Ship broken up.

Berlin
North German Lloyd

Builders: Armstrong, Whitworth & Co, Newcastle
Originally the Swedish-America Line, *Gripsholm*
17,993 GRT | 573 x 74 feet
Passengers: 127 first; 482 second; 948 third; crew 360

1924	November 26, launched
1925	November 21, maiden voyage Gothenberg–New York

1940-46   Used by international Red Cross exchanging prisoners and wounded
1946-52   In Swedish America Line service
1954   Joint ownership Swedish America and North German Lloyd, in service Bremerhaven–New York
1955   German ownership completed and ship renamed the *Berlin*, 18,600 GRT, passengers 98 first; 878 tourist class
1966   November 26, arrived at La Spezia, Italy for breaking-up.

Braemar Castle   Union Castle Line
Builders: Harland & Wolff, Belfast
17,029 GRT   576 x 74 feet
Passengers: 552 cabin class
1952   April 24, launched
          November 22, maiden voyage London–round Africa
1965   Cruising only
1966   January 6, arrived at Faslane for scrapping.

Bremen   North German Lloyd
Builders: Deschimag, AG 'Weser', Bremen
51,656 GRT   938 x 102 feet
Passengers: 800 first; 500 second; 300 tourist; 600 third; crew 990
1928   Launched
1929   July 16, maiden voyage Bremerhaven–New York wins Blue Ribband from the *Mauretania*
1939   *Bremen* in New York at outbreak of war, returned empty to Germany
1941   Burnt out at her dock in Bremerhaven.

HMY Britannia
Builders: John Brown, Clydebank
5,769 GRT   412 x 55 feet
Crew: 21 officers; 256 men
1953   April 16, launched
1954   Maiden voyage to Tobruk with Prince Charles, Princess Anne, where Her Majesty the Queen & Prince Philip embarked for their first voyage aboard after the first Commonwealth tour of the reign
1990   *Britannia* in full commission and continuing to undertake world voyages.

Britannic   White Star Line
Builders: Harland & Wolff, Belfast
26,943 GRT   712 x 82 feet
Passengers: 504 cabin; 551 tourist; 493 third; crew 500
1929   August 6, launched
1930   June 28, maiden voyage Liverpool–New York
1934   White Star & Cunard merge forming Cunard-White Star Line
1939   August 29, withdrawn for conversion to troopship
1947   Refit, passengers 429 first; 564 tourist; 27,666 GRT
1948   May 22, first post-war voyage Liverpool–New York
1960   December, sold for breaking-up at Inverkeithing.

Canberra   P&O Orient Lines
Builders: Harland & Wolff, Belfast
45,270 GRT   820 x 102 feet
Passengers: 548 first; 1,650 tourist; crew 900
1960   March 16, launched
1961   Maiden voyage Southampton–Australia–Round the world
1973   Permanent cruise ship
1982   April 9, sailed as troopship for Falklands war-zone
          July 11, returned in triumph to Southampton
          September 11, sailed on first post-war cruise
1987   Refitted and refurbished to higher standard
1990   Cruising from Southampton starting with a world cruise beginning in January.

Carthage   P&O S.N. Co.
Builders: Alexander Stephen & Sons, Glasgow
14,304 GRT   540 x 71 feet
Passengers: 177 first; 214 second
1931   August 18, launched
          December, maiden voyage London–Hong Kong, two funnels
1940   January, converted to armed merchant cruiser, aft funnel removed
1943   Reconverted as a troop transport
1948   Post-war overhaul completed – white hull. Passengers now 181 first and 213 second
          July 6, London–Hong Kong service
1961   June, arrived Japanese shipbreakers for breaking up.

Chusan   P&O S.N. Co.
Builders: Vickers-Armstrongs, Barrow
24,215 GRT   673 x 84 feet
Passengers: 475 first; 551 tourist; crew 572
1949   June 28, launched
1950   July 1, first voyage cruise from Southampton
          September 15, maiden voyage London–Bombay
1960   Service extended to round the world
1973   July 1, arrived in Taiwan for breaking-up.

City of New York   Inman Line
Builders: J.&G. Thomson, Glasgow
10,499 GRT   560 x 63 feet
Passengers: 540 first, 200 second, 1,000 steerage
1888   March 15, launched
          August 1, maiden voyage Liverpool–New York
1892   Wins Blue Ribband
1893   Sold to American Line, renamed *New York*
1898   Served in US Navy as cruiser in Spanish American war
1901   Refitted, one funnel removed
1914   Entered service New York–Liverpool route
1917   Served as armed transport
1921   Sold to Polish Navigation Co for New York–Danzig service
1923   Broken up in Genoa.

Columbus   North German Lloyd
Builders: Schichau, Danzig
32,354 GRT   775 x 83 feet
Passengers: 513 first; 574 second; 703 third; crew 733
1914   Laid down, as *Hindenburg*, work stopped for duration of war
1922   June, named *Columbus* but was unable to reach the water until August 12
1924   Maiden voyage Bremerhaven–New York
1927   Mid Atlantic breakdown with machinery destruction
1929   Refitted by Blohm and Voss now turbine steamship
1939   August, ship on cruise and obtains sanctuary in Vera Cruz
        December 19, challenged by British warship while attempting to return to Germany, scuttles herself, crew rescued by USS *Tuscaloosa*.

Conte di Savoia   'Italia', Flotta Riunite
Builders: CR dell' Adriatico Trieste
48,502 GRT   815 x 96 feet
Passengers: 500 first; 366 second; 412 tourist; 922 third; crew 786
1931   October 28, launched for Lloyd Sabaudo (transferred to Italia before completion)
1932   November 30, maiden voyage Genoa–New York
1939   Laid up near Venice
1943   September 11, attacked by allied aircraft and sunk
1945   Wreck salved – scrapped 1950.

Duchess of Bedford   Canadian Pacific
Builders: John Brown, Clydebank
20,123 GRT   601 x 75 feet
Passengers: 580 cabin; 480 tourist; 510 third; crew 510
1928   January 24, launched
        June 1, maiden voyage Liverpool–Montreal
1939   Converted to troopship
1947   March 3, renamed *Empress of India* during refit
        October, renamed *Empress of France*
1948   First post war voyage as an *Empress*. Passengers 400 first; 300 tourist
1960   Sold for breaking up.

Dunottar Castle   Castle Line
Builders: Fairfield Shipbuilding & Engineering Co., Glasgow
5,625 GRT   432 x 49 feet
Passengers: 360 in three classes
1890   May 22, launched
        October, maiden voyage
1891   Inaugurated companies sailing from Southampton in June
1911   Attended Delhi Durbar as cruise ship
1913   Transferred to Royal Mail, renamed *Caribbean*
1914   Converted to armed merchant cruiser
1915   September 27, foundered in heavy weather.

Edinburgh Castle   Union-Castle Line
Builders: Harland & Wolff, Belfast
28,705 GRT   747 x 84 feet
Passengers: 214 first; 541 tourist; crew 400
1947   October 16, launched
1948   December, maiden voyage Southampton–Durban
1976   March 5, last voyage with passengers
        June 3, arrived in Taiwan for breaking-up.

Empress of Scotland   Canadian Pacific
Builders: Fairfield Shipbuilding & Engineering Co., Glasgow
20,032 GRT   666 x 83 feet
Passengers: 458 first; 250 tourist
1929   December 17, launched as *Empress of Japan*
1930   June 14, maiden voyage Liverpool–Quebec
        August, made first line voyage Vancouver–Yokohama on intended transpacific service
1939   Converted for trooping
1942   Renamed *Empress of Scotland*
1948   Refitted for transatlantic service
1950   May 5, first post-war voyage Liverpool–Quebec
1958   Sold to Hamburg–Atlantic Line, renamed *Hanseatic*
1966   September 7, damaged by fire in New York
        December, broken up in Hamburg.

Empress of Asia   Canadian Pacific
Builders: Fairfield Shipbuilding & Engineering Co., Glasgow
16,908 GRT   592 x 68 feet
Passengers: 284 first; 100 second; 808 Asiatic steerage; crew 475
1912   Launched
1913   June 14, maiden voyage Liverpool–Hong Kong then in line service Vancouver–Yokohama
1914   Converted as auxiliary cruiser and later troopship
1919   Returned to owners after refit
1941   Converted to troopship
1942   February 5, attacked and sank by Japanese aircraft off Singapore.

Empress of Canada
original name *Duchess of Richmond*   Canadian Pacific
Builders: John Brown, Clydebank
20,022 GRT   600 x 75 feet
Passengers: 580 cabin class; 480 tourist; 510 third; crew 510
1928   June 18, launched
1929   January 26, cruising, Liverpool–Canary Islands and Africa
        March 15, maiden voyage Liverpool–St Johns
1940   Converted to troopship
1946   Returned to Fairfields for conversion as an *Empress*
1947   July 12, renamed *Empress of Canada*
        July 16, maiden voyage Liverpool–Montreal
1953   Burnt out at her Liverpool dock
1954   Raised and then broken up in Italy.

Europa   North German Lloyd
Builders: Blohm and Voss, Hamburg
49,746 GRT   941 x 102 feet
Passengers: 687 first; 524 second; 306 tourist; 507 third; crew 970
1928   August 15, launched
1929   When almost finished was damaged by fire
1930   March 19, maiden voyage, takes Blue Riband from the *Bremen*
1939   Converted for war as accommodation ship
1945   Seized by the US and used as military transport
1946   Handed to France and renamed *Liberte*, ran into wreck of the *Paris* and sank, during next few years salvaged and refitted
1950   August 17, maiden voyage as *Liberte* Le Havre–New York
1962   January 30, arrived at shipbreakers for breaking-up in La Spezia, Italy

George Washington
North German Lloyd

Builders: Vulcan, Stettin
25,570 GRT   723 x 73 feet
Passengers: 568 first; 433 second; 452 third; 1,226 steerage; crew 585

1908	November 10, launched
1909	June 12, maiden voyage, Bremerhaven–New York
1914	Interned in New York
1917	Seized by US Navy for use as transport
1920	January, laid up in Boston
	October, refitted for service
1921	First voyage New York–Bremen, under United States Lines colours
1931	Laid up
1940	Resumed service for US Navy
1942-43	Altered and repaired but not satisfactory
1947	Damaged by fire and laid up
1951	Another fire destroyed her and hulk sent for breaking-up.

Gothic
Shaw, Savill & Albion Line

Builders: Swan, Hunter & Wigham Richardson, Newcastle
15,902 GRT   561 x 72 feet
Passengers: 85 first class

1947	December 12, launched
1948	December 23, maiden voyage Liverpool–Sydney then London–New Zealand service
1951	Refitted as royal yacht by Cammell Laird for use by King George VI but not used due to death of the King
1953	Royal fittings reinstated for the world voyage undertaken by Queen Elizabeth II
1968	Damaged by fire during voyage, repaired but never fully
1969	August 13, arrived at Kaohsiung for breaking-up.

Himalaya
P&O S.N. Co.

Builders: Vickers-Armstrongs, Barrow
27,955 GRT   709 x 90 feet
Passengers: 758 first; 401 tourist; crew 631

1948	October 5, launched
1949	October 6, maiden voyage London–Sydney
1958	Service across Pacific to San Francisco
1963	Refitted as one class ship for 1,416 passengers
1974	November 28, arrived at Taiwanese shipbreakers.

Jervis Bay
Commonwealth Government Line

Builders: Vickers, Barrow
13,839 GRT   549 x 68 feet
Passengers: 12 first; 700 third; crew 216

1922	January 17, launched
	September 26, maiden voyage London–Brisbane
1928	Sold to White Star Line, managed by Aberdeen Line, registered in London
1931	Increased to 14,164 GRT, passengers decreased to 542 tourist
1933	Transferred to Aberdeen and Commonwealth Line, London
1939	September, fitted out as armed merchant cruiser
1940	November 5, caught by German surface raiders and sunk.

La Provence
C.G.T. The French Line

Builders:Penhoet, St. Nazaire
13,753 GRT   627 x 65 feet
Passengers: 422 first; 132 second; 808 steerage

1905	March 21, launched
1906	April 21, maiden voyage Le Havre–New York
1914	Converted to armed cruiser for French Navy
1916	February 26, torpedoed by German submarine U35 in Mediterranean with death toll of 930, crew and troops.

Leviathan
ex *Vaterland*   **Hamburg–America Line**

Builders: Blohm & Voss, Hamburg
54,282 GRT   948 x 100 feet
Passengers: 752 first; 535 second; 850 third; 1,772 steerage; crew 1,234

1913	April 3, launched
1914	May 14, maiden voyage Cuxhaven–New York
	August, interned at New York
1917	April 4, seized by USA
	July 25, handed over to US Navy as transport
	September 6, renamed *Leviathan*
1922	Reconstructed by Newport News Shipbuilding & Dry Dock Co for the United States Lines
1923	June 19, completes trials, passengers 940 first, 666 tourist, 1,402 third class
	July 4, maiden voyage New York–Southampton
1932	Laid up
1934	Four voyages to Southampton
1938	January 26, *Leviathan* sails from New York empty, bound for Scottish shipbreakers.

Lusitania
Cunard Steamship Co

Builders: John Brown, Clydebank
31,550 GRT   787 x 87 feet
Passengers: 563 first; 464 second; 1,138 third; crew 802

1906	June 7, launched
1907	September 7, maiden voyage Liverpool–New York, takes the Blue Ribband
1908	Loses title to *Mauretania* then regains it
1909	Loses Blue Ribband record to *Mauretania* permanently
1914	Remains in service on Liverpool–New York run but because of fuel economies runs at only 21 knots
1915	May 7, returning to Britain, *Lusitania* was torpedoed off the Southern Irish coast by German U-boat and sinks with massive loss of life, 1,198 people died.

Malwa
P&O S.N. Co.

Builders: Caird & Co., Greenock
10,883 GRT   560 x 61 feet
Passengers: 400 first; 200 second; crew 376

1908	October 10, launched
1909	January 29, maiden voyage London–Sydney
1917	Requisitioned and altered for trooping
1920	September 24, first post-war voyage
1932	May, sold to Japan for breaking up.

Manhattan   United States Lines
Builders: New York Shipbuilding Corp, Camden, New Jersey
24,289 GRT   705 x 86 feet
Passengers: 582 cabin; 461 tourist; 196 tourist class; crew 478
1931	December 5, launched
1932	August 10, maiden voyage New York–Hamburg
1940	European war stops service, ship used for cruising
1941	Renamed *Wakefield* and converted for trooping
1942	September 3, caught fire and towed to Halifax
1944	Rebuilt as troopship
1946	Laid up as reserve ship on Hudson
1964	May 27, sold for demolition, Union Metals & Alloys Corp, New York
1965	March 6, arrived at Kearny for breaking up.

Mauretania (II)   Cunard White Star Line
Builders: Cammell Laird, Birkenhead
35,738 GRT   772 x 89 feet
Passengers: 440 cabin class; 450 tourist; 470 third; crew 780
1938	July 28, launched
1939	June 17, maiden voyage Liverpool–New York
	December, laid-up in New York
1940	March 6, sailed to Sydney for refitting as troopship
1946	Recondition by Cammell Laird at Liverpool
1947	April 26, first post-war voyage Liverpool–New York
	June 10, service from Southampton–New York recommences, passengers: 475 first; 390 cabin; 300 tourist
1962	Painted multi-shade of green for cruising
1965	November 23, arrived at Inverkeithing, Scotland for breaking up.

Media   Cunard White Star Line
Builders: John Brown, Clydebank
13,345 GRT   531 x 70 feet
Passengers: 250 first; crew 184
1946	December 12, launched, first transatlantic liner built since end of war
1947	August 20, maiden voyage Liverpool–New York
1961	October, sold to Cogedor Line, Genoa, renamed *Flavia*
1969	Sold to Costa Armatori
1982	Sold, renamed *Flavian*, laid up Hong Kong
1986	Renamed *Lavia*
1989	Burnt-out in Hong Kong, broken up Taiwan.

Medina   P&O S.N. Co.
Builders: Caird & Co., Greenock
12,350 GRT   625 x 63 feet
Passengers: 460 first; 220 second; crew 400
1911	March 14, launched
	November 11, sailed on maiden voyage as Royal Yacht
1912	June 28, first line voyage London–Sydney
1917	April 28, sunk by U-boat.

Mauretania   Cunard Steamship Co
Builders: Swan Hunter & Wigham Richardson, Newcastle
31,938 GRT   790 x 88 feet
Passengers: 560 first; 425 second; 1,300 third; crew 812
1906	September 20, launched
1907	November 16, maiden voyage Liverpool–New York, breaks eastbound speed record
1909	Takes Blue Ribband for both directions and holds it for next 20 years
1915	June, converted as troop transport
1919	June 27, resumed passenger service
1921	Remodelled passenger accommodation and converted for oil fuel
1935	July 4, arrives at Rosyth for breaking-up.

Monarch of Bermuda   Furness Withy & Co.
Builders: Vickers-Armstrongs, Newcastle
22,424 GRT   579 x 76 feet
Passengers: 830 first; crew 456
1931	March 17, launched
	November 7, maiden voyage New York–Hamilton
1939	November, converted to troop transport
1947	During renovation work at Newcastle destroyed by fire, wreck bought by British government for use as migrant ship – refitted by J.I. Thornycroft & Co.
1950	First voyage as *New Australia*
1958	Sold to Greek Line, renamed *Arkadia*
1959	Maiden voyage Bremerhaven–Montreal
1966	December, arrived in Spain for scrapping.

Morea   P&O S.N. Co.
Builders: Barclay, Curle & Co, Glasgow
10,890 GRT   562 x 61 feet
Passengers: 407 first; 200 second; crew 307
1908	August 15, launched
	December 4, maiden voyage London–Sydney
1915	Converted to hospital ship, troop transport and then merchant cruiser
1919	Reconditioned for liner service to Australia and Far East
1930	Sold for scrapping in Japan.

Nieuw Amsterdam   Holland-America Line
Builders: Rotterdamsche Dry Dock Mij
36,287 GRT   759 x 88 feet
Passengers: 556 first; 455 tourist; 209 third; crew 694
1937	April 10, launched
1938	May 10, maiden voyage Rotterdam–New York
1939	Laid up at New York
1940	Placed under Cunard management and run as troopship
1946	April 26, first post-war arrival back in Rotterdam for rebuilding
1947	October 29, new maiden voyage Rotterdam–New York
1961	Modified as two class ship, passengers: 574 first; 583 tourist
1971	Used only for cruising
1974	January, sold for breaking-up in Taiwan.

Normandie
G.G.T. The French Line

Builders: Penhoët, St Nazaire
79,280 GRT   1,030 x 117
Passengers: 848 first; 670 tourist; 454 third; crew 1,345

1932	October 29, launched
1935	May 29, maiden voyage Le Havre–New York, broke speed record, took Blue Ribband from the *Rex*
1938	Loses speed record to the *Queen Mary*
1939	August 28, laid up in New York
1941	December 24, taken over by US Navy as transport, renamed *Lafayette* and work started on conversion to troopship
1942	February 9, fire broke out and eventually ship keeled over to become total wreck
1946	October 3, remains of the *Normandie* towed to Port Newark for breaking-up.

Olympic
White Star Line

Builders: Harland & Wolff, Belfast
45,324 GRT   882 x 92 feet
Passengers: 1,054 first; 510 second; 1,020 third; crew 860

1910	October 20, launched
1911	June 14, maiden voyage Southampton–New York
1912	Rebuilt after loss of *Titanic* with extra bulkheads and lifeboats added
1915	Converted to a troop transport
1918	May 12, attacked by U103 but unharmed, accidentally runs over attacking submarine sinking her
1919	Returns to Belfast for restoration after war work converted to oil fuel, passenger capacity changed to 750 first; 500 second; 1,150 third
1920	July 21, first post-war voyage
1934	February, White Star-Cunard Line merge
	May 16, collides with and sinks *Nantucket* lightship, 7 dead
1935	October 13, arrives at Jarrow for breaking-up.

Ophir
Orient Line

Builders: Robert Napier & Son, Glasgow
6,814 GRT   481 x 53 feet
Passengers: 230 first; 142 second; 520 third

1891	April 11, launched
	November 7, maiden voyage Tilbury–Brisbane
1901	February 27, sailed as royal yacht for around the world voyage
1902	January 3, resumes Orient Line service
1914	Requisitioned by the Admiralty as mail ship
	October 23, sailed on her last voyage to Australia
1915	Sold to Admiralty for £25,000 for use as armed merchant cruiser
1922	Sold for scrap and sailed to shipbreakers in Troon, Scotland

Orcades
Orient Line

Builders: Vickers-Armstrongs, Barrow
28,164 GRT   709 x 90 feet
Passengers: 773 first; 772 tourist

1947	October 14, launched
1948	Maiden voyage London–Sydney
1960	P&O Orient Line merge, *Orcades* on round the world route
1972	Laid up
1973	February 6, arrived in Taiwan for breaking-up.

Orontes
Orient Line

Builders: Fairfield Shipbuilding & Engineering Co., Glasgow
9,023 GRT   513 x 58 feet
Passengers: 320 first and second class; 323 third

1902	May 10, launched
	October 24, maiden voyage Tilbury–Brisbane
1914	Runs as usual despite war
1917	Requisitioned as troopship
1919	Returns to Orient Line service
1922	Laid up at Hull
1926	Sold to shipbreakers.

Orsova
Orient Line

Builders: Vickers-Armstrongs, Barrow
28,790 GRT   723 x 90 feet
Passengers: 681 first; 813 tourist; crew 620

1953	May 14, launched
1954	March 17, maiden voyage London–Sydney
1955	April, London–Sydney–San Francisco–London service
1960	May, owners become P&O Orient Line
1966	Under sole ownership of P&O, livery changed
1974	February 14, arrived at Kaohsiung to be broken-up.

Panama
Panama Railroad

Builders: Bethlehem Steel Co, Quincy
10,021 GRT   493 x 64 feet
Passengers: 202 first class

1938	Launched
1939	Entered service New York–Cristobal
1941	Taken over as an army transport – renamed *James Parker*
1946	Resumed passenger service, reverted to *Panama*
1957	Sold to American President Lines, renamed *President Hoover*
1964	Sold to Chandris Group for one class cruising in Mediterranean. Renamed *Regina*, 650 passengers.
1973	Renamed *Regina Prima*
1979	Laid up Piraeus
1985	Broken up Aliage-Izmir.

Paris
C.G.T. French Line

Builders: Penhoet St Nazaire
34,569 GRT   764 x 85 feet
Passengers: 563 first; 460 second; 1,092 third; crew 648

1913	Laid down, work stopped at outbreak of war
1916	September 12, launched
1921	June 15, maiden voyage Le Havre–New York
1929	Extensively damaged by fire, rebuilt
1939	April 19, destroyed by fire and keels over at her berth in Le Havre
1947	Wreck finally broken up.

Queen of Bermuda
Furness Withy & Co, London

Builders: Vickers-Armstrongs, Barrow
22,575 GRT   580 x 76 feet
Passengers: 700 first; 410 crew

1932	September 1, launched
1933	February 21, maiden voyage Liverpool–New York then on New York–Bermuda service
1939	October 28, taken over as armed merchant cruiser

1943   Refitted for trooping
1947   Returned to owners
1949   February, resumes service on Bermuda run
1961   Reconstructed with one funnel and modernised
1962   April 7, New York–Bermuda service resumed
1966   December 6, arrived at Faslane in Scotland for breaking-up.

Queen Elizabeth   Cunard Steamship Co.
Builders: John Brown, Clydebank
83,673 GRT   1,029 x 118 feet
Passengers: 823 first; 662 second; 798 tourist; crew 1,296
1938   September, launched
1940   March 2, almost complete, sailed directly from shipyard to
       New York without trials
       November, sails to Sydney and there fitted out as troopship
1946   March 6, released from government service
       October 16, sails on maiden voyage as Cunard liner Southamp-
       ton–New York
1968   Sails from Southampton for last time for Port Everglades
1970   Bought at auction, registered at Hong Kong, renamed Seawise
       University
1971   Sails from Florida to Hong Kong
1972   January 9, during refitting, fire destroyed the ship
       January 10, Queen Elizabeth keeled over and sank.

Queen Elizabeth 2   Cunard Steamship Co.
Builders: John Brown, Clydebank
65,863 GRT   963 x 105 feet
Passengers for transatlantic: 564 first; 1,441 tourist; reduced to one class
1,400 for cruising
1967   September 20, launched
1968   Series of failures on trials delays ships entry into service
1969   May 2, maiden voyage Southampton–New York
1982   May 3, requisitioned as troopship for Falklands conflict
       August 14, first post-war sailing
1987   Major rebuilding to become a diesel-electric ship
1990   Takes part in Cunard's 150th anniversary celebrations.

Queen Mary   Cunard White Star Line
Builders: John Brown, Clydebank
80,774 GRT   1,019 x 118 feet
Passengers: 776 cabin class; 784 tourist; 579 third; crew 1,101
1930   Laid down for Cunard
1931   Work stopped due to economic depression
1934   April 3, building resumed for new Cunard-White Star Line
       September 26, launched
1936   May 27, maiden voyage Southampton–New York
       August, takes Blue Ribband from the Normandie which won it
       again in 1937
1938   Queen Mary wins speed title and retains it for 14 years
1939   Laid up in New York
1940   Converted for trooping
1946   Handed back to Cunard
1947   July 31, first post-war voyage Southampton–New York
1967   Sold to city of Long Beach
       October 31, final departure from Southampton
1971   May 10, opened as museum and hotel after rebuilding
1990   Queen Mary taken over by Disney corporation and restoration
       continues, externally the ship is virtually unchanged from her
       days at sea.

Rangitata   New Zealand Line
Builders: John Brown, Clydebank
16,737 GRT   553 x 70 feet
Passengers: 100 first; 85 second; 410 third class
1929   March 26, launched
       November 22, maiden voyage Southampton–Wellington
1941   Converted as troop transport
1948   Refitted at John Brown & Co., passengers 123 first and 288
       tourist
1949   September 23, first post-war voyage London–Wellington
1962   July 21, arrived at Split, Yugoslavia to be broken-up.

Rawalpindi   P&O S.N. Co.
Builders: Harland & Wolff, Belfast
16,619 GRT   568 x 71 feet
Passengers: 310 first; 290 second; crew 380
1925   March 26, launched
       September 3, maiden voyage London–Far East
1939   September, requisitioned by Royal Navy and converted to
       armed merchant cruiser, one funnel removed
       November 23, attacked and sunk by two German battleships,
       270 crew killed.

Rex   'Italia', Flotta Riunite
Builders: Ansaldo, Sestri Pnente
51, 062 GRT   880 x 97 feet
Passengers: 604 first; 378 second; 410 tourist; 866 third; crew 756
1931   August 1, launched for Navigazione Generale Italiana, before
       completion the Rex becomes property of newly formed Italia
       Line
1932   September 27, sailed from Genoa at start of maiden voyage,
       damaged en route and voyage delayed for three days at
       Gibraltar
1933   Wins Blue Ribband
1940   Laid up at Trieste
1944   Attacked by RAF set on fire and eventually sank in shallow
       water
1947   Breaking-up commenced where she lay.

Southern Cross   Shaw Savill Albion
Builders: Harland & Wolff, Belfast
20,204 GRT   604 x 78 feet
Passengers: 1,160 tourist class
1954   August 17, launched
1955   March 29, maiden voyage Southampton–round the world
1971   Cruising from Liverpool until November when laid up in
       Southampton
1972   Laid up in River Fal, Cornwall
1973   Sold for further trading, renamed Calypso – refitted for cruising
1980   Renamed Azure Seas
1990   Cruising from USA.

Strathmore   P&O S.N. Co.
Builders: Vickers Armstrongs, Barrow
23,428 GRT   665 x 82 feet
Passengers: 445 first; 665 tourist; crew 515
1935   April 4, launched
       September 27, cruised London to Canary Islands
       October 26, maiden voyage London–Sydney
1939   Converted for trooping
1948   Refitted

1949   October 27, first post-war voyage carrying 497 first class and 487 tourist passengers
1961   Refitted to one class tourist ship
1963   Sold to Greek company as pilgrim carrier in Asiatic waters. Renamed *Marianna Latsi*
1966   Renamed *Henrietta Latsi*
1967   Laid up at Eleusis
1969   May 27, arrives at Italian breakers for breaking up.

Teutonic   White Star Line
Builders: Harland & Wolff, Belfast
9,984 GRT   565 x 57 feet
Passengers: 300 first; 190 second, 1,000 third
1889   January 19, launched as first armed merchant cruiser
        August 1, sailed to Spithead and naval review
        August 7, maiden voyage Liverpool–New York
1890   August, won Blue Ribband
1907   Home port transferred to Southampton
1914   September, commissioned by Admiralty as armed merchant cruiser
1921   July, sold to Dutch then German shipbreakers, broken-up at Emden.

Titanic   White Star Line
Builders: Harland & Wolff, Belfast
46,329 GRT
Passengers: 905 first; 564 second; 1,134 third; crew 900
1911   May 31, launched
1912   April 2, delivered as largest ship in the world
        April 10, sails on maiden voyage from Southampton bound for New York
        April 14, a few minutes before midnight the *Titanic* struck an iceberg
        April 15, 2.20 the ship sinks with the loss of 1,503 lives.

Uganda   British India Steam Navigation Co.
Builders: Barclay, Curle & Co, Glasgow
14,430 GRT   539 x 71 feet
1952   January 15, launched
        August 2, maiden voyage London–Beira
1967   Rebuilt as schools cruise ship with accommodation for 944 students and 320 cabin class passengers
1982   Requisitioned as hospital ship for service in war between Britain and Argentina for the Falklands
        April 19, sailed for South Atlantic
1985   Arrived in Falmouth for lay-up on River Fal
1986   May 20, sailed for Taiwanese breakers under the name *Triton*.

United States   United States Lines
Builders: Newport News Shipbuilding & Drydock Co.
53,329 GRT   990 x 101 feet
Passengers: 871 first; 508 cabin; 549 tourist; crew 1,093
1951   June 23, floated in Building Dock
1952   July 3, maiden voyage New York–Southampton, broke all speed records. The Blue Ribband has not been seriously contested for by any passenger vessel up to spring 1990 and the *United States* is the present holder. The Hales Trophy is held at the Merchant Marine Museum, Kings Point, New York and can be seen there
1969   November 8, laid up at Hampton Roads

1973   February, the US Maritime Administration bought the ship
1978   Sold to United States Cruises Inc.
1990   The *United States* still in lay-up and despite rumours of being made ready for further service, is becoming more run-down by the day.

Viceroy of India   P&O S.N. Co.
Builders: Alexander Stephen & Sons, Glasgow
19,648 GRT   612 x 76 feet
Passengers: 415 first; 258 second; crew 420
1928   September 15, launched
1929   March 29, maiden voyage London–Bombay
1942   November 11, serving as troopship *Viceroy of India* was torpedoed and sunk by U407 off North African coast at Oran.

RY Victoria & Albert (III)
1899   May, launched in Pembroke, 440 feet length overall
1901   July, commissioned
Built for Queen Victoria who never set foot aboard
Extensively used by King Edward VII and King George V
1915   Laid up for duration of First World War
1937   Was used at the Coronation review for King George VI
Was decommissioned and used as a depot ship in Portsmouth during Second World War
1955   Broken-up at Faslane
Furniture from the yacht was used in various ships chartered for Royal use during the early years of the century and finally installed permanently aboard the *Britannia* in 1953.

Washington   United States Lines
Builders: New York Shipbuilding Corp., Camden, New Jersey
24,289 GRT   705 x 86 feet
Passengers: 580 cabin class; 400 tourist; 150 third; crew 475
1932   August 20, launched
1933   May 10, maiden voyage New York–Hamburg
1940   January 13, first voyage New York–Genoa
        June, end of North Atlantic service, the *Washington* sailed as a neutral on voyages in American waters
1941   Renamed *Mount Vernon* and converted for trooping
1942   Sold to US government
1945   Renamed *Washington* and reconverted for tourist passengers only
1946   April 2, first post-war passenger voyage New York–Southampton
1951   October, laid up
1964   June 30, sold for breaking-up.

Windsor Castle   Union-Castle Line
Builders: Cammell Laird & Co., Birkenhead
37,640 GRT   783 x 93 feet
Passengers: 191 first; 591 tourist class; crew 475
1959   June 23, launched
1960   August 18, maiden voyage Southampton–Durban
1977   September, withdrawn from service after last arrival from South Africa
        September 15, sold to Greek John S. Latsis and left Southampton under the Panamanian flag and name of *Margarita L* on October 3.
1979   Converted to floating luxury hotel and based at Jeddah. Remains in use today.

Artists' Biographies

Allcot, John OBE (1888-1973)

Born in Derbyshire on November 13th 1888, the son of a master mariner. The family moved to Liverpool where, in due course, John apprenticed to a firm of lithographers, though he cannot have been there long as he went to sea at the age of 16 for eight years.

During this time his childhood interest in painting continued and in 1912 he went ashore at Sydney, New South Wales, and set up as an artist. He never left the area, living at various times at Mossman, Bowral and Manley. He was elected a fellow of the Royal Arts Society in Sydney and in 1970 was made an OBE for services to the arts.

He died in Sydney on July 13th 1973.

Beck, Stuart RSMA (born 1903)

Oils, watercolours and acrylics, all marine subjects and some landscapes, usually including lakes or rivers. Stuart Beck studied at Rochester School of Art. He went to sea in any type of ship or boat whenever possible. He started painting at the age of seven using his mother's oils on a piece of shoe box. He served in the RNVR as a technical illustrator for instruction purposes from 1941-46.

A marine technical illustrator for many years, he exhibited at the RSMA inaugural exhibition in 1946 and regularly since then. Stuart Beck lives at Lymington, Hampshire, England.

Becket, Charles

No information available.

Bergen, Claus (1885-1964)

Born in Stuttgart on April 4th 1885, Claus Bergen was the son of Fritz Bergen the illustrator and portrait painter. He attended the Munich Academy under Karl von Marr and became a book illustrator. He then studied in England and America. Around 1910 he was working in Munich and Dusseldorf.

In 1914 he became marine painter to Kaiser Wilhelm II and the German Naval Command and made paintings of the high seas fleet and of the Battle of Jutland in 1916. After the war, he again visited America and on his return continued to paint marines. A lot of his commissions were from public bodies and the paintings are of an impressive size.

He is thought to have died in Garmisch on October 4th 1964.

Bohrdt, Hans (1857-1945)

Hans Bohrdt was a completely self taught artist, never having any academic training. Nevertheless, he became one of the most eminent marine artists in the Kaiserreich. He was a friend of the Kaiser whose patronage ensured the artist's exposure to the buying public.

Brangwyn, Sir Frank William RA, RWS, PRBA, RE, HRSA, HVPSMA (1867-1956)

He was the son of a Welsh church architect who ran a workshop for ecclesiastical furnishings in Bruge where Brangwyn was born on May 13th 1867. Such early art training as he received he got from his father. He came to London with his family in 1875 and he practised drawing at the Victoria and Albert Museum.

From 1882-84 he worked in William Morris' workshop. In 1885 he had his first painting hung at the Royal Academy. Frank Brangwyn was much more than a marine painter, he is best known for his huge frescos, one of which was on the Canadian Pacific liner *Empress of Britain*, and sank with her. He was also a designer of furniture and an engraver.

He was elected ARA in 1904 and an RA in 1919. He died at Ditchling in Sussex on June 11th 1956.

Brenet, Albert (born 1903 in Harflour, France)

Albert Brenet is especially known as a painter of ships, parades, fire engines and animals in motion. He was awarded the Chevalier de la Legion d'Honour for his work in publicising the French navy during the war. He worked for many years producing the covers for the Moran tug company's house magazine 'The Towline'. He is also famous for his many fine paintings of French Line ships, especially the fabulous *Normandie*. His great portrait of the United States liner *Leviathan* was especially commissioned by Frank Braynard to be the cover of his six volume opus on that incredible ship.

Albert Brenet paints in watercolour and egg tempera which allows for a fluidity not possible when working with oils. His painting of the coronation procession of King George VI and Queen Elizabeth was bought by the late Queen Mary and is today in the royal collection.

Albert Brenet lives in Paris and is still painting.

Burgess, Arthur James Wetherall RI, ROI, VPSMA (1879-1957)

Born in Bombala, New South Wales on January 6th 1879 he studied art in Sydney and, after he came to England in 1901, at St Ives in Cornwall. He exhibited at the Royal Academy from 1904 and the Royal Institute of Oil Painters, the Royal Institute of Painters in Watercolours and the Paris Salon. He worked as an illustrator for the Graphic, the Illustrated London News and the Sphere, and for the Australian government in the First World War. He was a founder member of the Society of Marine Artists and its vice-president. He died in London on April 16th 1957.

Card, Stephen J. MNI

Stephen Card was apprenticed to the Glasgow firm of Denholm Ship Management Limited. He spent thirteen years at sea as a navigating officer, eventually commanding his own ship before coming ashore as Harbourmaster in Bermuda. He started painting nautical scenes in his spare time and in 1984 Captain Card retired to pursue a career as a marine artist.

Stephen Card's work has been published in the shipping periodical Sea Breezes and in the Commutator, the journal of the Titanic Historical Society. He is represented in the permanent collections of the American Merchant Marine Museum, Kings Point, New York, the Holland America Line, the Norway Caribbean Line and the Royal Caribbean Cruise Lines. He has been commissioned by the Cunard Line to paint ships of their present fleet for use as brochure covers, and a number of his large oils of famous Cunarders of the past now grace the public rooms aboard the *QE2* and in the Captain's suite. His work is avidly collected and is found in many corporate and private collections in Bermuda, the United States and in Europe. Noted maritime author and historian Frank O. Braynard, hailed him as a new master.

Stephen Card is a self taught artist, still only in his mid-thirties. His is a prodigious talent that seems destined for a place in the proud history of nautical art.

Conor, William (1881-1968)

William Conor was primarily a painter of portraits and figure subjects. Born in Belfast on May 7th 1881, he studied at the Belfast School of Art, also in London and Paris.

He exhibited at the Royal Academy, the Royal Hibernian Academy to which he was elected an academician, the New England Art Club, the Paris Salon and galleries in the United States.

William Conor died on February 5th 1968, at Belfast.

Copnall, Frank T. (born 1870)

Frank Copnall was born on April 27th 1870. He was really a portrait painter and was a member of the Liverpool Academy and the London Portraits Society. He was also president of the Liverpool Art Club and Liverpool Sketching Club. He exhibited at the Royal Academy and the Royal Society of Portrait Painters. His fine painting of the *Mauretania* hangs at the National Maritime Museum, Greenwich, and is the only marine by him in any public gallery.

Dawson, Montague FRSA, RSMA (1875-1973)

Born in Chiswick, London, Montague Dawson was the son of Henry Thomas Dawson an engineer and keen yachtsman who also painted marines and was the grandson of Henry Dawson the landscape painter. Early in his life Montague Dawson and his family moved to Smugglers House on Southampton Water and had every opportunity to indulge an inherited interest in ships.

Although he never went to art school, he inherited a flare for painting and in 1910 he joined a commercial art studio in Bedford Row, London, where he worked on posters and illustrations. At the outbreak of the First World War, he joined the Royal Navy and it was as a naval officer in Falmouth that he met Charles Napier Hemy who had a powerful influence on his work. During this time too, he supplied illustrations for publications in The Sphere. These were normally in monochrome.

In the Second World War he again worked for the Sphere, supplying them with pictures of historical events of the war. After the First World War he set up as a painter and an illustrator concentrating on historical subjects and portraits of deep water sailing ships, usually in a stiff breeze and a high sea. In the early 1930s Montague Dawson lived at Milford-on-Sea in Hampshire and he exhibited occasionally at the Royal Academy between 1917 and 1936. He also exhibited regularly at the Society of Marine Artists between 1946 and 1964 and was an elected member. He was also a fellow of the Royal Society of Arts.

He died at Midhurst, Sussex on May 21st 1973.

Demuth, Charles (1883-1935)

Charles Demuth was born in Lancaster, Pennsylvania and because of ill health and the artistic leanings of relatives, his well to do family encouraged him to pursue painting rather than joining the family business.

He first studied at the School of Industrial Art in Philadelphia and then at the Pennsylvania Academy of Fine Arts. Between 1912 and 1914 he was in Paris studying at the Academie Colarossi and Academie Julian. His early works, mostly watercolours, betray the influence of Marin and the Fauves, particularly Matisse. His paintings are well represented in some of the world's greatest museums, including the Metropolitan Museum of Art in New York and the Gallery of Fine Arts, Columbus, Ohio.

Desoutter, Roger Charles FRSA (born 1923)

Roger Desoutter paints in oils, mostly of sailing ships, coastal scenes and estuaries. He is also a landscape painter specialising in snow scenes.

He is a life long yachtsman and boat owner and from 1942-45 was an engineer on the staff of Sir Frank Whittle who was engaged in design and testings of the first jet engines. He has exhibited at the RSMA from 1974 and also at the Society of Aviation Artists from 1955. His works are shown in many London and provincial galleries.

He lives at Beaconsfield in Buckinghamshire.

Dixon, Charles (1872-1934)

Born at Goring-on-Thames on December 8th 1872, Charles Dixon was the son of the genre and history painter Alfred Dixon, and he himself developed a taste for historical subjects though always of naval interest. He was an illustrator and worked for the Illustrated London News, The Sphere and The Graphic.

Watercolour was his favourite medium and he liked to do large ones very quickly. He exhibited at the Royal Academy from 1889 with pictures hanging most years. He also exhibited at the New Watercolour Society. In 1900 he was elected a member of the Royal Institute of Painters and Watercolours.

He died at Itchenor, Sussex, on September 12th 1934.

Dufy, Raoul (1877-1953)

Raoul Dufy was born in Le Havre and retained throughout his career an attachment to harbours and boats which he expressed in both oil paintings and watercolours. He studied art in Paris at the Ecole des Beaux-arts and in 1905 adopted the brilliant colour gamut off the Fauves under the influence of Matisse.

His activities included designing silks and tapestries in association with the Bianchini Ferier silk factory at Lyons and he was employed on other forms of decorative art but he was also prolific in pictures of occasions of pageantry and pleasure by land and sea.

He visited England in the 1930s painting numerous pictures of yachts and regattas at Cowes. They were complimentary to his studies of regattas at Le Havre and Deauville. He was awarded the international prize for painting at the Venice Biennale in 1952 but died in the following year at Forcalquier in the Basses-Alpes. Works by him are in the Musee dArt Moderne, Paris, the Tate Gallery, London and the Museum of Modern Art, New York, and numerous private collections.

Everett, Herbert John (1876-1949)

Herbert Everett was born on August 18th 1876, he was the son of the Rector of Dorchester but had his first lessons in painting whilst on a visit to Munich. In October 1896 he moved to London to study at the Slade School of Art.

In May 1898, after leaving the Slade, John Everett shipped aboard the sailing ship *Iquique* as a passenger but entered in the ships books as a seaman with a token payment of a shilling a month. During the voyage, Everett had sketched extensively and he is unique in that a large part of his output consists of deck scenes on the ships he sailed on, painting mainly yachting and port scenes, many of them in France.

During the First World War he became particularly inspired by the dazzle painted methods of camouflaging ships which were invented by the artist Norman Wilkinson. After the war he would paint extensively in the Surrey Docks then frequented by the big sailing ships. In the 1930s he would make sea voyages each year but now in steamers and spent much of World War Two in Hertfordshire and his work of this period is mostly landscape. He never sold any of his work and lived on a gradually diminishing private income. At the Slade he had been thought of as perhaps the most promising of a remarkable class.

John Everett died in London in 1949 and left all his marines to the National Maritime Museum, Greenwich. The bequest amounted to 1,700 oil paintings and about twice as many drawings and engravings. He never tried to sell any of his work.

Gribble, Bernard Finegan RBC, SMA (1873-1972)

Born on May 10th 1873, Bernard Gribble was the son of the architect of the Brompton Oratory and was educated at the College of St Francis Saviour at Bruge. He then trained at the Royal College of Art, South Kensington and became a specialist in maritime history.

In 1912 he was made marine painter to the worshipful company of shipwrights. He exhibited at the Royal Academy, the Paris Salon and the Society of Marine Artists of which he was a member.

His early work is signed Bernard F. Gribble, later work is signed without the F.

French, Howard Barclay (1906-1987)

Howard French lived for most of life in the town of Cuttingsville, Vermont, and served with the United States Merchant Marine Academy during the early days of America's involvement with World War Two. He painted at least three very large works during this time.

He was a retiring person, who had very few shows and was never a member of any artistic associations. His work was important because of its precision and accurate proportions. He knew ships inside out as only a great marine artist does. A biographical sketch of him can be found in Who's Who in American Art, Volumes I-V.

Jacobsen, Antonio Nicholo Gasparo (1850-1921)

Antonio Jacobsen worked from a studio in West Hobokan, a suburb of New York. He was the most successful of the late 19th and early 20th century American ship portraitists and many of his works were commissioned from European sea captains and owners, thereby finding their way to European collections.

His work is to be found in many private and corporate collections and in international maritime museums, including the Altonaer Museum, the National Maritime Museum, Greenwich, the Maritime Museum, Cronburg Castle, the New Bedford Whaling Museum, the Peabody Museum of Salem which have forty-seven signed works and the Mariners Museum Newport News which is estimated to possess 275 of his paintings and drawings.

Jarvis, W. Howard RSMA (Birth date unknown-1964)

Howard Jarvis specialised in marine subjects, painting mostly in oils. He exhibited at the RSMA inaugural exhibition in 1946 with two pictures, and regularly thereafter until 1964, where he had a posthumous exhibit. He painted a number of famous yachts including the *Bloodhound* and the *Lutine*. He lived near Liss in Hampshire.

Marschall, Ken (born Whittier, California, 1950)

Ken Marschall specialised in paintings of the *Titanic*, becoming an acknowledged expert in all aspects of the ship and its disaster. He was a consultant for the movie 'Raise the Titanic' and has worked as a special effects artist for the Hollywood film industry for many years. In partnership with a colleague, he started his own studio in California.

Ken Marschall was involved with Doctor Robert Ballard's rediscovery of the *Titanic* wreck in 1986, subsequently painting many images of that discovery for books, magazines and films.

His paintings of ocean liners can be found in many museums and private collections throughout America.

Marsh, Reginald (1898-1954)

Reginald Marsh was born in New York, both of his parents were artists and Marsh learned to draw whilst still a child. The realist tradition of illustration claimed his professional interest for a decade before he turned to painting and he worked as an illustrator for Vanity Fair, Harpers Bazaar and the New York Daily News. He also did drawings for some of the more radical political journals.

Marsh himself was especially attracted by the circus and by the more perverse or lowly aspects of city life. The dock areas of New York with the ships and great liners were among his favourite subjects.

His works can be seen in most of the great museums of the world including the New York Whitney Museum and the New York Metropolitan Museum.

Muller, William

William Muller grew up in New York City in the 1940s where he developed a passion for the colourful steamers still operating within and from that port. He was especially fascinated by the majestic side wheelers which still plied the Hudson River. Eventually serving as quartermaster pilot on the last of them, the famous *Alexander Hamilton*. During this time he perfected his skills as an artist while painting the great liners which were fast disappearing from the scene.

Today William Muller is recognised as a master in his field, with his work being seen in many of America's most prestigious art museums, including the Peabody Museum of Salem, the Forbes Collection, New York, the Philadelphia Maritime Museum and the South Street Sea Port Museum in New York. He is also represented in many corporate collections throughout the world. He is a founding director and a fellow of the American Society of Marine Artists and is an adviser to the National Maritime Historical Society. He is also an elected member of the Society of American Historical Artists.

William Muller's work is currently represented by the Mystic Maritime Gallery at Mystic Sea Port Museum, Connecticut.

Muncaster, Claude Graham PRSMA, RWS, ROI, RBA (1903-1974)

Born at Sutton, Surrey on July 4th 1903, Claude Muncaster was the son of the landscape painter Oliver Hall. His decision in 1923 to change his name to an old family one of Muncaster was made partly to avoid confusion with his father as an artist.

In the 1920s he made several voyages as a deckhand. He went to Australia in a steam tramp and arriving in Hobsons Bay, Melbourne and found there the four masted barque *Olivebank*, one of Ericsson's last grain ships. He shipped aboard her and so became a Cape Horner. As a result of this experience one of his specialities became deck scenes and sailing vessels. During the Second World War, Muncaster became a Lieutenant Commander RNVR and a camouflage adviser to the Admiralty.

He first exhibited at the Royal Academy in 1920, under his original name Graham Hall. He also exhibited at the Society of Marine Artists and was elected its president following the death of Charles Pears in 1957.

Nevinson, Christopher Richard Wynne (1889-1946)

Richard Nevinson was born in London, the son of a writer. He attended the Slade School of Fine Art for four years from 1908 and started to exhibit at the Friday Club and the Allied Artists Association between 1912 and 1922.

He lived and studied in Paris for two years before the First World War, meeting and being influenced by Modigliani, Severini and other young futurists. On his return to London, he became a founder member of the London group and helped to publish the futurist manifesto in 1913 with Marinetti. His inclusion in the short-lived vorticist movement was the British attempt to form a modern school of painting, separate from the strong influences coming from the continent.

During the war he served in France from the outbreak in 1916, becoming an official war artist in 1917. His war paintings were exhibited in London with great success in 1918. At the end of the war he exhibited in New York working on more traditional lines having renounced futurism.

In 1939 the Royal Academy elected him an associate. His work is to be seen in many galleries and is enjoying a reappraisal of merit. Nevinson is now considered in the forefront of British artists of the mid 20th century.

Padday, Charles Murray RI, ROI (1890-1940)

Murray Padday painted in both oils and watercolours, mostly of marine coastal scenes and some landscapes. He lived on the south coast from 1895 at Bosham, Hampshire and in Folkestone, Kent from 1928. He exhibited many marine subjects at the Royal Academy from 1890.

Pansing, Fred (born 1844)

Born in Bremen, the son of a manufacturer, he went to sea when he was 16. After 5 years, during which time he began to draw and paint, he emigrated to America and set up as a marine painter and ship portraitist. He was working into the first quarter of this century and his pictures are of a high quality. Examples of his work can be seen at the Mariners Museum at Newport News, the Peabody Museum of Salem and in the collections of shipping companies and private individuals throughout Europe and America.

Pears, Charles PSMA, ROI (1873-1958)

Charles Pears was born in Pontefract, Yorkshire on September 9th 1873. He was educated at East Hardwick and Pomfret College and later became a professional illustrator who contributed to the Illustrated London News, The Graphic and Punch.

During the First World War Charles Pears held a commission in the Royal Marines and was also an official war artist to the Admiralty. In the Second World War he worked for the war artists commission. These war paintings were of events and actions but not actual things he saw himself. He was a keen yachtsman and an expert on ships and brought a high degree of technical accuracy to his work. He had an unusual technique in the handling of a seascape. He was the first president of the Society of Marine Artists later to have the prefix Royal. Many of his First World War pictures are in the Imperial War Museum and those done in the Second World War divided between the National Maritime Museum, Greenwich and the Imperial War Museum, London.

Shoesmith, Kenneth Denton (1896-1939)

Kenneth Shoesmith was born at Halifax, Yorkshire but was brought up in Blackpool. In 1906 he went as a cadet to HMS *Conway*, a training ship which was then moored in the Mersey and Shoesmith spent most of his spare time drawing the passing ships.

He was largely self taught but did subscribe to a correspondence course called Revival of Useful Art League. In 1909 he joined the Royal Mail Company as a junior officer and continued in the merchant marine until the end of the First World War by which time he found his duties as a Chief Officer allowed him too little time to paint. He became a professional artist living in London and specialising in poster designs, mainly for shipping firms and especially for the Royal Mail Lines.

He had his first one-man show in Belfast in 1921 and exhibited at the Royal Academy and the Paris Salon. In 1925 he was elected a member of the Royal Institute of Painters in Watercolour and he was also a member with the British Society of Poster Designers. The highlight of his career was perhaps his being chosen in 1935 as one of the artists to paint murals in the great new Cunarder *Queen Mary*. His work was strongly influenced by that of Frank Brangwyn.

Kenneth Shoesmith died in Hampstead Garden suburb in London on April 6th 1939. In 1974 his widow, Mrs Sarah Shoesmith, bequeathed all the drawings and posters which he had kept to the Ulster Museum in Belfast.

Smoothy, Derrick

Derrick Smoothy was born in 1923 at Rochford, Essex and educated at the old Elizabethan port of Leigh-on-Sea on the Thames. He has always been a great admirer of the works of the late, great Kenneth Shoesmith, both were gold medallists of the Royal Drawing Society at an early age, and both went to sea worldwide for some years.

During the heyday of the steamship he worked regularly as a poster artist for most of the great steamship companies. He now specialises in oils and watercolours, exhibiting in the United Kingdom and USA, including the John Stobbart Gallery in Boston, Massachusetts. His works may be seen at the Parker Gallery, London, the Royal Society of Marine Artists Exhibition in the United Kingdom, and at the Peabody Museum in Salem, Massachusetts.

Derrick Smoothy engages in the whole spectrum of marine art, including 19th century shipping, paddle steamers and liners of the 20th century.

Spurling, Jack (1871-1933)

Jack Spurling painted in oils but mostly in watercolours. His marine subjects were very finely drawn, especially of ships under full sail. He went to sea and learned about ships and salt water first hand. He painted about eighty covers for the magazine Blue Peter and many steamships commissioned by shipping companies, especially the P&O group where many of his paintings still hang today.

Stobart, John RSMA (born 1929)

John Stobart was born in Leicester on December 29th 1929. He studied first at the Derby College of Art from 1946-1950 and then at the Royal Academy school from 1950-56.

He first exhibited at the Royal Academy in 1952 also at the Royal Society of British Artists and the Society of Marine Artists. He was elected to the Society of Marine Artists in 1956. He lived at Farnham, Surrey in the 1960s where he studied to specialise in paintings of historic deep water sail, at which time he achieved a very finished expertise.

John Stobart now lives at Potomac Falls near Washington where he specialises in carefully researched American maritime scenes.

Thorp, William Eric RSMA, PS (born 1901)

William Thorp was born in London and educated in the City of London School. He studied art under Herbert Dicksee and Herbert Schroder. At the age of seventeen he was elected to the Artists Society, the youngest member ever, and in 1917 joined the Langham Art Club where one of the members was the marine painter Arthur Burgess. In 1947 Eric Thorp was one of the founder members of the Wapping Group and its president for the first five years.

He was elected to the now Royal Society of Marine Artists in 1958 and the Pastel Society in 1952. He has also exhibited at the Royal Academy.

y Torres, Raphael Monleon

A Spanish artist who worked in Madrid, flourishing in the late 19th century. A master of marine subjects. No data can be found about his life or where his work is exhibited. Commissioned to paint the liner *City of New York* in 1888 by her builders J&G Thomson for their Glasgow offices.

Waugh, Frederick Judd (1861-1940)

Frederick Waugh was one of America's best known maritime artists. He was born in Bordentown, New Jersey and attended the Pennsylvania Academy of the Fine Arts and the Academy Julienne in Paris. He lived in Europe from 1892-1907 where he had considerable success as an illustrator, also painting figure compositions in a turn of the century decorative manner, before taking up seascapes.

He eventually returned to America and settled in Cape Cod earning national fame for his brilliantly realistic understanding and depiction of rocks, waves and foam. In the 1930s, he was awarded the popular prize at the Carnegie International Exhibition for a number of years in succession.

Frederick Waugh was passionately interested in water and rocky shorelines. This was his special subject and frequently the ships in his paintings are decidedly incidental to his work. A brief essay on his life can be found in the Britannica Encyclopedia of American Art.

Wilcox, Leslie (born 1904)

Leslie Wilcox was born at Fulham, London in 1904. He was a self taught artist who had nevertheless very strong claims to be the doyen of British marine artists.

His main interest was in historical subjects and he was a member of the Royal Institute of Painters in Watercolours and the

Royal Society of Marine Artists. He also exhibited at the Royal Institute of Oil Painters and the Royal Scottish Society.

Wilkinson, Norman CBE, PRWS, RI (1878-1971)

Norman Wilkinson was born in Cambridge on November 24th 1878 and from the age of eight to fourteen he was a chorister at St Pauls Cathedral and after two years at Berkhampsted School. He went to live with his mother at Southsea, Hampshire where his passion for ships and the sea convinced him that he wanted to become a marine artist.

At the Portsmouth School of Art he obtained an Art Master's certificate and he also studied in St Ives. He made some voyages in coastal colliers and one deep water voyage before settling in London as an illustrator. His first drawing to be accepted by the Illustrated London News was in 1898 and he continued to work with them until 1915 when he got a commission as an assistant paymaster in the Royal Naval Reserve.

He was present at the Dardanelles campaign in 1917. In his new rank of Lieutenant in the Royal Naval Volunteer Reserve he commanded a motor patrol boat. It was at this time that he put forward the idea of dazzle painting ships as a means of confusing the aim of German gunners and torpedomen and this was generally adopted by both the naval and merchant fleets.

He was one of the best known poster designers for shipping and railway companies. His first poster was in 1903. A keen yachtsman he was made honorary marine painter to the Royal Yacht Squadron in 1919, he was also interested in aeroplanes and was a painter in that direction too. Thus, when the Second World War broke out in 1939, he became inspector of camouflage, with the rank of Air Commodore. He was president of the Royal Society of Painters and Watercolours and the acknowledged doyen of British marine painters.

Norman Wilkinson was commissioned by most of the great British passenger ship companies to paint portraits of their ships during the 1920s and 1930s, and it is in the remaining offices of those shipping companies that most of his great liner paintings can be seen today.

Wyllie, William Lionel RA, RI (1851-1931)

William Wyllie was born in London on July 6th 1851. He was first a student at Heatherleys Art School then joined the Royal Academy school in 1865. He exhibited his first painting at the Royal Academy in 1868 and in 1883 his picture of the Thames at Greenwich, called 'Toil, Litter, Grime and Wealth on a Flowing Tide', was purchased for the Chantrey bequest. The subject of this painting, tugs working barges, was something of an innovation as artists had formerly concentrated on the more decorative types of vessels. However, Wyllie's obsessive love for the sea and anything that floated on it embraced every type and size of vessel and moved him to cover every aspect of the working river which set a fashion for other artists to follow.

In 1889 he was elected an associate of the Royal Academy. His oils were never as high in quality as were his watercolours, which was his favourite medium. He was also a skilful engraver. His output was prodigious.

When he died in 1931 the watercolours in his studio were purchased for the proposed National Maritime Museum at Greenwich, and on counting these it was found that they numbered five thousand. One of William Wyllie's last tasks was his work as a member of the committee supervising the restoration of HMS *Victory* to her Trafalgar state in a drydock in Portsmouth dockyard. He exhibited regularly at the Society of British Artists, the New Watercolour Society and the Grosvenor Gallery. He died at Hampstead on April 6th 1931.

Zeeden, Walter (1891-1961)

Walter Zeeden's early life was spent as a railway engineer until 1932 when he began illustrating books on maritime subjects. His talents propelled him to the forefront of German marine art, becoming particularly well known for his watercolours. The great trans-atlantic shipping company, North German Lloyd, commissioned him in the 1930s to paint their greatest liners.

Abbreviations

ARA	Associate Member of the Royal Academy		RBC	Member of Royal British Colonial Society of Artists
CBE	Commander of the British Empire		RE	Royal Society of Painter-Etchers and Engravers
FRSA	Fellow of the Royal Scottish Academy		RI	Member Royal Institute of Painters in Watercolours
HRSA	Honorary Member, The Royal Scottish Society		RNVR	Royal Naval Volunteer Reserve
HVPSMA	Honorary Vice-President, Society of Marine Artists		ROI	Member Royal Institute of Oil Painters
MNI	Member of the National Institute		RSMA	Royal Society of Marine Artists
OBE	Order of the British Empire		RWS	Member of the Royal Watercolour Society
PRBA	President, The Royal British Academy		VPMSA	Vice President, Society of Marine Artists
PRSMA	President of Royal Society of Marine Artists			
PS	Member of the Pastel Society			
PSMA	President of Society of Marine Artists			
RA	Member of the Royal Academy			
RBA	Royal British Academy			

With the exception of the Royal Academies, nearly all the artistic societies in the United Kingdom which carry the prefix 'Royal', started without it.

Afterword

by Frank O. Braynard, Curator, American Merchant Marine Museum

Ever since my father brought home in 1925 a sumptuous poster showing the *Duilio* racing through the Atlantic I have loved marine paintings. The *Duilio*, while not my very top favourite of all time, has remained as one of my choice ocean liners ever since. I do not even know the artist, but that picture inspired me as few others ever have and the thought of a fine big book honouring the marine artists who painted great liners has always excited me. Now it is happening, and we have the spirit, the push and the many fine contacts of Kenneth Vard to thank. When he asked for my help in a small way, I was delighted. When he suggested that he would like an "Afterword" from me I was overjoyed! This is a book that will get a top place in my 5,000 ship book library in Sea Cliff. This is a work that has been a long time in the anticipating and will, I trust, be the beginning of a new appreciation of marine artists who painted great liners. There is room for many more books of this kind and I only hope they are done with the zest and style of Kenneth Vard.

With 80 reproductions between its two covers, Kenneth Vard's newest work will appeal to many thousands of ship lovers, to countless more thousands of artists and art lovers, and to those who have travelled on the great liners shown – as well as on their sisterships and companion ships of the various lines. I just hope that the book will be properly merchandised, so that it can be enjoyed through many editions by the very large areas of the "big public" to which I know it will appeal. Part One – the section of liner portraits – will draw thousands of young readers into the book's beauties. I can just imagine the young reader delving into this section and making his selection of favourite ocean liners from its rich assortment of colourful queens of the sea. Then Part Two – what a superb idea! I can list in my mind at least half a dozen great liners which played a part in British Royal cruises – thinking especially of the two-stacked *Medina*. And what an opportunity for the artist – with escorting craft of all kinds and the great parades at Spithead. Part Three – liners in warpaint – offers another wonderful spread on which to display liner paintings. I am thinking particularly of the canvas by Frederick J. Waugh, that painter of heroic water and wave scenes, who actually played a major part in designing the camouflage for the *Leviathan* and then was asked to make a painting of her under escort by old four-piper destroyers in World War I. The final section, decidedly important and much needed, will honour painters using liners as their main theme but not necessarily being known as liner artists. Again, my mind surges over a great number of outstanding works that fall into this important category. What a marvellous division. Each of these four groupings cries for a full book. Perhaps the success of this first effort will generate the interest in four more – each a spellbinder, each a work of art in this marvellously broad field, this almost untouched field of great art.

One final word, for those who bemoan the end of the liner era: Let me offer a spirited word of disagreement and hope. More great liners are being built today than ever. We are just entering the largest liner-building era of all time. Imagine six new ships of greater gross tonnage than the *QE2*! And don't let the sad comments of those who wish they could have lived a generation or two earlier worry you. I am positive that the generations which follow us will say the very same thing about our generation. True, the outline of some of our newer ships is a bit shocking, quite different, not at all traditional. But there are youngsters now learning to draw who will win inspiration from this Kenneth Vard masterwork. And they will paint these new ships – will love their bows, their sterns, their strange (perhaps) smokestacks and superstructures, and will leave us a heritage of new ocean liner art that will be well worth recording in a dozen new books of modern ocean liner paintings. Perhaps, gentle reader, you are one of them! Have fun.

Bibliography

I have scoured the following books in the course of my research. Many more have been dipped into over the years, whose titles escape me now but the contents of which are forever engraved on my memory. I am indebted to all the authors who have taught me so much. To them, and to the authors of the following books go my heart felt thanks.

The Decorative Arts of the Mariner by Gervis Frere-Cook, published by Castle and Co. Ltd., 1966

Art and the Seafarer by H.J. Hanson, published by Faber and Faber, 1966

Marine Painting by William Gaunt, published by Secker and Warburg, 1975

Spurling Sail and Steam by Warren Moore, published by Grosset and Dunlop, New York 1980

Dictionary of Sea Painters by E.H. Archibold, published by Antiques Collectors Club Ltd., 1980

20th Century British Marine Paintings by Denys Brooke-Hart, published by Antiques Collectors Club Ltd., 1981

A Dictionary of British Marine Painters by Arnold Wilson, published by F. Lewis Ltd., 1967

Early American Moderns by Mahonri Sharp Young, published by Watson-Guptill Publications, New York, 1974

The Ocean Liner by Richard B. Oliver, published by Cooper-Hewitt Museum, New York, 1980

Grand Luxe by John Malcolm Brinnin and Kenneth Gaulin, published by Bloomsbury, 1988

British Marine Painting by A.L. Baldry, published by The Studio Ltd., 1919

The Dictionary of British Artists 1880-1940, compiled by J. Johnson and A. Greutzner, published by Antiques Collectors Club, 1976

Port Out Starboard Home by Anna Sproule, published by Blandford Press, 1978

Merchant Ships of the Solent Past and Present by Bert Moody, published by Kingfisher Railway Productions Ltd., 1988

The Elizabeth by Neil Potter and Jack Frost, published by George G. Harrop and Co. Ltd., 1965

The Atlantic Ferry by C.R. Benstead, published by Metheun and Co. Ltd., 1936

White Star by Ray Anderson, published by J. Stevenson and Sons Ltd., 1964

Captain of the Queens by Captain Harry Grattidge, published by E.P. Dutton and Co. Inc., 1956

Great Passenger Ships of the World by Arnold Kludas, Volumes 1-6, published by Patrick Stevens, 1972+

Fifty Famous Liners by Frank O'Braynard and William H. Miller, published by Patrick Stevens, 1982

Normandie by Harvey Ardman, published by Franklyn Watts, 1985

The Liners by Terry Coleman, published by Alan Lane, Penguin Books, 1976

US Passenger Liners Since 1945, by Milton Watson, published by Patrick Stevens, 1988

Famous Ocean Liners by William H. Miller, published by Patrick Stevens

The Sway of the Grand Salon by John Malcolm Brinnin, published by Macmillan, 1972

The Only Way to Cross by John Maxstone-Graham, published by Macmillan, 1972

Ocean Liners by Robert Wall, published by William Collins Sons and Co. Ltd., 1978

Sail, Steam and Splendour by Byron S. Miller, published by Angus Robertson, 1977

Ocean Liners of the 20th Century by Gordon Newall, published by Bonanza Books, New York, 1963

Majesty at Sea by John H. Shaum Jnr. and William H. Flayhart III, published by Patrick Stevens, 1981

Shipping Wonders of the World by Clarence Winchester, published by the Amalgamated Press Ltd.

P&O A Fleet History by Stephen Rabson and Kevin O'Donahue, published by the World Ships Society, 1988

The Liners of Liverpool by Derek M. Whale, Parts 1-3, published by Countywise Ltd., 1988

The Royal Yacht Britannia by Andrew Morton, published by Orbis, London

The Wonder Book of Ships by Ward Lock & Co. Ltd.

RMS Queen Mary by David F. Hutchings, published by Kingfisher Railway Productions, 1986

P&O's Canberra by Neil McCart, published by Kingfisher Railway Productions, 1989

150 Years of Southampton Docks by Bert Moody, published by Kingfisher Railway Productions

Atlantic Queens by Clive Brooks, published by Haynes Publishing, 1989

Bon Voyage by John Malcolm Brinnin, published by Thames and Hudson, 1982

The Patient Speaks by C.M. Squarey, published by Thomas Cook & Son Ltd., 1955

Shipbuilders to the World by Michael Moss and John R. Hulme, published by the Blackstaff Press, 1986

Tramps and Ladies by Sir James Bissett, published by Angus and Robertson, UK Ltd., 1959

The Grand Days of Travel by Charles Owen, published by Windward-Webb and Bower

Picture History of the Normandie by Frank O'Braynard, published by Dover Publications Inc., New York, 1987

Passenger Liners by Lawrence Dunn, published by Adlard Coles Ltd., 1961

The Great Liners by Melvyn Maddocks, published by Time Life Books, 1978

The Frantic Atlantic by Basil Woon, published by Knopf, 1927

Lives of the Liners by Frank O'Braynard, published by Cornell Maritime Press, 1927

Cunard White Star Liners of the 1930s by Richard P. de Kerbrech and David L. Williams, published by Conway Maritime Press, 1988

Seven Centuries of Sea Travel by B.W. Bathe, published by Barrie and Jenkins, 1972

Ocean Liners of the Past - Reprints from the Shipbuilder, published by Patrick Stevens, 1971+

Lusitania by Colin Simpson, published by Longwan, 1972

A Million Ocean Miles by Sir Edgar T. Britten, published by Hutchinson, 1936

Acknowledgements

Without the assistance of the following, this book would not have been possible.

My thanks to Stephen Drew for his time and expertise in photographing paintings in the collections of the Furness Withy Group, Caledonia Investments PLC and paintings from the collections of private individuals. Mr Arun Gujaran for editing my manuscript so assiduously and Pauline Moore for her patience in converting my text into artwork; Mr Paul Barnes of Caledonia Investments PLC for his help in arranging access to the Union Castle collection; Bert Moody; David Hatchard; Mr Richard Alexander of the Furness Withy Group for his enthusiastic support and assistance; Mr Stephen Rabson and Mrs Mardi Esterkin of P&O who gave up so much of their time searching for transparencies of paintings from the P&O picture collection and getting them to me with time to spare. To Mr Eric Flounders of Cunard who, with great kindness, listened to and delivered most of what I requested, which was a lot; Captain Stephen Card who greatly encouraged me in all manners nautical, apart from his greatly appreciated contribution on matters artistic. To Captain John Treasure-Jones an old and valued friend who strode like a colossus on the bridges of so many of the world's greatest liners, to him I am indebted for writing the foreword of this book, and for many pleasant voyages and times spent aboard ships under his command. My sincere thanks to Mr Martin Anglesea of the Ulster Museum of Art in Belfast who offered the Kenneth Shoesmith archives for my inspection and delight and Mr Frank O. Braynard, curator of the American Merchant Marine Museum for his hospitality and infectious enthusiasm which will never be forgotten, I thank him for obtaining transparencies of paintings in his collection, his breadth of knowledge in the subject of shipping leaves me breathless and for doing me the honour of writing the afterword of this book.

I must also acknowledge my indebtedness to the forgotten men of Harland and Wolff's shipyards in Belfast who, so many years ago, gave me, when only a lad, tea out of a billy can and helped to sneak me aboard fabulous liners for a wide eyed look. It was they who instilled in me an interest in ships which has been the pleasure and passion of my life. To all the museums and art galleries I have visited, to the writers of shipping books and the painters of ships, my thanks for a lifetime's education and pleasure, and to the men and women who manned the liners on which I sailed on many a fabulous voyage, my undying gratitude.

To Hamza Arcan for the book's logo and John Geary, photographer from the American Merchant Marine Museum; Andrea Owens from Liverpool University; Cunard Archives Department; Arnold Kludas and Doctor Scholl from the German ships museum Bremerhaven, my sincere thanks.

Finally, to my publisher, Roger Hardingham, goes my gratitude and appreciation for his empathy and faith in this project.